CLARENDON LIBRARY OF LOGIC AND PHILOSOPHY

General Editor: L. Jonathan Cohen, The Queen's College, Oxford

SLIPPERY SLOPE ARGUMENTS

The Clarendon Library of Logic and Philosophy brings together books, by new as well as by established authors, that combine originality of theme with rigour of statement. Its aim is to encourage new research of a professional standard into problems that are of current or perennial interest.

General Editor: L. Jonathan Cohen, The Queen's College, Oxford.

Also published in this series

Slippery Slope Arguments

DOUGLAS WALTON

CLARENDON PRESS · OXFORD
1992

Oxford University Press, Walton Street, Oxford OX2 6DP
Oxford New York Toronto
Delhi Bombay Calcutta Madras Karachi
Petaling Jaya Singapore Hong Kong Tokyo
Nairobi Dar es Salaam Cape Town
Melbourne Auckland
and associated companies in
Berlin Ibadan

Oxford is a trade mark of Oxford University Press

Published in the United States
by Oxford University Press, New York

British Library Cataloguing in Publication Data
Data available

Library of Congress Cataloging in Publication Data
Walton, Douglas N.
Slippery slope arguments/Douglas Walton.
p.   cm. — (The Clarendon library of logic and philosophy)
Includes bibliographical references and index.
1. Fallacies (Logic)   2. Ethics.   I. Title.   II. Series.
BC175.W36 1992   168—dc20   91-23498
ISBN 0-19-823925-4

Typeset by Pentacor PLC, High Wycombe, Bucks.

Printed in Great Britain by
Biddles Ltd,
Guildford & King's Lynn

For Karen, with love

Acknowledgments

FUNDING for the research for this monograph was provided by the following awards: a Killam Research Fellowship from the Killam Foundation of the Canada Council, a Fellowship from the Netherlands Institute for Advanced Study in the Humanities and Social Sciences (NIAS), and a Research Grant from the Social Sciences and Humanities Research Council of Canada.

A summary of some parts of this work was presented as an Invited Lecture for the Department of Discourse and Argumentation Studies at the University of Amsterdam in the International Symposium on Argumentation Theory on October 27, 1989. For many useful discussions and comments following this talk, I would especially like to thank Eveline Feteris, Bart Garssen, and Francisca Snoek Henkemans. Members of the Research Group (Nucleus) on 'Fallacies as Violations of Rules for Argumentative Discourse' contributed many insights and useful pieces of advice during the ten months we worked together during 1989–90 at NIAS. My thanks to Rob Grootendorst, Agnes Haft van Rees, Scott Jacobs, Sally Jackson, Frans van Eemeren, Agnes Verbiest, Charles Willard, and John Woods. When an invited lecture in the NIAS Lecture Series on the slippery slope fallacy was given by the author on November 30, 1989, many interesting questions and criticisms were proposed. I would especially like to thank Paul Alexander, Graham Bush, Robert Druce, and Robert Sider.

For discussions, correspondences, and/or publications that were influential in shaping my perspectives on the slippery slope argument, I would also like to thank Tony Blair, Trudy Govier, Ralph Johnson, and Erik Krabbe. This research was also aided by a study leave granted by the University of Winnipeg and by the excellent research facilities and supportive ambience of NIAS during my Fellowship-in-Residence in Wassenaar. My thanks to Susan Crighton, the producer of *Family Matters*, for supplying a transcript of the panel discussion on research on human embryos televised on BBC-1 on February 2, 1990.

I am most grateful to Amy Merrett for word-processing this work, including all the figures and tables, with such care and accuracy, through the several drafts.

Contents

Illustrations

1

Introduction and Perspectives

A SLIPPERY slope argument is a kind of argument that warns you if you take a first step, you will find yourself involved in a sticky sequence of consequences from which you will be unable to extricate yourself, and eventually you will wind up speeding faster and faster towards some disastrous outcome. A good example was the argument used to support the majority opinion in the recent U.S. Supreme Court decision not to ban burning of the American flag as a criminal act. Justice William J. Brennan, Jr. argued that any ruling to ban physical desecration of the flag would lead to further cases that would 'enter territory having no discernible or defensible boundaries.' Wouldn't the court then have to consider prohibiting the burning of state flags, or the Constitution? Justice Brennan worried that in order to evaluate these choices, the court would end up imposing its own political preferences to suppress all kinds of unpopular protests. This kind of outcome is dangerous in a democratic country where freedom of speech is important.

Another recent case was a public discussion on the ethics of medical research on human embryos. An opponent of allowing researchers to do experiments on an embryo for the first fifteen days of its existence argued that once this was allowed, the researchers would improve their techniques, and having gotten a foot in the door, would push the boundaries back further and further, eventually ending up by doing all kinds of experiments on embryos at advanced stages of development. This outcome was clearly regarded by the speaker, and presumably by his audience, as dangerous and undesirable.

It is characteristic of all slippery slope arguments that a dangerous outcome of some contemplated course of action is warned of. But the slippery slope argument is more than just a warning. The dangerous outcome is put forward as a reason for not taking a first step in the contemplated course of action. It is an argument put forward by a speaker to persuade a hearer not to take this first step, on the grounds of the consequences that may follow.

Many textbooks on informal logic and critical thinking have a section on the slippery slope argument, where it is often treated as a fallacy. However, this book takes a case study approach which concludes that in some cases, the slippery slope argument can be used correctly as a reasonable type of argumentation to shift a burden of proof in a critical discussion, while in other cases it is used incorrectly. Four types of slippery slope argument are identified and analyzed in the four central chapters of the book. Each chapter presents guidelines that show how each type of slippery slope argument can be used correctly or incorrectly in a particular case.

One type of slippery slope argument warns that if some new step is taken, tried, or allowed, it will function as a precedent, which will set another precedent, and then another, until 'all hell will break loose.' This variant of the argument is also known as the (thin edge of the) wedge argument, the camel's nose in the tent argument, and the foot in the door argument.

Another type of slippery slope argument consists in the use of the rejoinder 'There is no cutoff point,' when an argument contains a key term that is vague, and the proponent of the argument is having difficulty defining the term in a precise but non-arbitrary way. This variant was known to the ancient Greeks as the 'heap' argument (sorites) or 'bald man' argument (*falakros*), because it could be used to prove the non-existence of heaps or of bald men (paradoxically) (see Chapter 2.1). It has also been called the continuum argument, in recent times.

A third type of slippery slope argues that once some action is carried out, it will cause a second event, that will in turn precipitate a causal sequence of worse and worse consequences. This variant has been called the domino argument, or the 'this could snowball' argument (in colder climates). It has also been called the 'genie in the bottle argument,' implying that a genie is an unkind force that will run out of control, causing harm, and once it has been released from its bottle, there will be no way to get it back in.

Sometimes a full-scale slippery slope argument will combine all three of these variants as subarguments to suggest that given a favorable climate of social acceptance, one first step, if taken, will trigger a contagious sequence of steps, ultimately leading to a 'parade of horrors.' A horror like 'the police state' or 'Nazi death squads' may be cited as the final outcome.

1. The Three Basic Types of Slippery Slope Argument

In the spring of 1989, the justices of the U.S. Supreme Court debated a decision that could overturn the precedent-setting case of *Roe* v. *Wade* that had stood for the beginning of legalized abortion in the United States. Charles Fried, Special Assistant U.S. Attorney General, argued that the Supreme Court should overturn the ruling of *Roe* v. *Wade,* by using an analogy of a thread and a cloth. Frank Susman, a lawyer representing abortion clinics in Missouri, took the opposing point of view, arguing that the *Roe* v. *Wade* ruling should be sustained. A segment of the dialogue, excerpted in *Newsweek* (May 8, 1989, p. 19), is quoted below.

Case 1.1

FRIED. We are not asking the court to unravel the fabric of unenumerated and privacy rights . . . Rather, we are asking the court to pull this one thread . . .

SUSMAN. I think [Fried] is somewhat disingenuous when he suggests to this court that he does not seek to unravel the whole cloth of procreational rights, but merely to pull a thread. It has always been my personal experience that when I pull a thread, my sleeve falls off.

It is not a thread he is after. It is the full range of procreational rights and choices that constitute the fundamental right that has been recognized by this court . . .

Cleverly, Susman turned Fried's own analogy back against him by transforming it into a slippery slope argument, saying that, in his experience, when he pulls a thread, his whole sleeve falls off. This is a slippery slope argument, because Susman is arguing that once we take the first step of overturning *Roe* v. *Wade,* '[t]here is no stopping,' and our whole 'range of procreational rights' will be lost. The thrust of Susman's argument is that to avert this unacceptable outcome, we must reject Fried's argument.

Slippery slope arguments sometimes have to do with the setting of precedents, like case 1.1 above, where the context of the discussion was a legal debate. However, the type of slippery slope argument most commonly cited in the 'new wave' (contemporary) informal logic textbooks is a causal argument. In this kind of slippery slope, there is a causally related sequence of events which could happen, where one event leads to the next. Sometimes called the *domino argument,* this version warns against which will be the first step in a chain of causes and effects that will ultimately lead to some horrible outcome, at the end of the chain.

The case most often cited in the contemporary textbooks concerned worries before and during the era of the American involvement in Vietnam, that the fall of Vietnam to the communists would lead to expanded communist domination to neighboring countries. Kahane (1971: 61), for example, cited a sequence following from the fall of South Vietnam through the rest of Southeast Asia, to India, Japan, and Australia. To wind up the argument, Bob Hope was quoted[1] as predicting, 'those Commies would have the whole thing, and it wouldn't be long until we'd be looking off the coast of Santa Monica.'

This type of slippery slope argument is often treated as a fallacy, although many texts recognize that the kind of argumentation involved need not be used fallaciously in every case. Kahane (1971: 62) warns 'sometimes that first step will lead to the rest; sometimes it won't.' Other texts warn about confusing what *might* happen with what *will* happen. However, there is vast disagreement, and very little in the way of serious attempts to explain how to tell the difference between the fallacious and non-fallacious cases of slippery slope reasoning.

Some logic textbooks stress a distinctively different kind of slippery slope argument which arises through the existence of borderline cases made possible through the use of vague terms or concepts. Fogelin (1987: 72), cites the following case, an argument that, paradoxically, seems to go from true premises to a false conclusion.

Case 1.2

> If someone has one cent, he is not rich.
>
> If someone is not rich, then giving him one cent will not make him rich.
>
> Therefore, no matter how many times you give a person a cent, he will not pass from being not rich to being rich.

---

[1] According to Kahane (1971: 61) Bob Hope was quoted from a *New York Times Magazine* article, 'This is Bob (Politician–Patriot–Publicist) Hope,' by Anthony J. Lukas, Oct. 4, 1970, p. 86.

What's wrong with this argument? Despite a large and growing philosophical literature on the subject, this has turned out to be a hard question to answer definitively. At present, it remains open to debate as a problem or paradox.

As Fogelin (1972: 72) points out, the problem stems from the vagueness of the term 'rich.' There are some clear cases where we can say an individual is definitely 'rich' or 'not rich,' beyond dispute. But there is also a grey area in between, where we can't definitively say, one way or the other. Even if we try to stipulate a definition, by specifying an exact cutoff point in dollars and cents, our criterion could be attacked as arbitrary (see Chapter 2.8).

The paradoxical nature of this kind of argument has been known since the ancient Greeks, who sometimes called it the 'heap' or 'bald man' argument, as noted above, because it could be used to prove that there are no heaps or bald men. It can be exploited as a tactic to attack someone who has used a term or concept that is vague, by insisting that since there is no precise cutoff point, their argument can be driven to extreme and absurd conclusions.

How the heap argument, and the slippery slope argument generally, became included in the list of fallacies in the modern textbooks is something of a mystery. Aristotle did not include the slippery slope argument in his original list of fallacies, and Hamblin (1970) makes no mention of it as a recognized type of fallacy. It is not mentioned in DeMorgan's collection of fallacies (1847), and it appears to be only rarely mentioned in the older logic textbooks, becoming fairly common only in recent ones.

Traditionally, the slippery slope argument, in the form of the heap, was treated as a sophism in the sense of a paradox or logical puzzle, rather than as a sophism (or sophistry or fallacy) in the sense of a tricky or deceptive argument that could be used to get the best of an adversary in a contested argument. The best explanation of how it has evolved from the former to the latter status is found in Alfred Sidgwick's little-known text *Elementary Logic* (1914: 151).

Sorites. This 'fallacy' is also important, though it has no place in Aristotle's lists, and is usually classed along with a few miscellaneous tricky arguments, on special points, that have been preserved from ancient times. It should be described rather as a source of difficulty than as a fallacy. . . . In its modern forms we generally call it the difficulty of 'drawing the line.'

Even the term *sorites* itself is ambiguous and potentially confusing, as used in the history of logic. According to Sidgwick (p. 151),

It gets its name from *sorites,* a heap, because the original form of it was the difficulty of saying how many grains of sand constitute a 'heap' when you begin with a number so small as not to deserve the name, and then add a grain at a time till the difficulty arises.

But the term sorites is also traditionally used in logic to refer to a chain of subarguments, where the conclusion of one has the role of a premise in the next one. For example, according to Whately's *Elements of Logic* (1836: 119), a sorites is a form of argument where 'you have a string of Syllogisms . . . in which the Conclusion of each is made the Premiss of the next, till you arrive at the main or ultimate Conclusion of all . . .' This idea of stringing together a longer sequence of linked subarguments in a chain with an ultimate, single conclusion is in fact highly characteristic of sorites arguments generally. So even the distinction between the two traditional concepts of a sorites argument contains the potential for serious confusion.

   Was Sidgwick right to describe the sorites as more a 'source of difficulty' than a fallacy? Although the majority of the logic textbooks have treated the causal type of slippery slope as the fallacy, some, including Scriven (1976) and Fogelin (1987) have viewed the slippery slope fallacy as being essentially the same kind of argument that is in the sorites. But the sorites is a paradox, a sophism in the sense of being a puzzle. To show how this type of paradox is, involves, or leads to a fallacy, in the sense of being a deceptive tactic of argumentation used to get the best of an adversary in an argumentative dispute, is a job that remains to be done.

2. The Combined or Full Version

In recent times, the slippery slope argument has become a common and powerful technique of argumentation in applied ethics. Issues in biomedical ethics, in particular, have provided a fertile area for this kind of argument. A classic kind of case concerns disputes on the subject of euthanasia.

   The setting of one dispute of this sort arises from the conflict of opinions between those who favor 'quality of life' to argue on humane grounds, in certain cases, for a relaxing of prohibitions on acts or omissions that might shorten human lives. The opposed point of view favors the principle of 'sanctity of life' as inherently valuable in itself (vitalism), and sees any qualifications, restrictions, or exceptions as a suspicious rhetorical ploy to erode or debase traditional values.

In a study paper on this issue, written for the Law Reform Commission of Canada, Keyserlingk (1979: 22) described how the vitalists have been very suspicious and mistrustful of qualifications proposed by the quality of life exponents, assuming 'the results will be an opening of the floodgates to an ever decreasing respect for human life, a substitution of subjective and shifting values and tastes for an absolute unchanging norm.' The expression of such reservations by the vitalist point of view takes the form of the slippery slope argument, characterized by Keyserlingk as follows.

Case 1.3

The argument is that once some form of killing, letting die or altering of human life is legitimated in a particular instance, though it may be compassionate, sometimes morally justifiable or at worst a minor evil in itself, if allowed and applied generally it will, despite goodwill and the best available safeguards, lead to wrongs of ever increasing magnitude. Therefore it is best not to take that first step, not to put that first wedge or foot in the door. (p. 22)

In this expression of the argument, the precise source of the predicted 'snowballing' is not explicitly stated. But it is indicated that the problem is the worry that any exceptions to the traditional prohibitions will become 'legitimated . . . if allowed and applied generally,' so that they will be taken as precedents which will lead to 'wrongs of ever increasing magnitude.' The worry seems to be that allowing exceptions will set precedents that will run rampant, despite 'the best available safeguards.'

But this worry seems to be only a part of the argument. Another aspect of it comes out in a statement of it quoted directly by Keyserlingk (p. 22) from the words of one of its exponents, Rostand (1973).

Case 1.4

Above all I believe that a terrible precedent would be established if we agreed that a life could be allowed to end because it is not worth preserving since the notion of biological worthiness, even if carefully circumscribed at first would soon become broader and less precise. After eliminating what was no longer human, the next step would be to eliminate what was not sufficiently human, and finally nothing would be spared except what fitted a certain ideal concept of humanity.

This text of argument adds another factor that underlies the sequence of escalation supposedly behind the slippery slope. Not only would a dangerous precedent be set, but the notion of 'biological worthiness' would become 'broader and less precise.' This is a linguistic or conceptual expansion—what was 'carefully circumscribed' at first would become vague—a grey area. This chipping away of the conceptual limits of a concept would, according to the words of case 1.4, pass through a sequence of steps, until a final value, a 'certain ideal concept of humanity' is the outcome. This final outcome has scary connotations—it sounds like some kind of elitist, utopian ideal.

The next stage of the slippery slope argument involves filling out this scary outcome more specifically by drawing a historical analogy to the 'Nazi parade of horrors.' Keyserlingk (1979: 23) expresses this part in the following terms.

Case 1.5

After all, under the Nazi regime euthanasia and experimentation may have begun with 'humane' intentions, and may not have been initially racist. But gradually, step by inevitable step, voluntary euthanasia for the terminally ill evolved into involuntary euthanasia imposed upon anyone determined to be useless to society or an enemy of the state, including the mentally retarded and especially Jews.

This part of the argument is clearly based on an analogy between two social contexts—that of the Nazi state and the present social situation of North America in the 1980s. And it is also based on a particular historical interpretation, or explanation, of how the Holocaust came about in Nazi Germany. Both these subarguments are highly controversial, certainly to historians, sociologists, and others who try to explain such things. Indeed, both claims would appear to be broadly empirical in nature, depending on all kinds of historical and social facts and interpretations.

Putting the whole chain of argumentation together from the various linkages and subsequences comprised of all three cases above, we get an argument that combines four different kinds of linkage. As noted already in the discussions of case 1.4 and case 1.5 above, respectively, there is a precedent slippery slope subargument and a sorites-type slippery slope subargument involved.

But throughout the whole sequence, there also appears to be a causal sequence of events implicit, whereby one action leads to another action. First there was compassionate shortening or altering of human life by voluntary euthanasia, but with safeguards. Then there was the step to eliminating 'what was not sufficiently human' by 'imposing' involuntary euthanasia on 'anyone determined to be useless.' Then there is the step to doing away with anyone thought to be an 'enemy of the state,' which leads to the Final Solution of the Nazi police state. This progression appears to have underlying it a causal sequence—one kind of action is actually causally instrumental in producing the next one.

There is also a fourth kind of linkage underlying this chain of developments. Each stage of what becomes permitted as a practice in a society leads to the evolution towards the next stage by becoming an accepted kind of action in that social context. As one act becomes less and less the exception that has to be argued for as acceptable in a particular case, a social climate of opinion sets in which makes it easier for the next stage to arise as a real possibility. As what is tolerated in a society changes, the possible becomes the plausible.

Historians are now debating controversial ethical and historical questions of how millions of people came to be exterminated in death camps by an organized bureaucracy for mass murder—the Nazi killing machine organized and set into action during the Second World War. Did the early Nazi programs of sterilization and euthanasia function as first steps that later led to killing of perceived political enemies on a wider scale, and then eventually to the Jewish Holocaust? Or was the extermination of the Jews Hitler's primary, driving obsession? Or even if the latter, could there have been a slippery slope from those first steps to a wider acceptance of killing by those of the German people, who might otherwise have fought harder against such policies? Were the early programs of sterilization and euthanasia Hitler's way of introducing anti-life policies in order to facilitate acceptance and set the bureaucratic structures of the Third Reich in motion for the mass murders of the death camps?

These historical questions have been sharpened by the finding of Lifton (1986: 22) that there were five identifiable steps in the sequence through which the Nazis carried out their program of 'life unworthy of life.'

(1) Coercive sterilization.
(2) The killing of 'impaired' children in hospitals.
(3) The killing of 'impaired' adults, mostly from mental hospitals.
(4) The killing of 'impaired' inmates of concentration camps.
(5) Mass killings, mostly of Jews.

One way or the other, it does appear that there were some elements of slippery slope argumentation implicit in the planning and persuasion sequence of this series of actions, as it came to be realized in the Third Reich. If historians probe into how this came about, it might help us to be more aware of and vigilant towards the possibility that something comparable might happen again in similar historical circumstances.

Analysis of the full slippery slope argument as a kind of reasoning that can be correct or incorrect, strong or weak, valid or fallacious, is therefore a job of some importance in evaluating historical controversies, and in evaluating argumentation on moral dilemmas and disputes generally. This would appear to be a job for practical logic, or the analysis of argumentation as an applied task, rather than a purely theoretical job for formal logic. For the full slippery slope argument is a broad type of argumentation that requires taking different kinds of evidence into account, in order to evaluate it. Not only may it require historical evidence, and presumptions about what social groups accept as plausible in the context of a particular era, but it incorporates all three of the prior types of slippery slope argumentation.

The method of this monograph will be to begin with the narrower tasks of analyzing each of the three basic types of slippery slope argument—the sorites type, the causal type, and the precedent type—using Descartes's method of breaking a problem into component problems by compartmentalization, and then putting the parts together.

3. Four Previous Developments

There were four previous developments in the field of argumentation research that established basic methodological presumptions enabling this project on the slippery slope as a distinctive type of argumentation to go ahead. The first was Govier's (1982) classification of the slippery slope argument into four basic types. This classification has been one methodological basis of the present monograph, and it is the author's contention that the Govier typology has been borne out by the cases and strengthened by the results of this further research into the subject.

The second development was the finding of Perelman and Olbrechts-Tyteca (1971: 282) that the slippery slope argument (called the 'argument from direction' by them) can be usefully viewed as a response to another type of argumentation tactic they called 'the device of stages' (see Chapter 7.3). Perelman and Olbrechts-Tyteca showed how the slippery slope argument can be viewed as a very common and natural response to a distinctive kind of situation or challenge in argumentation. By fitting the slippery slope argument into the ebb and flow of natural patterns of argumentation, they gave me an important clue and insight into how the slippery slope works, allowing the development of normative guidelines for both defending and attacking this type of argument in a systematic manner. Before we can evaluate slippery slope arguments, we first of all have to see how they function as effective tactics in particular types of situation. Out of these insights, the present analysis arose, adopting a pragmatic approach to studying how the slippery slope works as a technique of everyday argumentation.

The third development was the analysis of the critical discussion as a normative model for the pragmatic analysis of argumentative discourse by van Eemeren and Grootendorst (1984). This development in turn arose from the work of Searle (1969), which analyzed concepts of argumentative interaction as speech acts, and that of Grice (1975), who approached the analysis and evaluation of arguments as cooperative contributions to a conversation where the speakers follow maxims of politeness to contribute jointly to a common goal of discussion. Grice also put forward a concept of implicature which is used in the present monograph as a basis for the concept of conditional presumption, an important method-ological tool in the analysis of slippery slope argumentation.

By seeing the critical discussion as a rule-governed structure with clearly expressed goals and procedural rules, van Eemeren and Grootendorst took an important step towards making a systematic study of the informal fallacies possible. In this framework, fallacies can potentially be analyzed as types of violations of rules for reasoned discussion in argumentative discourse. This approach requires that the structural analysis of fallacies must have an interpretation component and an analysis component, as well as an evaluation component which rules whether the argument in question is correct or fallacious in a particular case. This approach makes it clear that interpreting the given text of discourse is a crucial and necessary part of making a determination of whether a particular argument can rightly be judged to be an instance of a fallacy like the slippery slope or not.

The fourth development was my own analysis of practical reasoning as a distinctive type of argumentation in Walton (1990). This development was necessary because it provided the general framework in which slippery slope argumentation can be seen as a legitimate, proper, and common species of goal-directed, knowledge-based, action-concluding reasoning in its own right. As such, it can be seen to have a legitimate function in a deliberative discussion between two parties where one party is considering a contemplated action and the other party is taking up contra-argumentation by warning of a possible risk or danger of the consequences that could ensue from this course of action.

The analysis of practical reasoning as a distinctive species of argumentation not only made possible the discovery of the cond-itions under which the slippery slope argument can be used reason-ably in some cases, but it also made possible the systematic study of the conditions which can enable us to critically question slippery slope arguments as weak, or even fallacious, in other cases.

At the same time, viewing slippery slope argumentation as a species of practical reasoning had important methodological implica-tions, because it suggested a realignment of the whole task of evaluating an argument as fallacious towards studying the uses of argumentation relative to the real circumstances of a particular case.

4. Summary of Main Theses

The purpose of this work is the evaluation of slippery slope arguments as correct or incorrect. This task is taken to be one that is practical, because the goal is to evaluate particular cases of slippery slope arguments as they are used in argumentation in natural language in discourse on disputed subjects. It follows that the task will also be taken to include elements of the interpretation and analysis of the given text of discourse in a particular case. However, the primary emphasis will be on evaluation of the argument as correct or incorrect. And in particular, it is important to test the presumption made by so many of the logic textbooks that the slippery slope argument is a fallacy, i.e. a species of incorrect argument.

It will be found throughout this work that the methods best suited to this task are pragmatic, meaning that they study how an argument is used. At the same time, the methods used are dialectical, in that they take into account the context of dialogue in which the argument is used. Hence, to use the current expression, the analysis will be pragma-dialectical in nature.

Through analysis and evaluation of the numerous cases of slippery slope argumentation, several main theses will crop up again and again. To aid the reader, it may be useful to state these main theses, below, gathering them together in a unified outline form in a single statement which lists the key properties of slippery slope arguments. Slippery slope arguments are characteristically:

(1) uses of practical reasoning;

(2) used in a context of dialogue, meaning that they are bilateral, involving a *proponent* and *respondent*;

(3) negative arguments from consequences;

(4) defeasible;

(5) of varying degrees of strength or weakness, but rarely outright fallacious;

(6) often effective in shifting the burden of proof.

These six theses are novel because they put the task of evaluating slippery slope arguments in a new and different perspective. Slippery slope arguments will be evaluated as successful or unsuccessful, correct or incorrect, in relation to the use to which they have been put in the given context of dialogue in a particular case of their use.

This type of context is typically a conflict of opinions between two or more parties on how to proceed with some contemplated or proposed course of action. For example, the conflict might be a political or ethical controversy concerning some policy which is being discussed. Typically, the one participant in the discussion is considering opting for this policy, or taking a step of action in the direction of it, while the other is counselling against the policy. In other words, the one participant in the dialogue is taking a *pro* point of view, the other a *contra* point of view.

Such a dialogue is about actions, and therefore the kind of reasoning involved is practical reasoning—it is a problem of how to proceed prudentially in a given set of circumstances where an agent must make a choice based on some explicit or implicit set of goals or priorities. The problem in such cases is one of possible future consequences that will or may flow from a given projected course of action. Thus the *contra* arguer in a slippery slope argument is saying to the other party, 'Don't do this, because if you do, it will lead to consequences which will have a bad outcome for you!' In the way it is used then, the slippery slope argument is a species of negative argument from consequences.

The future consequences of a contemplated action (especially in complex cases of moral and political issues) cannot be known in advance or predicted absolutely. Arguments about such consequences, therefore, have a speculative yet practical nature. In order to be correct or reasonable, they should not be seen as having to meet a perfect, deductive ideal of never admitting of counterexamples. Nor are they best conceived as inductive arguments that predict an outcome based on probability. These practical arguments involve a kind of presumptive reasoning that makes them best seen as relative to the specific circumstances in a given situation. Such arguments are always based on presumptions that are inherently defeasible, or open to reasonable rebuttal. In order to be successful, they have to be just strong enough to shift a burden of proof in a balanced dialogue. The target requirements for success of slippery slope argumentation should reflect this practical and dialectical nature.

A defeasible argument is tentative and provisional, because it is based on presumptions that may, in the future, turn out to be false. But even so, in the absence of definite knowledge to settle an issue, and given a practical need to go forward with some action or policy soon, defeasible argumentation may be the best basis for action a person can reasonably go ahead with in a particular situation. Defeasible argumentation can therefore be reasonable where it has taken the relevant presumptions into account in building a convincing case for concluding that the thesis on one side of a disputed issue is more convincing than the opposed thesis. The question may be one of how strongly convincing it needs to be to settle the issue as a basis for a provisional conclusion which is a reasonable guide for practical action. The key thing about slippery slope arguments is that the strength of commitment required to make such an argument reasonable should be judged by the context of dialogue rather than by some abstract and context-free standard of deductive or inductive correctness.

The textbooks have tended to treat the slippery slope argument as a fallacy, generally. Some textbooks portray it as a type of argument that is inherently fallacious, while others present it as a kind of argument that is, if not always a fallacy, one that may generally or most often be presumed to be fallacious. The fifth thesis of this work goes against the standard treatment of the slippery slope argument. Through the subsequent case studies in this work, it will be found that slippery slope arguments are most often strong or weak in particular respects, but they are rarely so bad that they deserve to be called fallacious.

This thesis is related to two others. First, once slippery slope arguments are accepted as being inherently defeasible in nature, there is less of a tendency to evaluate them by unrealistically high standards of correctness. Having adopted this perspective, there is less of a tendency to automatically classify a faulty or weak slippery slope argument as fallacious.

Second, there is the question of the meaning of the word 'fallacy.' If this word is taken to denote a serious charge in argumentation, it may be wise to resist the tendency to classify every argument that is open to criticism as 'fallacious.' The issue at stake here is a broad one for the study of fallacies generally. But the slippery slope argument is an especially interesting case in point.

The sixth main characteristic of slippery slope arguments is that they are often effective in shifting a burden of proof. This means that the standard of correctness of a slippery slope argument should be sought in its use in contributing to a dialogue exchange. Success is to be sought in establishing a stronger case than the opposed argumentation. An argument is correct, in such a context, if it meets strong enough requirements for a good argument to shift the burden of proof against the other side. Of course, such a shift is provisional on the response of the other side. So a successful argument of this sort is, by its nature, defeasible. Even so, the argument can be said to be correct (good, reasonable) to the extent that it successfully meets the right requirements of burden of proof for the type of dialogue it is supposed to be a part of.

5. The Pragmatic Perspective on Arguments

Whether the slippery slope argument ought to be classified as a fallacy, and how we ought to judge whether particular instances of this kind of argument are fallacious or not, are questions that depend very much on what is meant by the term 'fallacy,' as noted in Section 4 above.

In the modern era, a fallacy has come to be explained (Hamblin 1970, ch. 1) as an argument that seems valid but is not. The term 'seems' inappropriately suggests a psychological interpretation instead of a normative analysis of what is a fallacy. And the term 'valid' inappropriately suggests a semantic interpretation, oriented towards truth and falsity relationships in a designated set of propositions.

This semantically oriented concept of fallacy did not turn out to be very happy or successful in helping us to understand the fallacies and deal with them constructively and in a useful manner. The trend, until recently, was to seek formal, semantic models of valid argument that the 'fallacious' arguments failed to conform to. But this approach never got very far, because the existing formal systems of logic turned out to be of little or no practical use for this purpose, and even turning to non-standard or 'deviant' logics did not appear to take us far enough to be as useful as one might have liked (Woods and Walton: 1989).

The next step was to turn from semantic models of argument to pragmatic (Gricean) models of interactive argumentation governed by collaborative rules of politeness in speech-act conversational exchanges. This approach, so far, is appearing to prove much more fruitful. Van Eemeren and Grootendorst (1984) proposed the idea that fallacies should be thought of as violations of rules of a critical discussion. At the same time, Walton (1984) advocated the idea that fallacies could be studied as inappropriate or incorrect moves in dialectical models of dialogue where the goal of each participant is to persuade the other participant that a particular proposition, called the *thesis* of that participant, is true, according to the rules for that model of dialogue. This pragmatic and dialectical approach—now called the pragma-dialectical school of thought—has proved much more fruitful in producing more useful accounts of the various informal fallacies.

The pragma-dialectical method results in a different approach to evaluating slippery slope arguments from previous analyses in the literature. According to this viewpoint, an argument is seen as a dynamic exchange, a sequence of pairs of moves in a dialogue between two or more participants in an argumentative discussion. The particular argument given, a particular case, is evaluated by mapping a normative model of dialogue onto the given text and context of the particular case.

Many different kinds of normative model of argumentative discussion have been recognized in the literature (Walton 1984; van Eemeren and Grootendorst 1984), but several of these are particularly relevant to the study of slippery slope arguments. Each normative model has a set of procedural rules that define what should be permitted as a move in that type of discussion. Each type of dialogue has a goal, and the participants have tacitly or explicitly agreed to collaboratively support, or at least not to hinder, the goal of a discussion. An argument can be evaluated as good, reasonable, or correct insofar as it supports the goal of an exchange. An argument can be evaluated as fallacious, erroneous, or incorrect to the extent that it hinders or frustrates the goal of the discussion. After Grice (1975), such failures are deemed to be social failures, failures of politeness in helpfully contributing to a collaborative social activity.

One important type of dialogue is called the *persuasion dialogue* (Walton 1984) or the *critical discussion* (van Eemeren and Grootendorst 1984). In this type of dialogue, there are two participants. One participant has a thesis (conclusion), a particular proposition that he has the job of proving. The other participant can have two different kinds of role, depending on the kind of critical discussion it is, in a particular case. In one kind of critical discussion, the second participant has the job of casting doubt on the arguments of the other participant, by asking questions. In another kind of critical discussion, the second participant has the stronger obligation of himself positively proving a thesis which is the opposite of the first participant's thesis. The obligation, or burden of proof in the second type of dialogue, called a *dispute,* is stronger for the second participant than in the first case (Walton 1984; van Eemeren and Grootendorst 1984).

Usually the two participants in an argumentative discussion are called the *proponent* and the *respondent* where the former has the positive role of proving something, or where his role as initiator or supporter of an argument is to be emphasized. However, where an asymmetrical distinction of roles is not necessary or appropriate, they can simply be called *Black* and *White,* or otherwise designated by arbitrary names.

Negotiation dialogue is quite different from persuasion dialogue, because the goal is not to convince the other party that your opinion is true or plausible. Instead, the goal is to maximize one's share of some commodity that is subject to disputed ownership, and the method is one of bargaining by making offers and concessions. Negotiation dialogue is called *interest-based conflict* by Moore (1986: 74), and described as 'disputants collaborating to compete for the same set of goods or benefits.' Perelman and Olbrechts-Tyteca (1971: 282) have observed that the slippery slope argument is often used in negotiations between representatives of management and workers when one side does not want to yield to the other side.

A third type of dialogue is the *expert consultation,* where a layperson in a particular domain of knowledge seeks the advice of an expert on what he (the layperson) should do in a problematic situation. In this type of discussion, the goal is to move to a conclusion which recommends a particular course of action as the best prudential advice, based on the knowledge available, relevant to the particular situation of the layperson. This kind of discussion often has to do with causal reasoning, as the participants must try to forecast and evaluate the seriousness of the possible consequences of a particular line of action being considered. Good consequences support the argument for a proposed action. Bad consequences go against it. What counts as 'good' or 'bad' depends on the goals of the agent.

Slippery slope arguments sometimes arise in a context that leads to a secondary dialogue of expert consultation because it is difficult to predict the consequences of actions, and, especially in connection with controversial social policies, experts are often consulted as a source of advice.

Usually, however, the primary context of a slippery slope argument is *deliberation,* where an individual (or group) is trying to decide whether or not a particular, contemplated action is prudentially reasonable or not. Where slippery slope arises, such cases often involve controversial social policies on issues of human deliberation, like abortion or euthanasia, for example. The kind of reasoning in such cases is practical reasoning, which involves goal-directed evaluation of the practical thing to do in a particular situation.

Deliberation is the most common primary context of practical reasoning, and also the use of the slippery slope argument, which is a species of practical reasoning. But deliberation, especially in cases where controversial social policies are concerned, often takes place in a secondary context of critical discussion, which, in turn, can be connected to a third context of expert consultation.

After examining many cases, we will come to see, in this monograph, that the slippery slope argument is commonly used in critical discussion arising from deliberation to try to persuade someone not to do something he is contemplating. In many instances, as such, it is a reasonable argument, fulfilling a legitimate function in an argumentative dialogue.

6. Stages of Argumentative Dialogue

Any argumentative discussion has four stages (van Eemeren and Grootendorst 1984: 85–7). In the *opening stage,* participants agree to take part in a particular type of discussion. Any discussion can be identified with a *speech event,* the particular social or institutional framework in which the rules are codified. For example, if the argument is to take place as part of the trial proceedings in a criminal court, the particular rules of procedure for that type of speech event will be quite different (and also more strictly and explicitly codified, in certain respects) than an argument that is an everyday conversational discussion about politics or the weather.

At the *confrontation stage,* the goal of the dialogue is set, so that it is made clear what the problem, question, or difference of opinion is. All argumentative discussion is to resolve an initial conflict or difference (*stasis*), and the nature of this conflict is specified at the confrontation stage.

The *argumentation stage* is the part of the argument where there is a sequential exchange of views or moves by both parties, where each party tries to carry out his obligation in the discussion. Finally, the *closing stage* is the point where either the goal of the dialogue is fulfilled, or the participants agree to close the sequence of exchanges anyway.

The pragmatic approach is different from, but complementary to the semantic approach to the logic of arguments which stresses the truth or falsity of individual propositions in an argument. In the semantic approach, an argument is simply a designated (arbitrary) set of propositions. One is designated as the conclusion, others as premises, but no real weight is put on the idea that the conclusion is a *claim,* supported by the premises (or whatever the purpose of the argument is supposed to be). This is a pragmatic idea, relating to how the argument should, or is meant to be *used* in a context of reasoned discussion.

The slippery slope turns out (according to the analysis of it as a type of argumentation in Chapter 6) to be a kind of argument that can fulfill a proper function at the argumentation stage of a discussion. As such, it is a practical argument used to alter presumptions in a deliberative discussion to negatively question, or rebut, a contemplated course of action by one of the participants in the discussion. But it will also turn out to be the case that proper understanding of the slippery slope as a fallacy involves key references to other stages in such a discussion.

It will be shown, in Chapters 6 and 7, how the slippery slope argument arises naturally in a particular type of situation in the opening and confrontation stages of a discussion. Responding to the slippery slope argument effectively and critically, in a particular case, involves knowing and understanding this initial situation. The first phase of the slippery slope argument has often been called the 'wedge argument' or 'camel's nose in the tent argument,' because it involves the first step in a gradual sequence or continuum. Indeed, the slippery slope argument can be perspicuously seen as a kind of response to a real or potential situation where an opponent is pushing forward by small stages in a longer sequence to overwhelm you by gradual degrees.

We can get an initial glimpse of how this tactic works through an example. An article in *Newsweek* reporting on trends towards the harmonizing of taxes in a global economy discussed the value-added tax or VAT as a case in point (Frankel, Thomas, and Morrison 1989). According to the article, the VAT in Europe currently ranges between 12 percent in Spain to 25 percent in Ireland. Although some countries, like the United States, do not have a VAT, other countries outside Europe have recently brought in this tax, as noted in the quotation below.

Case 1.6

Countries outside Europe have also embraced VATs or consumption taxes. Japan recently established a 3 percent tax on purchases. Though it sounds negligible, the tax is a case of allowing the camel's nose into the tent: more will follow (Frankel, Thomas, and Morrison 1989: 47).

This argument can plausibly be interpreted as a slippery slope argument insofar as it proposes that once the 3 percent VAT is established, the government is very likely to raise it to higher levels. The suggestion is that once you let a small VAT in, it will then harmonize with the VAT rates of other countries by rising. To the extent that the argument is suggesting that a high VAT is a bad thing, or something you should avoid if you can, it is a slippery slope type of argument, warning you about that first step of 'letting the camel's nose into the tent.'

What is especially interesting about this case it that it suggests the possibility of a kind of gradualistic tactic on the part of governments. First they get a lower-rate VAT in, a small rate like 3 percent, that voters may not object to very strongly. Then once this rate has been established, and the tax becomes a reality and controversy over bringing it in has died down, you can raise it by small degrees. Each small raise, by itself, may (hopefully for the proponents of the VAT) not appear too objectionable to be 'pushed in.'

Where such a gradualistic possibility exists in a situation at the opening or confrontation stages of a discussion, this is exactly the basis out of which the slippery slope arises as a useful and effective argument to overcome your opposition by degrees. To understand practically how to criticize or rebut the slippery slope argument— or so it will be shown in Chapter 7—you need to understand this kind of initial basis, how it arises, when it arises, and how to counter it.

The closing stage of discussion also turns out to be important as part of the analysis of the slippery slope fallacy put forward in this monograph. The slippery slope argument, when it is used reasonably in a dialogue to shift presumption to the other side, normally has an open quality as a species of argumentation. Even where it shifts a weight of presumption successfully, it leaves openings for rebuttal.[2] Yet in some cases, the argument is advanced too aggressively in a tactic of trying to close off these possibilities of refutation in advance. The tactic here is one of premature, improper closure. Evidence of the use of this tactic will turn out to be a key indicator of the existence of a slippery slope fallacy.

The present monograph not only adopts a pragma-dialectical approach to the study of the slippery slope fallacy but carries it one step further. The slippery slope fallacy is analyzed not only as a violation of a rule of reasonable dialogue, but as a characteristic type of argumentation tactic that is used to subvert or hinder the dialogue by conveying the idea that further discussion would be pointless.

According to the new view advocated here then, a fallacy is to be understood as a particular type of argumentation tactic which can in some cases be used correctly to fulfill or advance legitimate goals of reasonable discussion, but is used in a particular case at issue as a systematic type of argumentation tactic to try to subvert the goal of the discussion and unfairly get the best of the other party.

---

[2] See the account of defeasibility in Sect, 8 below.

This new conception of fallacy captures some of the traditional idea of fallacy, but is in many respects a deviation from current preconceptions and a return to the Aristotelian conception of fallacies as sophistical refutations or unfairly combative tricks used in reasoned dialectical argument between two parties, a proponent and a respondent or opponent.

7. Fallacies as Sophistical Refutations

The pragmatic point of view sees argumentation as a linked sequence of subarguments that moves in a certain direction, ideally towards the realization of a goal of dialogue. Because of its emphasis on argumentation as an orderly exchange of interactive moves between two (or more) participants in a sequence, this perspective is *dialectical,* in the ancient Greek sense of this word.

The dialectical method originated with the Sophists, who advocated the technique of question and answer as a way of resolving conflicts of opinion on disputed issues of the time (Kerferd 1981: 32). This technique developed into the technique used by Socrates in the early dialogues called the *elenchus.* Robinson (1953: 7) described the *elenchus* as the method of 'examining a person with regard to statements he has made, by putting to him questions he has made, calling for further statements, in the hope that they will determine the meaning and truth-value of his first statement.' Characteristically, Socrates started with a big question, like 'What is justice?' and then moved to a series of smaller and smaller questions, until the respondent found himself embarrassingly trapped into having conceded some contradiction or absurdity. Consequently, Robinson (1953: 7) also recognized a secondary meaning of *elenchus* which means refutation, or cross-examination that ends in refutation. In this sense, the dialectical method, as developed and used by Socrates, character-istically involved a two-person sequential argumentative exchange that is similar to the technique of *reductio ad absurdum,* where one party starts from a second party's initial assumption, and reasons through a sequence of inferential steps to some 'absurdity,' a proposition that is clearly unacceptable to both parties, or to any reasonable person.

This procedure sounds as if it could be negative and destructive, but Socrates emphasized his maieutic function of assisting in giving birth to new insights and ideas in this kind of discussion. The respondent himself actually produces the idea, however, because it was formerly implicit within his thinking in a cloudy or inchoate form, and the Socratic discussion merely helped him bring it out of himself by articulating and sharpening it, and the reasoning behind it, through the course of the discussion. The real goal of this kind of dialogue then is not to defeat the other party in verbal combat, but to help sharpen or clarify the other person's own deeply held, but initially obscure position on a controversial issue.

Plato portrayed dialectical reasoning as the method to seek knowledge of what is true and unchanging, and disparaged any kind of opinion-based reasoning as characteristic of the Sophists, a group he despised (ostensibly because they accepted fees for their lectures and teaching services). Aristotle distinguished between *demonstration,* or scientific reasoning based on premises known to be true, and *dialectical reasoning,* or question–reply discussion based on premises that are generally accepted opinions (either popularly accepted opinions or expert opinions of 'the wise'). In dialectical reasoning, a proposition is refuted if it leads to absurd or self-contradictory consequences. Aristotle worked out rules for dialectical reasoning, and offered practical advice on the best techniques to use, in his three major works on argumentation, the *Topics, Rhetoric,* and the *De Sophisticis Elenchis (On Sophistical Refutations).*

One of Aristotle's most important contributions to this field, especially in the third work, was to describe certain characteristic types of errors or fallacies in dialectical reasoning which he called 'sophistical refutations.' For Aristotle refutation was a kind of argumentation that is an interactive sequence of questions and replies in a rule-governed dialogue structure where two parties reason together for some purpose. A sophistical refutation for Aristotle was an effective kind of argumentation technique, trick, or tactic used to unfairly defeat your opponent by violating a rule of the dialogue.

Linguistic difficulties have compounded the current confusions about the meaning of 'fallacy.' Greek had no precise synonym for this word (Hamblin 1970: 50), and it is often translated as 'sophism' or 'paralogism'. The Latin word *fallacia,* meaning 'deceit, trick, artifice, stratagem, craft, or intrigue' according to

Lewis and Short (1969: 721) is descended from the Greek word *sphal,* meaning 'cause to fall,' either in sports (e.g. Homer uses it to refer to wrestling) or by verbal tactics of argumentation.[3] On the other hand, the word 'sophism' is often taken to mean something quite different. In the Middle Ages, particularly, sophismata were paradoxes or logical puzzles, often involving inconsistency, or logical absurdities, like the heap argument. Yet throughout the evolution of the standard treatment of this field in the logic textbooks and treatises, right up to the present, 'the fallacies' have come to be identified (somewhat superficially) with Aristotle's original list of fifteen or so types of sophistical refutation. As Hamblin (1970) showed, the fallacies evolved historically from Greek times into the current logic texts through additions to and deletions from Aristotle's list through the centuries. However, the pragmatic Greek roots of the concept of fallacy as a sophistical refutation in a question–reply dialogue structure of orderly disputation faded into obscurity, especially as modern logic came to be dominated by a semantic conception of argument.

Now with the advent of pragmatic methods of analysis that have very recently begun to come to prominence, a reevaluation of the concept of fallacy can take place that can make the idea have some sense as a component of an informal logic. According to this pragmatic conception, a fallacy can only be properly understood as a technique of argumentation, and evaluated as a violation of normative rules of reasoned argumentation, in relation to a community of argument users who have come together to engage in a conventional, institutional, or rule-governed structure of interactive dialogue.

But even beyond this, we need a new approach to the concept of fallacy that goes back to the Greek roots of the idea of sophistical refutation, and back to the etymological origins of the word 'fallacy,' meaning a verbal tactic or deceptive trick that can be used to cause someone to 'fall down' in argument. Not only is a fallacy a violation of a rule of reasonable dialogue, but beyond that, it is a special kind of deceptive tactic or technique that can be used to unfairly defeat an opponent in reasonable dialogue by exploiting a rule or rules of the dialogue.

---

[3] The author is indebted to Paul van der Laan for this account of the etymology of 'fallacy.'

The prospect of this new approach means that the standard treatments of the logic textbooks cannot be taken for granted as the best word on how to analyze or evaluate fallacies. To study fallacies, we should look at how the arguments that supposedly contain them are actually used as skilled (or fumbling) techniques to carry out goals of dialogue in a particular context of discussion. This undertaking requires a case study approach that views each individual case as part of an extended sequence of interactive argumentation in a context of discussion.

Of course, concentration on particular cases can make the classification of fallacies less clear-cut, and more needing to be mindful of the individual circumstances of a given case. DeMorgan (1847: 276) argued that it is impossible to classify fallacies, because there is 'no such thing as a classification of the ways in which men may arrive at an error' (quoted by Hamblin 1970: 13). A good point is made here—it is not possible to classify exhaustively all the possible ways of exploiting a rule of dialogue, because there are no limits to ingenuity in this regard.

Fallacies are often hard to track down, classify, and categorize into simple types of errors of argumentation because each fallacy can occur in an unlimited number of ways. The reason is that a fallacy is a misuse of a basically reasonable kind of argumentation in a particular case. A fallacy is more than a violation of a rule of reasonable dialogue. It is a clever way of exploiting a rule of collaborative discussion in order to get the best of a trusting co-participant who presumes that all other participants are following the expectations of the discussion. But this can be done in many ways, for there is no limit to the number of ways in which a rule of discussion can be exploited.

Levinson (1983) made a comparable point by citing an important general reason why the communicative power of language can never be reduced to a set of conventions for the use of language.

The reason is that wherever some convention or expectation about the use of language arises, there will also therewith arise the possibility of the non-conventional *exploitation* of that convention or expectation. It follows that a purely conventional or rule-based account of natural language usage can never be complete, and that what can be communicated always exceeds the communicative power provided by the conventions of the language and its use (p. 112).

It follows from this general principle about language use that the study of the tactics of how a type of argument is used in a particular case will always be an important part of the study of fallacies. For fallacies are not just violations of rules of reasonable discussion. They are also clever tactics for the exploitation of conventions and expectations in reasonable discussions.

8. The Tip of the Iceberg Theory

The current ways of identifying and classifying fallacies need to be rethought. Currently, when identifying a fallacy, the textbooks describe extreme, but highly visible, even spectacular instances of arguments that have gone so badly wrong that they appear ridiculous. These are the top one-tenth of the iceberg. But the problem is that the same kind of basic argument as the type classified as fallacious can also be used in many more typical cases of argumentation (the bottom nine-tenths of the iceberg) in a way that is not so bad that we could honestly be justified in calling it fallacious. In this bottom range of cases, some of the arguments are reasonable (correct). But many more of them are weak—open to critical questioning—but not 'fallacious.'

Using a new approach we need to rethink the concept of fallacy, redefining a fallacy as a basically reasonable type of argument which has been used in a bad or corrupted way in a given instance, so that it only appears to be good rather than having the reality of being a good argument. In other words, every good kind of argument, which can be used reasonably to further legitimate goals of dialogue, also has potential for misuse. A fallacy then may be characterized as a good type of argument which has been used wrongly in a particular instance. But some wrong uses of arguments are blunders or non-serious errors of one kind or another—violations of rules of reasonable dialogue that are not so bad that they deserve to be called fallacies. A fallacy is a very serious misuse where there is a systematic underlying abuse of this particular type of argument by twisting around its proper function altogether to use it as a tactic to subvert or even close off the dialogue in an improper way. The fallacious uses are the sometimes highly visible, but (normally) relatively unusual tip of the iceberg.

Through the analysis of many case studies of slippery slope argumentation, it will be argued in this monograph that slippery slope arguments are sometimes correct (reasonable, good, strong) arguments, and in other cases are incorrect (erroneous, weak, bad) arguments. It will also be argued that a weak slippery slope argument—one open to legitimate critical questioning—need not necessarily be a fallacious slippery slope argument. The pragmatic method of the analysis will identify characteristic argumentation schemes (see van Eemeren and Kruiger 1987), which represent correct uses of the slippery slope argument in a context of discussion, and critical questions matching each of these argumentation schemes.

The slippery slope is shown to be a *defeasible* argument, meaning (Levinson 1983: 13) that it is subject to cancellation by features of the context. As Levinson (p. 13) puts it, such features 'interact with or arise from assumptions made by participants in the context . . .' In Chapters 6 and 7, an analysis of the slippery slope argument is presented which shows how this kind of argumentation arises within a framework of initial presumptions in a particular case, and is used by one participant in a dialogue to shift a weight of presumption against the side of an opposed participant. The argument is defeasible when used in this way because even if it is successful in shifting the weight of presumption required to make its point, it can still be open to legitimate rebuttals by the respondent it has been used against.

The defeasibility of the slippery slope argument has important implications for the general project of devising guidelines to aid in determining when instances of this argument should be judged to be fallacious or incorrect.

One important thing about this new approach is that it postulates a difference between a fallacious argument and an argument that is judged incorrect because it is weak or inadequately supported. To say an argument is fallacious is a particularly strong type of criticism, claiming that the argument is systematically flawed, and can therefore be refuted as a particularly tricky, inappropriate, and unfair argument to use in that context of discussion. Thus there are many weak and incorrect arguments that are mere blunders and self-destructive moves in argumentative discussions that may be arguments that 'seem valid, but are not' but are not properly classified as fallacious.

The slippery slope argument, in its more extreme, i.e. fallacious forms, is used as a tactic to try to suggest that you will be locked in to a sequence of consequences with no turning back, once you have made an initial step. The suggestion is that once you have made the initial step, you are irrevocably committed. An analogy would be to a person who has inadvertently locked his keys into his car. Once the unfortunate step of locking the door was taken, there was no turning back. The commitment, once made, was not easy to reverse.

But most arguments, as Gilbert (1979: 100) put it, are more like staircases than slippery slopes—at each step we can decide whether we want to go further down or not. The case studies of this monograph will reveal the dialectical nature of slippery slope arguments by showing that they always have two sides. They will often turn out to be weak arguments that could be defended, even though they have specific critical defects, rather than fallacious arguments. In most cases, even though legitimate critical questions could be asked, the slippery slope argument is not so badly wrong that it deserves to be categorized as fallacious.

9. The Language of Fallacies

As noted above, it has become traditionally accepted practice to write in the textbooks of the slippery slope fallacy in a way that implies that the slippery slope argument is either always fallacious, or can generally be presumed to be fallacious. This established usage immediately creates a linguistic difficulty, given the thesis of this book that slippery slope arguments are sometimes fallacious, but usually not. It may seem to the reader that the argument of this book is the contradictory assertion that the slippery slope fallacy is not really fallacious.

The traditional tendency to presume that the slippery slope argument is always fallacious may even have some linguistic causes. It could well be that speakers of English have a tendency to classify the slippery slope argument as a fallacy because the adjective 'slippery' carries strongly pejorative connotations in the context of argumentation. A 'slippery' arguer is a kind of quarrelsome or sophistical arguer who 'weasels' out of his commitments and cannot be fairly 'pinned down' in a dialogue. By analogy, it may seem that a slippery argument, piece of reasoning, or text of discourse is one that, by its very nature, must contain fallacious and deceptive subarguments woven into it.

Given these connotations of the word 'slippery,' thesis (5) of this book (see Section 4, above), that some slippery slope arguments are reasonable and fallacy-free arguments, has to be stated carefully. If you think of a slippery argument as a fallacious argument, then for you thesis (5) could be reformulated as the following thesis.

(5R) Some slippery slope arguments are slippery arguments, but it is by no means the case that all slippery slope arguments are slippery arguments.

The subtlety of (5R) rightly suggests that thesis (5) is meant, at least to some significant degree, as a novel proposal which requires linguistic reforms in the traditional categories of logic. Thesis (5) is not meant to imply that a fallacy is, in some cases, not fallacious. It is meant to imply that the slippery slope argument is sometimes, but not always a fallacy.

The case studies worked out in this book indicate that some reform is needed, and that a new approach to the slippery slope fallacy is required. But there are a number of alternative positions that could be taken with respect to the status of slippery slope arguments as fallacies. Slippery slope arguments could be said to be (*a*) never fallacies, (*b*) sometimes fallacies, or (*c*) always fallacies. The traditional logic often seems to suggest (*c*), or at least to imply that generally, slippery slope arguments can be presumed to be fallacious, in the absence of evidence to the contrary. This is an approach we will reject, even though the classification of slippery slope as a type of fallacy will not wholly be rejected.

Alternative (*a*) is not inherently implausible. Indeed, given the finding of so many non-fallacious cases of slippery slope argumentation in this work, (*a*) does turn out to be an option that has some plausibility. Option (*a*) could be supported by citing the finding that most bad slippery slope arguments are just weakly supported arguments. These arguments are not worthless, or beyond redemption, and do not deserve to be categorized as fallacious.

On the other hand, it will emerge from the case studies of this book that some instances of the slippery slope argument are so bad, so deeply flawed that they could rightly be called fallacious. But it could be argued that in cases of this sort, the defect is a kind of fault that is not unique to slippery slope arguments. For example, the fault might be an inadequately supported premise. But lots of arguments suffer from this fault, yet are not slippery slope arguments. Approach (*a*) is borne out, on the grounds that there is no single fallacy that is peculiar to slippery slope argumentation.

This approach is based on a good point. Slippery slope arguments, when they do go wrong, can exhibit a variety of different faults. Even so, (*a*) will not be accepted as the best point of view. It will be argued instead that, in some cases, the slippery slope argument has been used in such a way that it exhibits an underlying serious flaw in its execution, such a serious and bad abuse that we can say that it has been deployed as a sophistical tactic of argumentation, and can rightly be evaluated as a slippery slope fallacy. Approach (*b*) then is partially in agreement with the traditional classification of slippery slope as a fallacy, even if it does not go the whole way of (*a*).

But how can a slippery slope argument be a fallacy if there is no specific or unique fault in every such argument that makes it a slippery slope fallacy? The answer lies in how the slippery slope argument was used as an argumentation tactic in a given context of dialogue, according to the evidence of the text of discourse. The argument is fallacious only if used in such a way that it goes contrary to the goals of dialogue the arguers are supposed to be engaged in. And the slippery slope argument has its own distinctive and characteristic ways of being used to obstruct the legitimate procedures of reasoned dialogue. It will be seen how there are four different types of slippery slope arguments. But they share common features of use as a method of attempting to convince someone not to undertake a proposed course of action being critically discussed.

10. A New Theory of Fallacy

Quite clearly, the slippery slope fallacy is only one fallacy among many that have been traditionally recognized—(see Hamblin

1970, ch. 1, where the standard list of traditional fallacies is outlined). Any analysis of this one fallacy will be conditional upon a general theory of fallacy, to some extent. This is not the place to promulgate or defend such a general theory,[4] but some brief remarks on fallacy theory will be helpful to provide perspectives.

In Section 7, it was seen how the Aristotelian concept of fallacy as sophistical refutation portrayed a fallacy as an intentional tactic of deceptive argumentation used as a trick by one participant in a dialogue to unfairly get the best of another participant in the verbal exchange. The concept of fallacy here explicitly contained the idea of intentional deception by an arguer.

The modern idea of fallacy which has become dominant in the recent logic textbooks has tried to remove this idea of intentional deceit completely, recasting a fallacy as an invalid inference—a kind of formalistic flaw in an inference from premises to conclusion. In this modern conception, the Greek dialectical notion of an argument as an interaction between dialogue partners has been expunged. The only trace of it remaining is the psychological appendage that a fallacy is an argument that *seems* valid.

This historical evolution of the notion of fallacy poses a dilemma for the fallacy theorist—which is better, the Greek idea of fallacy as deceptive tactic or the modern idea of fallacy as invalid inference?

Although, in English, the word 'fallacy' covers both ideas, in some languages there are two different words for each meaning. German is such a language.

According to *Duden* (1981: 2637), *Trugschlusz* is used in logic to refer to the use of deceit (*Täuschung*) or trickery (*Überlistung*) by one partner in dialogue (*Gesprächpartner*) to make the other draw the wrong conclusion. The aspect of intentional deceit involved in a *Trugschlusz* is made explicit in the *Brockhaus* entry (1974: 49), where the word intentional (*absichtlich*) deceit is used. According to this entry a *Trugschlusz* is a type of wrong inference (*Fehlschlusz*) where the wrong conclusion is made to be drawn by one partner in dialogue, through the use of trickery or deceit. According to *Harrap's Standard German and English Dictionary* (Jones 1967: 25), a *Fehlschlusz* is an incorrect, wrong conclusion

---

[4] The author has formulated such a theory in a forthcoming book, tentatively entitled *Argumentation Tactics*.

or a 'wrong inference.' In logic, this term means fallacy or paralogism, but outside logic, it means 'unsuccessful shot' or 'bad shot' (p. 25). According to a native speaker of German the author consulted (Sigwart Lindenberg), this word naturally refers to failures of correct argument or inference where no intentional deception of one party by another is (necessarily) involved.

It is possible to accommodate this linguistic dualism by recognizing two types of fallacy. The sophistical tactic type of fallacy involves a context of dialogue where a proponent is abusing some particular type of argumentation tactic to get the best of the other unfairly while only appearing to conform to the rules of the dialogue. The error of reasoning type of fallacy involves a faulty inference of some kind from premises to a conclusion. The second type of fallacy is a kind of failure within a set of propositions to meet some standard of correct inference. No essential reference to a dialogue, proponent, or respondent is required to evaluate this type of fallacy.

This binary classification could be a nice basis for categorizing the traditional fallacies. *Ad hominem* and *ad verecundiam*, for example, would seem to come out better if analyzed as sophistical tactics types of fallacy. Whereas fallacies like affirming the consequent, biased statistics, *post hoc,* and other formal or inductive kinds of error, could perhaps fit nicely into the errors of reasoning category.

Before discussing this program for the classification of fallacies any further, however, it should be realized that, as the distinction stands, it is highly problematic. Hamblin (1970: 264) warned against psychologism in the study of the fallacies, emphasizing that a participant's commitment to a proposition as expressed in dialogue should not be identified with that participant's belief that the proposition is true. According to Hamblin, we do not necessarily believe everything we say, but one's saying something (in the proper context of dialogue) should commit him to it subsequently, whether he is known to believe it or not. What should be important in deciding whether a speaker's argument is fallacious is not the psychology of the speaker's actual beliefs. Instead, the evidence for or against such a charge should be sought in reconstructing what the speaker said, according to the evidence of the text of discourse of the dialogue, and the normative rules for the type of dialogue that the speaker was supposed to be engaged in.

Van Eemeren and Grootendorst (1984: 6) also warned against psychologism in the study of fallacies, arguing that it is important to guard against the 'internalization of the subject' of critical argumentation. They propose the avoidance of such 'psychologizing' in critical evaluation of allegedly fallacious argumentation by concentrating on the *expressed* opinions of an arguer. Van Eemeren and Grootendorst (p. 6) suggest that a critic should focus on the statements made by an arguer in the course of a discussion, instead of focusing on the 'thoughts, ideas and motives which may underlie them.' According to this wise advice, it should not be required, in order to prove that somebody's argument is fallacious, to show that this person had an actual intent to deceive his opponent (or anyone else) when he framed his argument. Nor should it be required that the argument seemed valid to the person it was intended to convince, or to anyone else. To build such mentalistic requirements into the concept of fallacy would be a bad form of psychologism. It would make the task of nailing down a charge of fallacy focus inappropriately on internal motives of an arguer, instead of focusing properly on the external evidence of the text of discourse in a dialogue. A psychologistic theory would be a wrong turn as a program for the analysis of fallacies.

From this perspective, the distinction between a *Trugschlusz* and a *Fehlschlusz* type of fallacy is problematic, as it stands, posing a dilemma for the fallacy theorist. For the *Trugschlusz* notion clearly requires the intent to deceive by argument, making it psychologistic. It captures the Aristotelian notion of the deliberate sophism—the intentional perpetration of a deceitful trick or fraudulent move in argumentation by a perpetrator on a victim. On the other hand, the *Fehlschlusz* notion is too weak, by itself, to do justice to those fallacies requiring a dialectical context, to be properly understood or evaluated. Moreover, it doesn't do justice to the fact that not every invalid argument is fallacious. Some are just faulty or weak arguments. But if you add the notion of seeming validity to strengthen it, then it too appears to have become unfavorably psychologistic.

The solution is to carefully redefine the two basic types of fallacy so that both are pragma-dialectical rather than psychologistic concepts. The sophistical tactics type of fallacy should be defined as the misuse of a particular type of argumentation tactic in such a way that the technique of argumentation actually used, according to the textual evidence, goes against the proper goals of the type of dialogue the participants are supposed to be engaged in. This is a dialectical conception of fallacy, requiring a background context of dialogue for the argument to be fallacious. It is also a pragmatic conception which defines a fallacy as the use of a tactic in argumentation. Such tactics can be used well or badly, constructively or obstructively in a dialogue.

How does the element of deception come in here? Argumentation tactics can be used correctly to fulfill legitimate goals of dialogue. But the very same type of tactic can also be used incorrectly, or abused in various ways. In such a case, because of its similarity to a correct use in the context of dialogue, such an argumentation move could appear quite persuasive and legitimate to the uncritical audience or respondent. Such arguments do not fool everybody, nor are they always intentionally meant to deceive anyone. But because they have some characteristics of correct use (which makes them very convincing, as arguments), they tend to be quite tricky, deceptive, and powerfully effective for persuasion.

The error of reasoning type of fallacy is a matter of propositions following from other propositions or not by some standard of correct inference. It could be a deductive standard, an inductive standard, or, for example, a standard of practical reasoning (see Walton 1990). To determine whether an error of reasoning has been made, no essential reference to the context of dialogue is needed, once it has been determined which standard is appropriate. But how can you determine whether the error of reasoning is a fallacy, as opposed to simply being a faulty or weak argument?

The answer is that the concept of seeming correctness should be brought in, not in a psychological, but in a pragma-dialectical way. It is not required that a fallacious argument of this type should seem valid to the actual respondent to whom it was directed. But to be a fallacy, it must be close enough in the way it was presented, in the text of the argumentation, to a kind of argument that would be correct in meeting the appropriate standard of correct reasoning. So reconstrued, seeming correctness is no longer a psychological concept, but a matter of resemblance in use to some correct type of inference.

Whether this new pragma-dialectical approach to the study of fallacies is a good theory that will lead to useful methods of analysis and evaluation of argumentation remains to be seen. The point at issue in the present work is the project of studying the slippery slope fallacy. The case that will be made here is that the slippery slope fallacy is best analyzed, and evaluated in particular cases, as a sophistical tactics type of fallacy. A strong indication that this line of approach will be taken is already evident in thesis (2) in the list of theses in Section 4 above (and thesis (6) as well).

In this work, it will be argued that the slippery slope fallacy has elements of the error of reasoning type of fallacy in its core structure. One can appreciate this connection already by recalling thesis (1) from Section 4 above, the thesis that slippery slope arguments are uses of practical reasoning. Practical reasoning, as will be shown in Chapter 3.4 has a structure of characteristic premises and a conclusion. As such, errors of practical reasoning can occur when the requirements of this structure are not in a given case.

However, it will emerge very clearly, again and again, in the subsequent chapters on the various types of slippery slope arguments, that a fully adequate account of the slippery slope fallacy requires close attention to many key aspects of how this type of argument has been used in a given context of dialogue. In short, an additional major thesis is that the slippery slope fallacy is a prime example of the sophistical tactics type of fallacy. To fully understand how the slippery slope argument is used as a fallacy, it is necessary to analyze it as a sophistical tactic used in a context of dialogue.

2

The Sorites Slippery Slope Argument

MANY logic textbooks do not mention the slippery slope argument at all. Of those that do, the majority cite the causal type of slippery slope argument and classify it a fallacy (or a tricky argument that can be fallacious). These texts identify the slippery slope fallacy with the causal type of slippery slope argument.

A few texts treat the slippery slope fallacy as an argument essentially having to do with the use of vague terms in reasoning, and these texts generally bring in the ancient sorites or bald man argument as related to the problem. Two texts in particular, Scriven (1976) and Fogelin (1987), have taken some useful steps in indicating how the paradox of the sorites argument is related to the practical problem of dealing with slippery slope fallacies in contexts where reasoning with a key vague term is evidently the source of the problem.

However, the link between these two things has never been made clear. It is clear that slippery slope arguments are often aided and made possible through the use of vague terms or concepts in argumentation. But exactly how this works has not been made clear. Despite the tendency of the textbooks to treat slippery slope arguments as fallacious, it has become evident that this is probably not correct, and that some arguments of this type can be reasonable, given the right context of discussion.

In this chapter, beginning with some historical origins of the sorites paradox, we will look at a series of case studies indicating that some slippery slope arguments of this type are better than others. Our aim, in the end, will be to provide general guidelines for judging the good, the bad, and the fallacious.

1. Ancient Origins: The Heap and the Bald Man

Eubulides, a student of one Euclides, an older contemporary of Plato, is said to have been the inventor of many paradoxes. One of these sophisms was called the *heap* (sorites). If you take one grain away from a heap, it makes no significant difference—you still have a heap. Each time you repeat this step, it makes no difference, because one grain is too small to make a difference between something being a heap or not. But repeated long enough, the conclusion of this reasoning will become absurd, for it will become obvious that what is left can no longer be described as a heap.

According to Diogenes Laertius (ii. 108), Eubulides originally expressed the argument in this form.

Case 2.1

Isn't it true that two are few? and also three, and also four, and so on until ten? Two however are few. So also ten are few. (quoted by Black 1970: 2)

Another, more explicit way of expressing the sophism was called the *bald man (falakros)*. According to Kneale and Kneale (1962: 114), this argument can be conveyed by the following dialogue-sequence.[1]

Case 2.2

Would you say that a man was bald if he had only one hair?
Yes.
Would you say that a man was bald if he had only two hairs?
Yes.
Would you . . . , etc.
Then where do you draw the line?

That the argument was naturally expressed by the Greeks in the manner of a two-party question–reply dialogue is significant. It suggests that not only is the puzzle a sophism in the sense that it appears to be a case of valid reasoning from true or apparently acceptable premises to an absurd or false conclusion. It is also a sophism in the sense that it can be used as a kind of tactic for attacking someone who is having difficulty drawing the line, or making a clear-cut line of demarcation between two things.

Cicero saw the potential of this sophism in applying to all kinds of arguments in everyday discourse.

---

[1] The Kneales (1962: 114 n. 4) cited three sources for the version of the bald man argument quoted in case 2.2: Diogenes Laertius, vii. 82; Cicero, *Academica*, ii. 49; Horace, *Epistulae*, II. i. 45.

No faculty of knowing absolute limits has been bestowed upon us by the nature of things to enable us to fix exactly how far to go in any matter; and this is so not only in the case of a heap of wheat from which the name is derived, but in no matter whatsoever—if we are asked by gradual stages, is such and such a person a rich man or a poor man, famous or undistinguished, are yonder objects many or few, great or small, long or short, broad or narrow, we do not know at what point in the addition or subtraction to give a definite answer. (Cicero 1951, quoted by Black 1970: 1–2).

The scope and implications of Eubulides' paradox are brought out clearly by Cicero's remarks. Since there is no way of knowing absolute limits on any matter in any discussion, a series of questions asked in gradual stages can be used to press ahead. When confronted with this kind of interrogation, we simply do not know at what point to give a definite answer. Cicero notices that not only is this kind of argument tactic difficult, or perhaps even impossible to defend against, but it is applicable on any subjects where there are no absolute limits to the demarcation of a concept —virtually everywhere.

2. The Sorites Paradox

The parameters of the sorites paradox as a logical problem can be brought out more perspicuously if we consider the following form of it. The sorites argument has two initial premises, a base premise, B_0, and an inductive premise, I. The case below represents the first step of a typical sorites argument.[2]

Case 2.3

(B_0) Every person who is 4 feet in height is short.

(I) If you add one-tenth of an inch to a short person's height, that person is short.

(B_1) Every person who is 4 feet and one-tenth of an inch in height is short.

---

[2] The example of the sorites argument presented here is similar to that given by Black (1970: 3). However, in Black's version there is an additional premise, 'Every man who is shorter than some short man is short.'

The conclusion of this argument, (B_1), follows from the two premises (B_0) and (I) by *modus ponens*. Hence the argument is deductively valid.

But the argument in case 2.3 above is just the first stage of the sorites argumentation. At the second stage, the inductive premise (I) can be applied once again, this time to the conclusion (B_1), which now functions as a premise for a new conclusion.

(B_2) Every person who is 4 feet and two-tenths of an inch in height is short.

Moreover, (B_2) can now be used as a new premise to which (I) can be reapplied to yield a new conclusion (B_3), and so forth, until eventually the argumentation will reach its final conclusion,

(B_n) Every person is short.

Now each single step in this chain of argumentation is an instance of *modus ponens*. It seems then by transitivity of deductive implication, the whole sequence of argumentation must be deductively valid reasoning.

But this appears to be paradoxical or sophistical. For although the original premises (B_0) and (I) appear to be true, the ultimate conclusion (B_n) certainly appears to be false. What has perhaps most often appeared paradoxical to logicians is the apparent need to deny the law of excluded middle—in this case, the proposition, 'Every person is either short or not short'—in order to reject the sorites argument. Odegard (1965) rejected the law of excluded middle on the grounds that the sorites argument is an exception to it.

Black (1970) concluded that while it is all right to reason with vague (loose) concepts, we can get into trouble doing this in borderline cases, where the logical rules cease to apply. King (1979) also located the problem in the inductive premise (like Black), and devised a kind of fuzzy logic for vague concepts which sets varying 'accuracy values' for the inductive premise at each step. The solutions of Campbell (1974) and Weiss (1976) have also concentrated on applying restrictions to the inductive premise.

As is the case with all sophismata, there are only three ways of dealing with, or trying to resolve the paradox. You can deny that the premises are true, deny that the argument is valid, or deny that the conclusion is false. In the case of the sorites argument, the conclusion appears to be clearly and incontrovertibly false. The argument is a chain of *modus ponens* inferences, which makes it hard to see how it could be denied that it is valid. This leaves the route of denying the truth of the premises as the most plausible opening of attack. Sainsbury (1988: 31) supports this observation by writing: 'An initial reason for rejecting the premises is simply the unattractiveness of the other possible responses.' One of the best-known approaches that takes this route is Fine (1975), who argued that not all of the premises should be regarded as true in the penumbral area of the sorites argument.

Sainsbury (1988)—who incidentally has presented a nice summary of the literature of proposed solutions to the sorites paradox—denies the premises by arguing that the tolerance principle fails in the penumbral area of the argument. The *penumbra* (p. 31) is the range of cases where an object either possesses a property or does not. The *tolerance principle* is the tendency to think if an object has a property, then a closely similar object should also be judged to have the same property. In our analysis of the paradox, we will use *grey area* as a synonym for penumbra, and use the term *consistency* (between cases) as an expression of the relation or judgment of the tolerance principle (see Section 5 below).

3. The Practical Problem of the Use of the Sorites Argument

The sorites argument is a fascinating logical paradox, but it may be hard to see (despite the indications given in Cicero's remarks quoted in Section 1) just how it is involved in real-life slippery slope argumentation that can be used to persuade people deceptively or insidiously to accept substantive conclusions on serious issues. Scriven (1976: 118) has presented an excellent example that brings out this connection very perspicuously.

Case 2.4

. . . you may be persuaded that torture is justified in the interrogation of suspected criminals or prisoners of war by somebody who points out that the line between physical and mental torture is not a sharp one, and that we obviously believe that imprisonment and interrogation are in some circumstances justified, so that we really are drawing an arbitrary line when we say that physical torture is not to be allowed; in addition to being arbitrary, this line handicaps the forces of right in their quest to stamp out evil. So we finish up by agreeing that using totally brutal methods of physical torture while interrogating (or standing by while our allies do it) is legitimate.

As Scriven (p. 118) notes, part of the technique used for persuasion in this case is the strategy of the sorites argument. The proponent has argued that there is no sharp line to be drawn between physical torture and mental torture, and has exploited the vagueness of the term 'torture' to push towards allowing physical methods of interrogation of prisoners.

Although we may be inclined to think of verbal, terminological, or definitional questions as trivial, it is clear that in this type of case (and many others like it), the decision, although partly verbal in nature, is very serious. Anyone put in the position of having to interrogate prisoners of war who might have crucial information (that could save lives) should be very attentive to the fine shades of the above distinction. It is a serious matter which could have very serious consequences.

Elaborating on the example initially presented in case 2.4, Scriven (1976: 119) went on to show how the slippery slope argument could be deployed or spelled out more fully.

Case 2.4a

The slippery slope argument involves saying that we already accept very long and exhausting interrogation, prison camp conditions, shouting at prisoners in the course of interrogation and probably shining strong lights in their eyes, and so on. It's only one step from these to a little cuffing around, or sticking the point of a knife into somebody, and only a step from that to chopping off a finger or shooting off an ear or tying a wire around the throat or applying an electric prod to the genitals.

The argument proceeds through a sequence of steps separated (it seems) one from the next only by a series of small differences. What seems to propel the argument along from one step to the next is the difficulty of seeing a clear demarcation between one step and the next, given the vagueness of the boundary between 'interrogation' and 'torture.'

As Scriven noted, such an argument could be used to justify brutal interrogation of a military prisoner, by combining it with moral arguments, e.g. the information extracted may be vital to saving the lives of our own soldiers (Scriven 1976: 122). So used, the slippery slope would be a bad argument that should be open to strong criticisms. But given the inherent vagueness and contestability of the key terms used in arguments on moral controversies, it may be hard to resist the slippery slope argument. It may be harder still to pin down exactly where and why it should be resisted, and to pinpoint the specific criticisms that should be brought to bear against it.

Part of the *modus operandi* of slippery slope argumentation on the issue of euthanasia (like case 1.3) involves the exploitation of the vagueness of key concepts. A case in point is the following familiar kind of dispute.

In this case, Lois and Clark are arguing about the morality of euthanasia. Lois takes the position that euthanasia should be allowed, but Clark is against it.

Case 2.5

LOIS. With all the respirators and other high-technology therapies in use in intensive care units these days, people can be assaulted with useless and undignified, painful, extreme hardships, unless euthanasia is permitted. Each of us has a right to refuse treatment not wanted or required.

CLARK. You are portraying euthanasia as 'passive euthanasia' or refusal to take treatment. But once patients are given the right to voluntarily ask for poison, or an injection from a physician, to end their suffering (as they are now allowed in Holland), the term 'euthanasia' becomes expanded to include active euthanasia as well. But once this step is taken, because it is hard or impossible to exactly define what is 'voluntary,' the next step is to allow termination of terminally ill or severely defective infants, with a guardian's and physician's consent. Once this is included, it too is classified as 'euthanasia.' From there you can see how it goes. Other kinds of patient can then be included in this category, until it becomes a convenient label for disposing of anyone who is a 'problem.'

Clark is using the slippery slope argument by citing the vagueness of two key distinctions—active euthanasia versus passive euthanasia and voluntary versus involuntary actions—in order to criticize the initial position put forward by Lois on the issue of euthanasia. Lois attempts to take a conservative position which gives patients the right to refuse extraordinary treatment in hospitals. But Clark extends the concept of euthanasia much further, by a series of steps linking comparable situations, to the eventual, dangerous outcome cited.

This is a typical type of slippery slope argument on euthanasia that has become familiar enough, but what is interesting to note here is how the exploitation of conceptual vagueness (typical of the sorites argument) is used as an adjunct in order to propel the respondent's argument down a slope that also has elements of causal and precedent argumentation.

It appears then that the sorites argument does have a practical dimension. It is more than a logical paradox of purely theoretical interest as a semantic difficulty. The mechanism of the sorites argument can actually be used as a powerful technique of persuasion in serious disputes where identifying fallacies is important.

Instead of concentrating on the semantic problem of making modifications to deductive logic in order to exclude the sorites paradox, it is also important to examine how sorites argumentation functions as a sophistical device of reasoned persuasion in a discussion. This pragmatic, rather than purely formalistic approach, concentrates on trying to understand how the sorites type of argument can function as a fallacy in argumentation. Perelman and Olbrechts-Tyteca (1971: 283) initiated this approach. They describe the *argument from direction* as a device used in negotiations, and other types of contentious dispute, to force the other party to yield by small degrees. In Chapter 6, this pragmatic program of analysis will be carried forward by putting the slippery slope argument in perspective as a species of argument from gradualism.

This practical approach has also been very effectively taken up by Govier (1982), who saw the sorites as only one kind of slippery slope argument, of which there are several important varieties. In contrast to the formal logicians, Govier expressed interest in the sorites argument primarily for its possibilities in generating fallacious arguments (pp. 307–8).

How then does the sorites type of slippery slope argument arise in a particular situation or conflict of opinion? How is it used as a vehicle of reasoned persuasion in such a context? And how can it go wrong or be misused as a kind of fallacy? To answer these practical questions, let us turn to a more detailed case study that has been the subject of recent controversies.

4. Verbal Disputes and Vague Concepts: The Abortion Case

The sorites type of slippery slope argument is most commonly used in everyday argumentation in situations where there is a problem, dispute, or conflict of opinions, and the issue turns on a key term that is vague, with the result that there is a difficulty of finding a fixed or single cutoff point along some contested continuum. Thus abortion and euthanasia are two areas of ethical controversy that provide precisely this kind of situation. With scientific and technical developments in life-support systems, problematic situations arise where 'life' is revealed as a vague concept that could be defined to support either one side or the other of a moral dilemma.

The sorites type of slippery slope typically centers around the definition of a contested term or concept. What launches it, or makes it an appropriate tactic of argumentation, is the kind of situation where one party in an argumentative discussion tries to promote his side of the argument by using a 'friendly' definition that tends to support his side, and to go against the other side. This can occur in negotiations, and other contexts of discussion, but it very often occurs in a critical discussion about values—for example, an ethical controversy about what is right or wrong in a morally problematic type of situation where there is controversy and heated disagreement. What typically occurs is that the substantive moral dispute turns to a verbal dispute on how a key term should be defined.

Some see such verbal disputes as trivial, as leading away from resolving the main or 'real' issue. But this is only sometimes an accurate criticism. In general, a participant in a critical discussion should have the right to advance a definition of a vague term, even if it tends to support his side of the case. But equally, the other party in the discussion should have the right to challenge the proposed definition, or to offer an alternative definition that he can give reasons for preferring.

Verbal disputes can be carried to excess, but in principle, they can be helpful in working towards resolving the issue in a critical discussion. The basic reason is that all natural-language argumentation involves the use of vague terms that are subject to clarification and definition.

The sorites type of slippery slope argument is one technique of exploiting a verbal dispute or problem of vagueness. The proponent uses it to ask the respondent where he can draw the line. If he can't draw the line, he can be pushed, by a slippery slope argument, into having to answer how he can reject drawing it in a way that is inimical to his own position.

Slippery slope arguments flourish where scientific or technical developments create new situations not covered by traditional terms, especially controversial terms like 'death,' 'life,' and 'person.' New options for defining these terms then become open to argumentation on issues of how the new technology should be used or limited. The abortion issue seems to be the most common example of this kind of argumentation.

In the following case Bob and Bertha are arguing about the morality of abortion. Bertha advocates the position that life begins at birth. Bob, however, thinks that the fetus must be 'alive' in the womb, during the latter stages of pregnancy.

Case 2.6

BOB. Surely the baby in the womb must be defined as a living person, with rights during these latter stages, because a surgeon can do intra-uterine surgery to correct the baby's heart defect, in some cases of this sort. The baby is the doctor's patient, therefore it must be a living person. Moreover, in many such cases, the baby, if delivered by Caesarian section, could be supported by intensive care, without the mother's support.

BERTHA. I don't agree with your position, because where do you draw the line? If the baby is alive in these latter stages near birth, then it is also alive in the earlier stages, where it cannot survive on its own, but where it has all the same features like a heart, lungs, limbs, and so forth. I don't see any point where you can draw the line, other than by having to admit that it could be 'alive' from the moment of conception (an absurd view).

In this discussion, Bertha has used the slippery slope argument to reduce Bob's argument to an untenable position. The way she has used this argument is similar to a *reductio ad absurdum* argument. She claimed that Bob can't draw the line in any non-arbitrary way along a continuum. Therefore, she argued, Bob is driven to draw the line at the lowest point in the continuum, if anywhere, and this view is absurd or untenable. Her conclusion seems to be that Bob's whole position on the issue of abortion is untenable.

One way out for Bob would be to try to draw the line at some point in the continuum, e.g. to declare that the fetus is a living person in the third trimester. This position too could be attacked by Bertha, but if Bob can present a defensible reason for drawing the line at that point, it would be an effective reply to Bertha's slippery slope attack.

Another way for Bob to respond would be to stand Bertha's argument on its head, by utilizing the following argument, quoted from Rudinow (1974: 173–4).

Case 2.6*a*

Birth is a morally insignificant event in the history of the born individual. As far as personhood and entitlement to treatment from the moral point of view are concerned, birth, which for the baby is a mere change of environment, is no more significant than the first birthday. But once birth has been demythologized, as well it should be, we are on the slippery slope. For no particular point between birth and conception is a point at which the person/non-person distinction can be non-arbitrarily located, because the differences in development between any two successive intrauterine points are so unimpressive.

Bob has replied to Bertha's slippery slope by posing a counter slippery slope which questions her criterion for drawing the line. Bob's argument appears to have the same reasoning as Bertha's. If her argument is reasonable, it seems that his should be too.

It seems, on the surface of the matter at any rate, that both slippery slope arguments are inherently reasonable. Bertha's argument questions whether Bob has any non-arbitrary way of drawing the line in order to sustain his position that a fetus is a person (who is alive). The burden of proof appears to lie on Bob's position, given that the current legal and customary view (while not unambivalent) tends to support the view that a baby is a person only after it is born. Therefore, Bertha's argument could perform a legitimate and useful function in a reasoned discussion on the abortion issue by shifting this burden of proof explicitly toward Bob's side of the argument to ask where he draws the line. Bob thinks that the fetus is 'alive' in the womb, so Bertha's question asks Bob to tell us when, in his view, it becomes 'alive.'

Bob's argument too seems reasonable, insofar as it has the function of shifting the burden of proof back onto Bertha's side of the contested issue, by asking her to specify what exactly is so morally significant about the moment of birth. The moment of birth is the accepted convention, but it does not follow that it is morally right or defensible, as a way of drawing the line. By questioning this presumption in a disputable case, Bob's slippery slope argument seems reasonable.

Either of these slippery slope arguments could become non-reasonable, or even fallacious, if it were to be phrased differently, or if it were to draw a different conclusion. In fact, the argument of case 2.6*a* above actually had the following conclusion when it was originally employed by Rudinow (1974: 174).

Case 2.6*b*

Consequently, we are forced to locate the beginning of human life at the point of conception.

If Bob had added this conclusion to his slippery slope argument of case 2.6a, he would have gone too far. By using the phrase 'we are forced,' he leaves Bertha no room to reply, other than by conceding a viewpoint she has already rejected as absurd, and which she would (presumably) want to reject anyway.

Once the sequence of argumentation has proceeded from case 2.6 through to the end of case 2.6*a*, it has reached the stage where there is a kind of deadlock between Bertha's argument and Bob's. Each has used a slippery slope argument against the argument of the other. Yet neither of their slippery slope arguments is fallacious. Indeed, both slippery slope arguments, up to that point, appear to be reasonable attempts to shift the burden of proof against the other side. Neither slippery slope argument is successful in that attempt. But neither appears to be inherently erroneous or illicit as a move in the context of the critical discussion on the abortion issue.

But when we reach the point in the sequence where Bob has added case 2.6b as his conclusion, it definitely seems appropriate to say now that Bob has committed a slippery slope fallacy. But why is that so?

Basically, there are two reasons. First, the slippery slope is essentially a tentative or open kind of argumentation used properly to warn someone not to take a first step. But Bob attempts to use it in a much stronger way, to refute Bertha by claiming to have definitely proved by the slippery slope argument that the beginning of human life is located at the point of conception. But his slippery slope argument cannot prove this conclusion—it is too weak an argument to bear that kind of heavy burden of proof. This makes Bob's argument weak or erroneous. But the second reason is that Bob phrases the conclusion in an even stronger way by using the conclusion 'we are forced.' This is an even more serious kind of failure which makes his argument fallacious.

Govier (1982: 308) agreed that the argument gotten by combining case 2.6a with case 2.6b is fallacious. Lamb (1988: 116) diagnosed the first basic error succinctly and accurately, in his critical comment on Rudinow's case.

. . . the slope argument in this context should not be taken to imply that human life begins at conception; it is simply directed against a position which makes a claim on behalf of any significant moment in the gestation process. If the conceptionist employs the slope argument to support the idea that the point at which life begins is conception, then he or she is drawing from the argument something which is not in it.

The proponent of the slope argument (represented by Bob's continuation of it in case 2.6b above) commits an error by trying to draw a conclusion out of the argument that is not really in it. This is a serious error, but it becomes a fallacy when the proponent tries to stick the conclusion down even more firmly by claiming that there are no alternatives to this conclusion so that, for all serious purposes, the discussion may be regarded as over. This preemptive move is a tactic that is seriously at odds with the methods and goals of critical discussion.

These cases indicate that the sorites type of slippery slope argument can be reasonable arguments in some cases, and unreasonable (or even fallacious) arguments in other cases. It seems that a slippery slope argument can be pushed too far, or posed in an overly aggressive manner that makes it go beyond the boundaries of good reasoning.

Before going on to the job of constructing general criteria to aid in sorting between the reasonable and the unreasonable uses of the sorites type of slippery slope argument, it is necessary to come to a better understanding of how this type of argument works as an effective technique of reasoned persuasion in a context of discussion. Traditionally, this undertaking would be classified as rhetorical, and therefore not a logical question. But if fallaciousness is to be defined pragmatically as the misuse of an inherently reasonable kind of argumentation as a deceptive technique to thwart the aims of a reasonable discussion, it becomes imperative to understand not only the semantic structure of the argument type in question, but how the argument is used and how it works in a discussion.

5. *Modus Operandi* of the Sorites Slippery Slope

A sorites argument, like the one in case 2.6, depends on the vagueness of a term that occurs in it. That much is obvious. But the real *modus operandi* of the sorites argument as a tactic of argumentation is more subtle. It depends on a term that is clear in some areas of application and is unclear in other areas. For any term, we need to distinguish between its *clear areas of application,* where the term definitely applies to the entities in that area or not, and its *grey areas of application* (or unclear areas), where it is not determined whether it applies or not. For example, in the area between 3 feet and 4 feet in height, or in the area between 6 feet and 7 feet in height, it is clear whether a person is short or not. In the first area, a person is definitely short. In the second area, a person is definitely not short. But there is a grey (penumbra) area in between where it is unclear whether a person can rightly be said to be short or not.

Now it is not just the existence of grey areas with respect to the application of a term that leads to slippery slope arguments of the sorites type. It is the fact that the transition point from the clear area to the grey area is also indeterminate or grey. As we proceed along the sequence of sorites reasoning from a step B_j to a next step B_k, we may know we are getting further from the clear area and closer (or perhaps into) the grey area. But we can never know exactly, at which single step, the transition has taken place. *The transition itself is grey.*

The proponent's tactic in the sorites type of slippery slope attack capitalizes on the greyness of the transition by trying to move forward along the continuum, because there is no single point which is the logical point to halt the attack. The respondent must resist, but the indeterminacy of the transition along the sequence of steps leaves him no guidance on where he should begin resistance. The slippery slope attack in sorites argumentation can be visualized as a movement from the left to the right side of Fig, 2.1. The proponent starts by gaining the respondent's commitment on a proposition where the answer is clear. For example, if he asks, 'Is a person who is 4 feet in height short?' the respondent must unhesitatingly answer 'Yes.' Once he has fixed definite commitments in the clear areas, the proponent then moves by small degrees toward the grey area. Here the reasonableness of continuing to give affirmative answers becomes less and less clear, but the proponent keeps exerting pressure on the respondent.

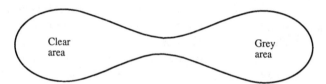

Fɪɢ. 2.1   Grey transition in the sorites argument

But how does the proponent exert such pressure? Can't the respondent simply reply 'I don't know?' as soon as he begins to feel that he is no longer definitely in the clear area where there is no doubt on how he should answer? Of course, it is possible for the respondent to do this, but in a critical discussion there is a burden or obligation on an answerer to take on commitments by giving an answer that seems right, and consistent with one's previous answers, even if there may be some doubts about whether one's answer is absolutely right, or uncontroversial. This obligation stems from the very nature of a critical discussion on a subject of controversy where, by the nature of the discussion, the evidence to conclude the dispute is lacking.

In a critical discussion, the proponent has a position, and the respondent has a position. Each party's position is the sum total of his previous commitments made during the course of the discussion. If either party makes a new commitment that appears to be inconsistent with any of his previous commitments, he can be challenged to resolve the apparent inconsistency. Indeed, such a challenge can be a strong form of attack in a critical discussion.

In sorites argumentation, the proponent can exert pressure because the respondent is open to attack if he is committed to the proposition that one object has a certain property, but is reluctant to commit himself to the proposition that some other object has the same property, even though the two objects differ only in some small, arguably insignificant degree. The proponent can then reply: 'Well, you have agreed that such-and-such a person is short, but now you don't agree that this other person is short, and he is only one-tenth of an inch taller than the first person?' The respondent appears to be in the illogical position of someone who changes his mind without any real reason to do so—not a reliable advocate, it would seem, who is consistently adhering to a coherent position.

Thus there are two primary factors that make the sorites type of slippery slope argument a powerful and effective technique of argumentation. First, the greyness of the transition continuum from the clear area to the grey area leaves no clear point of defense or resistance to the respondent. And second, the proponent can exert pressure, leveraged by the respondent's previous concessions, which he had no choice but to make in the clear cases, because the respondent has an obligation to give replies that make commitments if possible. In particular, the respondent is open to further serious attacks if he gives a reply that appears to be inconsistent with his previous replies.

The practical effectiveness of the sorites type of slippery slope attack is greatly enhanced by the penalty that attaches to the respondent in a critical discussion who tries to avoid answering a question that he should give a clear answer to by saying 'I don't know.' or 'I'm not sure about that.' This kind of evasiveness appears to be especially culpable where the respondent evidently should have an opinion on the question, judging by what we know of his position on the issue of the question.

The right pragmatic framework in which the sorites slippery slope argument arises then is a two-person dialogue on an issue of contention containing some key term which is part of what is being disputed. The goal of each participant is to get the other to make commitments or concessions that can be used for constructing arguments to show that one's own point of view can be proved. One quite legitimate technique or method of achieving this goal is to use an argument which proceeds by small degrees, namely a slippery slope argument.

But what makes this kind of argument fallacious? The answer is that it can be misused, or used incorrectly in a dialogue to violate the rules of a reasonable dialogue. Already our case studies have given us many clues indicating ways this can happen. For example, in case 2.6b, Bob went too far, claiming that Bertha is forced to locate the beginning of life at conception. His critical questioning of Bertha's position, legitimately sanctioned by his correct use of the slippery slope argument, became fallacious, or went beyond the boundaries of reasonableness, because he pressed ahead too hard.

To come to understand how the slippery slope argument can become fallacious in some instances, we need to see how this powerful (but, in principle, legitimate) kind of argumentation can be pressed ahead too aggressively in an attempt to subvert or close off reasonable dialogue. This entails seeing how the argumentation scheme for the sorites slippery slope can shift a burden of proof reasonably, but can also be challenged by critical questioning.

6. Argumentation Scheme for the Sorites Slippery Slope

Whether a slippery slope argument is used reasonably or unreasonably depends on the context of the discussion. The characteristic context in which the slippery slope argument arises involves an issue where there are two sides, a pro and a con. But the difference of opinion can be of two types. In one kind of case, one party is arguing for a thesis (conclusion) T, and the other party is doubting or questioning T. This kind of conflict of opinion is called a simple (single) dispute by van Eemeren and Grootendorst (1984: 80). In another kind of case one party is arguing for a thesis T, and the other party is arguing for the opposite thesis, not-T. Van Eemeren and Grootendorst (p. 80) call this second kind of case a compound (single) dispute. The difference between the two kinds of opposition is one of burden of proof. In the second kind of case, the second party has an obligation (burden) to prove not-T, in order to be successful in fulfilling his burden of proof. In the first kind of case, the second party only has to throw legitimate doubt on the argument of the other party, in order to meet his burden successfully in the discussion.

In the sorites type of slippery slope argument, there is a sequence of objects, or stages of development of an object, a_0, a_1, ..., a_i, ..., a_j, ..., a_n, and a certain property P, which some of the objects possess and others do not. In the abortion controversy, for example, the objects are the different stages of development of the entity that (at some disputed point) becomes a baby (person). Characteristically, the objects lie along a continuum which begins at a_0 and ends at a_n. The two points a_i and a_j are the cutoff limits in the continuum that may be agreed upon or designated by the participants in the discussion as representing the last clear cases where P is present or not. These two points may be subject to dispute, however, and characteristically, they are not determined by the participants. In the abortion dispute example, a_i could be the point of conception, and a_j could be the point of birth. That is, before conception, nobody claims that there exists a baby that is a person. And after birth, everybody is willing to agree that the organism can now rightly be called a (living) person. The problem is the contestability of the grey area between a_i and a_j. In case 2.6, both Bertha and Bob agree that before conception, whatever exists cannot be called a person. At least, that is not at issue. And likewise, neither of them wishes to contend that, after birth, the individual that exists is not a person. What is subject to contention is the extent and boundaries of the grey area in between.

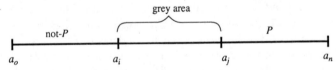

FIG. 2.2   Context of discussion for sorites slippery slope

The opposition, and the possible moves to exploit the vagueness of the grey area, can be viewed in the following terms. Bertha is trying to push a_i further in the direction of a_n. She argues that since there is really no clear cutoff point that Bob has opted for and defended, for all he knows or can argue for, the real cutoff point could be at a_j (birth). When Bob turned around, in case 2.6*b*, and used the slippery slope against Bertha, he was pressing in the opposite direction. He argued that since Bertha had not successfully defended a chosen cutoff point in the grey area, for all we know, or can concede to her position, the real cutoff point could be a_i (the point of conception).

However, a second interpretation is possible. Note that in the original argument, case 2.6, Bertha had taken the definite position that life begins at birth. Bob, however, was less definite. He claimed that the fetus must be alive in the womb, at some stages or other. But he did not stipulate a particular cutoff point (like the beginning of the third trimester) where life begins.

In this instance, the two parties are on a different footing, and the argument must always be evaluated (as strong or weak) with that in mind. For example, if Bertha tried to use the slippery slope to refute Bob's alleged argument that life begins at conception, such an argument should rightly be regarded as a fallacious slippery slope.

To determine the argumentation scheme for this type of argument generally, we divide the roles into a proponent and a respondent. The proponent is using the sorites slippery slope argument to attack the position of the respondent. The technique is for the proponent to take any clear case conceded by the respondent to have a particular property (or not) and then work, by small stages, into the grey area.

Let's look at one direction of arguing in Fig. 2.2. Suppose the respondent definitely agrees that some object $a_k(n \geq k \geq j)$ has property P. Next, he has to get the respondent to concede that some similar, neighboring object a_{k-1}, also has property P. Third, he has to work through the sequence, closer and closer to getting the concession that a_i has P. The closer he gets, the more doubt he throws on the respondent's argument. If he gets to a_i or beyond, he has successfully refuted the respondent's argument.

Here we should distinguish between strong and weak refutation of an argument. To refute an argument weakly is to throw legitimate doubt on it. To refute it strongly is to prove that the argument is untenable. The confusion between weak and strong refutation is essentially the kind of argumentation known traditionally as the *ad ignorantiam* fallacy. However, the *argumentum ad ignorantiam* is not fallacious in all cases (Walton 1989: 43–9). Essentially, this argument reflects the idea of how burden of proof works in critical discussion. If a proposition cannot be proved to be true, then it may be presumed to be not true (or not established), provided there has been plenty of room given to argue for it in a discussion, and all attempts have failed. Thus the slippery slope, in many instances, is a legitimate species of *argumentum ad ignorantiam,* where it does not necessarily try to claim the whole grey area for its side, but only tries to question the other party's claim to it.

When the sorites type of slippery slope argument is being used correctly to shift a burden of proof in a context of discussion, it takes the following form, with three characteristic kinds of premise.

Argumentation Scheme for Sorites Slippery Slope

Initial base premise	It is clearly beyond contention that a_k has P.
General inductive premise	If a_k has P, then a_{k-1} has P.
Reapplication sequence premise-set	A sequence of *modus ponens* sub-arguments linking premises and conclusions from the clear area through the grey area.
Conclusion	a_i may have P, for all we know (or can prove).

This argumentation scheme is implanted in a sequential fashion by continually reapplying the third premise-set as far as possible. The proponent of the slippery slope pushes ahead, in effect continually asserting to the respondent: 'You have no clear cutoff point, so you can't reasonably resist.' The intent is to drive the respondent to an ultimate conclusion that weakens or undermines his position.

However, even if the respondent picks a cutoff point, the sorites slippery slope can still be used to question the non-arbitrariness or clarity of the proposed cutoff point, using the same kind of reasoning. For example, if the respondent picks the beginning of the third trimester as the first point of viability, where life begins, the proponent can argue for the lack of significant difference between this point, and some point of development of the fetus just prior to that. So questioning the premises of a sorites slippery slope argument may not be convincing in a reasonable discussion unless it is done in a proper manner.

7. Appropriate Critical Questions

There are four basic ways of challenging a sorites slippery slope argument—you can challenge the initial base premise, you can challenge the general inductive premise, you can challenge any of the premises in the reapplication sequence, or you can challenge the appropriateness of the conclusion, in relation to the premises. This third kind of challenge was raised in connection with case 2.6*b* for example, where the conclusion was different from the weaker one that would have been appropriate to match the rest of the argument in the prior discussion.

Generally, however, the most problematic aspect of responding to a sorites slippery slope argument is to know how to best challenge the reapplication sequence premise-set. The respondent usually needs to question either or both of the base or inductive premises at some point in the sequence. But his problem is to know where is the best point to do that.

The basic reason that the sorites slippery slope is effective and powerful as a technique of argumentation is that it works by small, seemingly insignificant degrees to gain assent. Coupled with the factor of the vagueness of the predicate P, this gradualistic attack works so well because there appears to be no *single* point at which the respondent is clearly justified in beginning his resistance. Either way, if he resists too soon, or not soon enough, the proponent can follow up with additional attacks, held in reserve for this eventuality.

Going back to the diagram of Fig. 2.2, we can see that it is oversimplified in some important contexts of discussion in one key respect. The borderlines of the grey area can themselves be fuzzy or grey. In other words, in some cases, a_i and a_j are not single points, but continual—we sometimes know definitely whether we are inside or outside the grey area, but sometimes we don't. This feature is in fact characteristic of the kind of problem situation where the sorites slippery slope argument arises as a particularly powerful technique.

The problem is that the respondent has no way of knowing at what precise point he has definitely entered the grey area or not, in the sequence of concessions he is being asked to make. Neither does the proponent, for that matter, if the property P is inherently vague.

What this observation suggests is that we should think of the argumentation scheme for the sorites slippery slope not as consisting only of three premises, but as an extended sequence of linked premises and conclusions. Now generally, in a linked argument, the best strategy is to attack the weakest link, or the least plausible premise (Rescher 1976: 15). But the problem here is that if the respondent waits too long until the argument becomes highly implausible because the premises are very weak, it may be too late, because he may already have conceded 'incriminating' propositions. How can a reasonable respondent deal with this kind of attack?

The first thing for a respondent to do is to decide whether he is going to go for drawing the line at some particular cutoff point or not. If he is going to draw the line, then he will likely be called upon to defend the cutoff point he has chosen as being appropriate and reasonable for the context of the discussion. This leads to further questions and replies which are treated in the next section.

But suppose the respondent wishes to concede that the key term at issue is indeed vague. Then he is confronted with the slippery slope attack which pushes ahead, using consistency between closely similar cases to conclude, 'You can't really draw the line anywhere!' Here, the slippery slope argument is a powerful technique, and it is difficult to resist it.

The best strategy generally for a respondent in this instance is to begin to deny the reapplication sequence at some favorable point —it does not generally matter exactly where, but it should be towards the earlier stages of the grey area—by denying the applicability of consistency, even to closely similar cases, on the grounds that the property P is vague. The respondent, in other words, should insist on his right not to be bound to strict consistency in an area where whether the predicate at issue applies or not is vague. That is, he should argue that even though he has conceded that one thing a_m, for example, has property P, and another thing a_{m+1} is very similar to a_m, he is not bound by consistency to concede that a_{m+1} has P. He should reply that a_{m+1}

might have P, for all he knows, but that because of the vagueness of P, he should be free to doubt whether a_{m+1} definitely has P, and therefore he is going to exercise his right to decline conceding, or committing himself to the proposition that a_{m+1} has P.

This means that in a continuum where a key term is vague, and accepted by both the proponent and the respondent as vague, the respondent has a right not to be bound strictly by consistency between closely similar or indistinguishably adjacent points on the continuum in just the following sense: just because he has accepted one point as having a property, he need not be bound by consistency to accepting the next point as also having the same property. Of course, this right to deviate from strict consistency only applies where the property is vague, and is distinctive of the kind of case where the property is legitimately vague. In effect, this approach means that the respondent is denying the truth or acceptability of the premises at some point in the reapplication sequence.

The respondent's grounds for raising critical questions about the premises of the slippery slope argument should not center exclusively on a particular pair of premises in the sequence, however. He should demand that the argument be looked at in a holistic way, and point out that, because of the vagueness of the key term, it is arbitrary to fasten on any particular point in the reapplication sequence. He should reply: 'Any point in roughly this range (the grey area) will do. I have to begin to cease making definite commitments somewhere, so this is as good a point as any. I am not being unreasonably arbitrary in this selection. It is because of vagueness (which we both admit) that it is not known where the best point is to begin to stop making concessions. But I have to start somewhere, according to the dictates of reason. So provisionally, until the vagueness is clarified, here is the point I pick. Pick some other point (within the acceptable range of choices) and that would be all right too, if you prefer it.'

The proponent can persist in claiming that the respondent's choice of beginning point to raise critical questions is arbitrary. But this is not a reasonable move. The respondent can (and should) reply: 'Yes, it is arbitrary, but some reasonable degree of arbitrariness in choice here is appropriate and necessary (even inevitable) because of the inherent vagueness of the property at issue, as it applies to the range of cases in the continuum.' Where there is vagueness, there is reasonable arbitrariness versus unreasonable arbitrariness in a slippery slope dispute.

8. Precise Definition and Arbitrariness

One way to attack a slippery slope argument of the sorites type is to propose a precise definition of the vague term at issue. This move can certainly have the effect of resolving the problem posed by a sorites argument. Fogelin (1987: 72) puts this point very well, in connection with the use of the vague term 'rich' that occurred in case 1.2.

Case 2.7

If we laid down a ruling (maybe for tax purposes) that anyone with a million dollars or more is rich and anyone with less than this is not rich, then the argument would fail. A person with $999,999.99 would pass from not being rich to being rich when given a single penny. But, of course, we do not use the word 'rich' with this precision.

However, as Fogelin's last sentence above suggests, for this type of attack, there can be a good defense open in reply: 'Your definition is precise, but arbitrary!' The problem is that some terms are inherently vague, and any attempt to define them precisely seems bound to be open to a charge of arbitrariness.

Whether a definition is 'arbitrary,' and whether arbitrariness is objectionable, however, are questions that depend on the context of a discussion. In an everyday discussion about the question of whether excessive wealth is morally harmful, a definition stipulating that anyone with a million dollars or more is 'rich' could be attacked as arbitrary. On the other hand, to cite Fogelin's example, for tax purposes the same definition could be defended, perhaps, as reasonable, on various grounds. It could be argued that any precise definition would be arbitrary to some extent, and that drawing the line at one million dollars is as fair and reasonable as any precise definition that could be offered. Moreover, in this type of discussion, it could be argued that agreeing on a precise definition is both useful and necessary in order to arrive at fair conclusions about tax claims and audits. So putting forward a precise definition[3] is one way of dealing with a slippery slope argument of the sorites type, but whether it can be successfully defended as a correct way depends on the context of dialogue. The move to precise definition may lead to the charge of arbitrariness.

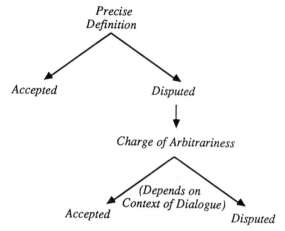

Fig. 2.3 The move to precise definition

The slippery slope argument is rightly used to pose the question 'Where do you draw the line?' But if the respondent takes this question literally, and proceeds to draw a sharp line at some particular point, the proponent may come back and attack such a reply on grounds that the criterion is arbitrary.

When this pattern of attach and defense transpires, the dispute becomes one of whether or not precise definition is appropriate or legitimate in the given context. For example, in university coursework, it is an accepted and necessary part of the procedure to draw sharp distinctions among numerical grades, and in particular, between passing and failing grades. Although this procedure has been attacked as 'arbitrary' from time to time, it is an accepted presumption in this context that precise judgments on a numerical scale, or scale of some accepted sort, are legitimate, necessary, and useful for the purpose of assigning credit for coursework. Of course, disputes about borderline cases do arise,

---

[3] Characteristically, the tactic of putting forward a precise definition of the key term on which a slippery slope argument depends is a move made by the respondent in order to refute the proponent's sorites type of slippery slope argument.

and the arbitrariness reply may arise here, even legitimately, in some cases. But generally, the need for precise definitions of 'pass' and 'failure,' and the acceptance of a grading procedure that incorporates some method of precise definition, places the presumption on the acceptability of precise definitions generally, and places a burden of proof on a participant in an argument who would use the arbitrariness reply.

Once the precise definition has entered the picture, it does not mean, in all cases, that the slippery slope argument disappears. As Chapter 4 will show, slippery slope arguments can occur where precise policy guidelines are already in place. But in some cases, precise definition can be a sufficient solution by itself.

Another way of dealing with sorites slippery slope arguments is to introduce a graduated method of precise definition that distributes outcomes or benefits so that not too much significance attaches to any one controversial borderline. This can effectively reduce incidents of disputed cases. A very clear example of how this practical method works in dealing with slippery slope problems has been presented by Fogelin (1987: 76).

Case 2.8

With a poverty program we can use a graduated scale based on need. Those with a greater need will receive more aid, and the aid will decrease as the cut-off point is approached. In this way, there will be only a small difference between those just below the cut-off point who receive minimal aid and those just above it who receive no aid at all.

But this strategy is only practical in some contexts of dispute. Where the outcomes cannot be put on a graduated scale of several borderlines, this method is of no use. Fogelin (p. 76) cites the case of decisions about capital punishment: 'since death does not admit of degrees . . . similar cases will be treated in radically different ways.' Thus the death penalty can be accused of a certain inevitable arbitrariness in decisions about which kinds of case come under it and which do not. This arbitrariness could perhaps be defended, or argued as a necessary evil in various ways. But it cannot be dealt with by introducing a graduated scale of 'partial executions.' The outcome or conclusion to be arrived at in this type of case simply does not admit of more finely graduated degrees.

9. What is the Fallacy?

The application of the argumentation scheme to the cases studied in this chapter have shown that the sorites type of slippery slope argument is a reasonable (correct) argument, in some cases. Or, at least, it can be used in a reasonable manner in a particular case to forward the aims of a reasonable discussion. But the slippery slope argument is known, or at least often portrayed, as a fallacy.

According to Govier (1982: 308), the type of reasoning involved in the sorites slippery slope argument is a fallacy that has the following structure. P is a property and x is a degree of difference between two cases.

Fallacy of Assimilation (Govier 1982: 308)
  (1) Case (a) is P.
  (2) Cases (b)–(n) form a series differing initially from (a) and then from each other, only by x.
  (3) Considered in itself, each difference of amount x is insignificant.
Therefore:
  (4) There is no difference between (a) and (b)–(n) with respect to P; all are equally P.

As an instance of this fallacious type of reasoning, Govier cited the abortion argument from Rudinow (1974: 173-4), quoted as cases 2.6a and 2.5b. But Govier did not attempt to explain why arguments having the form of argumentation cited above are fallacious. She only stated that proceeding by degrees on a 'conceptual spectrum' of argument 'does *not* imply that all cases spectrally arrangeable are equivalent' (p. 309). This is true, but it leaves the question of what the fallacy is unexplained.

In fact, the scheme described above as the fallacy of assimilation by Govier is generally a reasonable kind of argumentation, which only becomes fallacious when it is used (or misused) in specific ways. To begin to understand how it can be used reasonably to shift a burden of proof in some contexts of discussion, yet can be a fallacious argument in other cases, we need to see how this type of argumentation is used in the context of a vague term to shift a sequence of moves through a clear area of demarcation through a grey area and beyond.

Indeed, when all the proper steps in such a progression are put in, this kind of extended chain argument is deductively valid. It is a sequence of *modus ponens* arguments where the conclusion of one is a premise in the next subargument. Hence this type of argument is valid. To challenge it, a critical respondent needs to attack one of the premises, showing that the argument is weak, or lacks necessary support, in accord with the requirements of its argumentation scheme.

But there is a difference between a weak argument and a fallacious argument. A slippery slope argument, as we saw in case 2.6*b*, occurs where the proponent has pushed ahead too aggressively, trying to make his argument appear stronger than the evidence merits. This can occur by trying to substitute an inappropriately strong conclusion, as in case 2.6*b*, where Bob tried to conclude 'we are forced to locate the beginning of human life at the point of conception,' implying that one's opponent's contention has been strongly refuted, closing the discussion.

The use of the slippery slope argument in case 2.4*a* is not fallacious as such. But when the conclusion indicated at the end of case 2.4 is added as the conclusion which is supposed to be drawn from the argument, an error occurs. The error here is jumping to the conclusion that we should finish by agreeing to the use of 'totally brutal methods of physical torture' because the line can't be drawn between these methods and other methods we are already using, or have conceded as acceptable to use. The error here is promoting the leap to a conclusion that is too strong to be justified by the premises. This move is not warranted because the proper conclusion, as indicated by the argumentation scheme, should only be that the harsher physical methods may not be unacceptable, for all we know or the respondent has shown, given the respondent's acceptance of other methods that appear less harsh, but are not demonstrably different as physical methods.

Admittedly, case 2.4 seems like such a bad argument that it could be labelled 'fallacious' because any argument used to justify using brutal methods of physical torture has such a repugnant conclusion that we are bound to think that the argument must be badly wrong. But it is one thing to be nasty or brutal, quite another thing to commit a fallacy. Many arguments can be immoral, weak, disgusting, or even silly without necessarily being fallacious.

Evaluation of cases 2.4 and 2.4*a* is also complicated by the fact that the author is reporting on how an argument might plausibly be used against us to try to persuade us to agree that using brutal methods of physical torture while interrogating is legitimate. We do not have the actual text of such an argument given. Scriven is only reporting on how such an argument might be used. This lack of a definite text of discourse makes an exact evalutation of cases 2.4 and 2.4*a* as an argument impossible.

What can be said, however, is that the argument in cases 2.4 and 2.4*a* is not necessarily a fallacious slippery slope argument. It is a report of an argument that could have some weight in challenging someone who accepts harsh interrogation but not brutal physical torture to give some criterion to 'draw the line' or generally indicate the difference between these two things. Anyone who insists that there is a difference but can't articulate the difference clearly and adequately could certainly be open to critical questioning by the slippery slope argument. It does not follow, however, that he should at once capitulate and agree that using brutal methods of physical torture is legitimate.

In general, each case must be judged on it merits in its context of discussion, to evaluate whether the sorites slippery slope argument is reasonable, weak, or fallacious. Generally, such an argument is weak where it fails to reply adequately to appropriate critical questioning. It is fallacious where there is a tactic of pushing ahead too hard in order to try to choke off or subvert critical questioning. As our case studies indicated, this can happen in a number of ways. Although the slippery slope argument is often reasonable as a warning that some danger may occur, in some cases the language of the argument becomes inappropriately strong, claiming that this danger must occur, once the first step has been taken. The fallacy here is a confusion between, or illicit substitution of strong refutation for weak refutation.

Another form this fallacy takes is the tactic of pushing too hard to demand consistency even when a term is vague, especially once the argument has entered a grey area. In such a case, we need to ask whether or not the context of discussion is right for a precise definition. If a certain degree of vagueness is acceptable, or even inevitable, as in an ethical controversy, trying to force strict consistency of commitments where reasonable doubt exists may be fallacious as a line of argumentation.

10. Rights in Using Vague Terms and Proposing Definitions in a Discussion

The main lesson of that sorites slippery slope argument is that in a certain type of situation, a respondent should have the right to say 'No.' This type of situation is one where a key term in the discussion is inherently vague, so that it is unclear whether an individual thing a_j has a property P or not. Even though the respondent has just conceded that some closely similar thing a_i (which he admits is not significantly different from a_j, in the context) has P, he should nevertheless be reasonably allowed to refrain from committing himself to the proposition that a_j has P. This right is reasonable if a_j is in a grey area with respect to P.

The sorites type of slippery slope argumentation naturally arises in ethical controversies because the key terms in these kinds of dipute are inherently vague, and are open to attempts to push 'friendly' definitions by each side. Typically, in ethical controversies and dilemmas, a term may be clear enough in principle, as it occurs in a general policy or guideline, but applying it to a particular case may be controversial and difficult.

In case 2.4*a*, for example, the term 'physical torture' becomes hard to definitively apply when we are presented with the short step from shining a strong light into someone's eyes to 'a little cuffing around.' Shining a strong light in someone's eyes definitely has a physical effect on the prisoner. So how could we draw the line that says that this is acceptable but 'cuffing around' is not?

The problem here is that different people might, reasonably and defensibly even, draw the line at different places. One person, for example, might feel that 'cuffing around' is never acceptable, but the use of a strong light could be acceptable. But even here defining 'strong' and 'cuffing' could be problematic. Another person might draw the line in a different place saying: 'Yes, I will allow a little cuffing around, as long as it doesn't do any permanent damage to the prisoner.' Then the argument might shift to the issue of what constitutes 'permanent damage,' e.g. does this include mental conditions like post-traumatic stress? The issue has then shifted from one vague term to another. But there need be nothing wrong or fallacious about that shift. The discussion may be making progress.

In general, a participant in a critical discussion like an ethical controversy, where vague terms are likely to play an important part in the discussion, has a number of rights or freedoms in responding.

1. *Freedom to use vague terms.* A participant has a right to use a vague term if the term (despite its vagueness) is appropriate for the discussion. Of course, the other party has a right to ask him to be more precise, as well, or to define the term he has used.

2. *Freedom to define your terms.* A participant has the right to define a term in a 'friendly' way that supports his own point of view. Of course, definitions can be challenged, on various grounds. But they can also be reasonably defended on good grounds, in some cases.

3. *Freedom to use a defining criterion that is vague.* Inappropriate precision can be a hindrance to critical discussion. Vagueness is acceptable in some cases, within limits appropriate to the context of a discussion.

4. *Right to relax standards of strict consistency in vague contexts.* As stated at the beginning of this Section, a respondent should have the right to say 'No' to a commitment, even though he has committed himself to prior closely related points on a continuum.

The sorites slippery slope argument is a fallacy only when it is used as an unduly aggressive tactic in a discussion to try to prevent a respondent from the reasonable exercise of one of those rights in an argument.

To understand how sorites-type argumentation can be used fallaciously to put pressure on, or defeat an adversary in contested discussions, we need to see how this type of argumentation is characteristically used in arguments like that of case 2.6. Typically, in this kind of case, the proponent of the slippery slope attack tries to argue that the moment of birth is an arbitrary point to declare that a *person* has come into being. Characteristically, the proponent of this type of argument cites development in science and new medical techniques, like ultrasound, fetal surgery, and amniocentisis, which have shown that the developing fetus has many of the same 'human' characteristics that the baby has. This kind of evidence can be legitimately cited in an attempt to argue for continuity, in order to overcome the burden of proof set in place by the traditional presumption (embodied in law) that birth is the significant point to define personhood and its attendant legal and moral implications.

But any definition, however well entrenched, can be contested by reasoned argumentation. Scientific discoveries, for example, are continually leading to revised definitions of traditional terms. The proponent of the argument in case 2.6 is pushing for some earlier point, perhaps, though not necessarily conception, as the new proposed point of demarcation. Does this argument have to be a fallacy? Not necessarily. Whether it is weak or strong in a particular case depends on how much reasonable evidence has been adduced to support its premises, in the face of the criticisms put forward by the respondent who is opposed. This kind of argumentation is defeasible, and open to various kinds of criticisms (critical questions). Each side has particular rights and obligations. The arguments of each side can be stronger or weaker in specific respects. To call the sorites slippery slope argument a fallacy *per se* is therefore a massive oversimplification.

Consider an analogy with case 2.3. Suppose, for 'affirmative action' purposes—for example, for dispensing government benefits to 'short' persons who have been disadvantaged in the workplace because of 'unequal height'—a legislated definition of five-foot-two were to be set down as the cutoff point for short persons. Someone who disagrees with the fairness of this ruling could, using slippery slope argumentation of the sorites type, contest it as arbitrary on the grounds that she, as a person whose height is only one-tenth of an inch over five-foot-two, is being unfairly denied the benefit. She might argue that since there is a grey area in shortness, and since there is no really good reason for picking five-foot-two as the best cutoff point, the policy should be liberalized to include people up to and including a height of five-foot-five. A negotiation could ensue, each side giving its reasons for its proposed cutoff point, without either side having necessarily committed any fallacy.

In this type of dispute, it seems reasonable that each side's arguments should be evaluated on their merits. It would seem inappropriate to always have to classify the dissenter's argument as a fallacious sorites argument or fallacy of assimilation. Hence the idea of the sorites argument as a fallacy needs to be rethought.

3

The Causal Slippery Slope Argument

THE causal type of argumentation identified by so many logic textbooks with the slippery slope fallacy appears to be quite different from the sorites argument. Instead of proceeding by comparing pairs of closely similar (or indistinguishable) instances of a property, it proceeds by predicting a series of distinct events, each one of which, it is claimed, will cause the next one. But, in general outline, both are slippery slope arguments. In a pattern of use similar to the sorites argument, the causal version claims that an initial step or action will lead, through the sequence, to some dangerous or otherwise bad ultimate outcome. Both arguments are used to try to dissuade a respondent from taking the initial step.

1. The Textbook Accounts

The classic case is the *domino theory* type of argumentation so often used during the Vietnam war to support the 'hawk' point of view. The use of this type of case by Kahane (1971: 61) has already been cited in Chapter 1.1, where it was shown to have been treated by Kahane as a fallacy. However, there have been many different statements of the domino theory. Consider the following possible variant.

Case 3.1

If Vietnam falls to the Communists, they could use this base to infiltrate Cambodia. Once Cambodia falls, neighboring states could then be brought under pressure by the creeping Communist influences. Eventually, the whole of Asia could be under Communist domination.

In historical hindsight, this argument no longer seems so worrisome to many as it may have during the Vietnam war period. But it does seem excessive to call the version in case 3.1 a fallacy, or a fallacious argument. The argument in case 3.1 seems more like a prediction of a possible outcome of a series of hypothetical causal linkages. A prediction, even an implausible one, is not necessarily a logical fallacy.

What then is the difference between the heavily exaggerated version of the argument portrayed in Kahane, and the milder version of case 3.1? Could the causal slippery slope argument be non-fallacious in some cases?

Another classic case often cited in the textbooks concerns the controversy about the decriminalization of marijuana, a proposal that was once fashionable to discuss. Johnson and Blair (1983: 161–2) cite an example of such a discussion from an editorial of the *St. John's Evening Telegram*.[1]

Case 3.2

The federal proposal to switch cannabis from the Narcotics Control Act to the Food and Drug Act will probably be the first step leading to the eventual legalization of this 'soft' drug. Under the drug act the possession of marijuana or hashish will be punishable with a fine rather than with a jail sentence as called for in the narcotics act.

The penalties for trafficking, importing and cultivating the drug will still be stiff. However, it is hardly likely that judges will take as serious a view of a drug as they do of a narcotic, and in time the penalty for trafficking or importing will probably be a light fine and a ticking off by the judge. Then, in turn, the fine for possession will likely be dropped and it will be legal to have cannabis for personal use.

From there the next step is controlled manufacture and sale along the same lines as alcoholic drinks. Then the emphasis on the nature of the crime will switch to smuggling and bootlegging with the intention that the Crown gets its legitimate revenue from the sale of the drug. By that time, cannabis will probably be called joy candy or fun smoke or by some other euphemism.

If we seem to be moving too fast, remember that this is the usual way of softening up the law. We hope that when Health Minister Lalonde makes the change he will understand that he is opening the door to putting pot in every pocket.

In their analysis of the slippery slope argument in this case, Johnson and

---

[1] No date is given by Johnson and Blair for case 3.2.

Blair (p. 162) spell out seven stages that are links in sequence of argumentation.

(1) Marijuana put under Food and Drug Act;
(2) Possession punished by fine rather than jail; trafficking, importing, and cultivating punished stiffly;
(3) Judges take a less serious view of offenses against this law;
(4) The penalty for trafficking and importing becomes less severe—a light fine;
(5) Penalty for simple possession dropped; legal to possess marijuana;
(6) The manufacture and sale of marijuana controlled by the government;
(7) Emphasis changes from possession and trafficking to smuggling and bootlegging;
(8) Marijuana legal and in common use.

In evaluating the argument in case 3.2, Johnson and Blair point out that some of these links are weaker than others. Although some of the links are fairly plausible, others are very weak, and are not defended in the argument. In criticizing the argument, therefore, they opt for the method of attacking the weak links in the causal chain (p. 163). For this reason, they cite it as a case of the slippery slope fallacy.

Johnson and Blair, however, do not think that all arguments that have the same general form or outline as causal slippery slope arguments are fallacious. They indicate (p. 160) that assessing a proposed policy or course of action by showing that it leads to undesirable consequences is a legitimate kind of argumentation. The slippery slope fallacy only occurs where 'the causal projection is weak because one (or more) links in the causal chain is dubious, and either not defended or insufficiently justified' (p. 161). It seems then that according to Johnson and Blair, causal sequence arguments that predict a bad outcome are only instances of the slippery slope fallacy if one or more of the links in the causal chain are weakly substantiated or inadequately defended.

Govier (1982: 312) goes even further and claims that the causal slippery slope argument can be non-fallacious. She is of the opinion (p. 313) that 'there is nothing wrong, in principle, with arguments of this type, though many may be found which are based on entirely unwarranted empirical claims.' The structure of this type of argument she cites is the following.

The Causal Slippery Slope Argument (Govier 1982: 312)

(1) Action (*a*) is prima facie acceptable.

(2) Action (*a*) would, if performed, cause the occurrence of events e_1, e_2, ..., e_n.

(3) It is not desirable that the series of events e_1, ..., e_n occur.

(4) Therefore, action (*a*) should not be undertaken.

This type of argument seems as though it could be a (reasonable) argument in some instances. It appears to be a form of negative argument from consequences which has, in outline, the form of a *modus tollens* inference. It involves a conditional hypothesis of the form 'If A then B.' And because B is said to be undesirable, it is argued that A is also undesirable as a kind of action to be undertaken. Such an argument could represent the giving of good advice in some cases (see cases 3.3 and 3.4).

One small difference is that Johnson and Blair (1983: 164; see also Section 7 below) do not see the intervening events, e_1, e_2, ..., e_{n-1}, as undesirable, but only the ultimate outcome e_n. Generally, Govier is right that these intervening events tend to get more undesirable as the sequence proceeds. But Johnson and Blair are right that it is only necessary or essential for the final event to be undesirable, in order to have a causal slippery slope argument.

Waller (1988: 179) also claims that a causal slippery slope argument can be non-fallacious if the arguer proposing it has given good reasons to believe that bad effects will follow from the action in question. He cited the following persuasive case.

Case 3.3

Suppose we are considering whether to allow a manufacturer of hydraulic fluid to dump millions of gallons of PCB-contaminated wastes into a small stream. Someone who opposes such dumping might argue that the PCBs will run from that stream into a downstream river, will accumulate in fish, will pollute our drinking water with a known cancer-causing agent, and will eventually result in pollution of rivers, killing of wildlife, and severe hazard to humans who use the water downstream. (p. 179)

In this case 'we' (some group of people) are considering whether or not to allow a manufacturer to carry out a proposed action. Someone who opposes the plan puts forward the slippery slope argument above, citing a sequence of effects that, he claims, will ultimately lead to a situation that is hazardous to human life. Is the slippery slope argument a good reason for rejecting the proposed plan or not? Waller is suggesting that it could be, in a kind of case like 3.3 above.

This case certainly shows us that a causal slippery slope argument can be reasonable. But it also shows something else. Just because one or more of the links in the causal chain is weak, because it has not been defended or sufficiently justified, it does not seem to follow that the argument has to be fallacious. Perhaps it could be a reasonable, or at any rate non-fallacious slippery slope argument even if there are some good arguments against it. Perhaps a somewhat weak argument need not necessarily be a fallacious argument, and moreover, could perhaps even be a reasonably good argument, in a context of discussion.

Little, Groarke, and Tindale (1989: 240–3) present a clear and succinct account of causal slippery slope arguments which also contends that there can be good as well as bad slippery slope arguments of this type. As an example of good slippery slope reasoning, they cite (p. 241) an argument from Johnson and Blair (1983: 165), which was originally attributed to John Hofsess (*Maclean's,* October 1973).

Case 3.4

If you don't get into the habit of exercising regularly when you're young, you are less likely to keep exercising during your later 20s and your 30s, when career, home and family take up more and more time and interest. You'll then tend to become sedentary and physically unfit. That will set you up for various heart and lung diseases during middle age. No one wants to have a heart attack at 45 or 50, so to lessen that danger, you ought to get into the habit of regular exercise when you're young.

Little, Groarke, and Tindale (1989: 241) claim that this argument is a good (cogent) slippery slope argument, because the causal links are plausible. Johnson and Blair commented that the argument 'seems reasonable' because it is a 'probabilistic one rather than one delivered with iron-clad assurances.' They concluded: 'Not every argument that involves a projection into the future is a slippery slope argument.' Although more cautious about classifying case 3.4 as a slippery slope argument, at any rate they concede that it is not a fallacious argument.

Little, Groarke, and Tindale (p. 242) give the following example of a bad causal slippery slope argument, quoted from St. John of Chrysostom.

Case 3.5

[T]o laugh, to speak jocosely, does not seem an acknowledged sin, but it leads to acknowledged sin. Thus laughter often gives birth to foul discourse, and foul discourse to actions still more foul. Often from words and laughter proceed railing and insult; and from railing and insult, blows and wounds; and from blows and wounds, slaughter and murder. If then, thou wouldst take good counsel for thyself, avoid not merely foul words, and foul deeds, or blows, and wounds, and murders, but unseasonable laughter itself. (*Post-Nicene Fathers,* V. ix. 442)

This argument is classified as a bad slippery slope argument by Little, Groarke, and Tindale because the supposed causal connections between unseasonable laughter, foul discourse, railing and insults, etc., are weak and implausible. The distinction then, between the good and the bad slippery slope argument, seems to turn, in their view, on the question of whether it is plausible that the stated causal connections really hold.

The question of whether one event causes another is an empirical question. And the causal slippery slope argument generally takes the form of an empirical prediction that a series of events will cause each other in the future. This is an essentially empirical kind of argumentation which depends on evidence relating to the occurrence of events predicted in the future.

In this respect, the causal slippery slope appears to be quite different from the sorites slippery slope, because the latter turned out to be a subtle, logical kind of argumentation similar to mathematical induction and also to *reductio ad absurdum* in structure. It required subtle, logical considerations to see how it functioned as a fallacy. By contrast, the causal slope seems to be a good or bad argument simply depending on whether it can be backed up by empirical evidence. In case 3.4, for example, the relevant evidence is presumably a set of medical and statistical findings. In case 3.3, the evidence required to back up the slippery slope argument would presumably be in the form of biological, chemical, and environmental facts and knowledge. In other cases, the causal slippery slope argument depends on historical facts.

2. Dependency on Empirical Evidence

It is interesting to note that evaluations of a causal slippery slope argument can depend a lot on historical perspective. Slippery slope arguments that once were taken for granted as ridiculous arguments may not appear to have been so silly from the perspective of a subsequent era. The author of an early informal logic textbook, Chase (1956: 52), reminisced about his enthusiastic campaigning for women's suffrage as a young man.

Case 3.6

I said it would purify politics, end the rule of corrupt bosses, get the cigar smoke out of smoke-filled rooms, elect the best men, improve the public schools and public health, clean up the slums. My opponents on the soapbox were equally confident that the vote would destroy feminine charm, put women into trousers, reduce the birth rate, break up the home, and cause our forefathers, who said nothing about it in the Constitution, to turn in their graves.

From a viewpoint of hindsight, these consequences do not seem ridiculous or far-fetched at all, either the positive or negative ones. They refer to outcomes that, at least to some degree, and under some descriptions, have come true.

Chase, however, from a viewpoint of 1956, saw the argument in case 3.6 as an instance of the fallacy of the 'thin entering wedge' (slippery slope). He evaluated the argument as a shaky prediction that turned out to be fallacious.

Well, women got the vote in 1920 and what happened? Very little. The electorate was doubled with hardly any change in results; the Republic neither tottered nor reached the millennium. Few citizens now doubt that it is only fair and reasonable for women to have the right to vote. But my prediction of purified politics was as shaky as my opponents' vision of twenty-five million broken homes. (1956: 52)

But students using Chase's textbook now would not be so easily convinced that the argument in case 3.6 is fallacious.

Several comments need to be made on this case, however. One is that much depends on the wording used in the outcomes described in a slippery slope argument of this sort. In this case, metaphors are used, like 'turn in their graves,' and some of the predicted outcomes are described in an exaggerated form, e.g.

'clean up the slums.' However, if we tone down the language and the exaggerations, most of the outcomes cited have in fact occurred, in some form, or to some degree. So one possible source of fallacy here is the use of imprecise language. Another is the exaggeration of an opponent's conclusion (straw man fallacy).

Another possible source of error arises through the exaggeration of the role of the cited cause. The granting of the right to vote to women was not sufficient, in itself, for all the outcomes cited. But it was a causal factor which no doubt contributed to the development of these outcomes, as part of larger trends in America, and other countries as well.

Another important comment concerns the time frame of the prediction in a slippery slope argument. Viewed as a short-term prediction of immediate outcomes, as Chase portrays the argument, case 3.6 can be refuted as an argument that didn't turn out to be correct. This refutation can even be based on empirical evidence to the effect that certain events did not occur. However, in fact the argument as stated in the text of case 3.6 above is not bound to any specific time frame. And, of course, it could be criticized on these grounds as vague, and so forth. But in fact, for all we can say on the evidence of the given text, the argument could possibly be meant to be a long-term prediction, with some uncertainty about the question of exactly when these consequences might actually come about. As such, it is far from obvious that it is a fallacious argument on grounds of being a slippery slope.

As noted by Schauer (1985: 382), slippery slope arguments have often been exaggerated so that they can be sneered at, and portrayed as ridiculous fallacies: 'Many slippery slope claims, whether in law or in popular discourse, are wildly exaggerated. As a result, it is possible for the cognoscenti to sneer at all slippery slope arguments, and to assume that all slippery slope assertions are vacuous. But things are not quite so simple.' But as Schauer goes on to note, slippery slope arguments are not always purely logical. They are often strongly empirical in nature. As such, they can be weak or strong, fallacious or reasonable, depending on the empirical evidence given (or not given) to support them. Once they are portrayed in a less exaggerated manner of presentation, it may be far from obvious that a presumption of fallaciousness, in general, can be taken for granted.

Instead of condemning causal slippery slope arguments as

fallacious because they seem to go against the popular trends or opinions of a particular era, a harder look needs to be taken at the kind of evidence they are based on as reasoned arguments. The problem is to see how empirical evidence is introduced and utilized in a critical discussion.

According to van Eemeren and Grootendorst (1984: 166), participants should begin any critical discussion with a list of propositions that are jointly accepted, called their *jointly shared starting point.* One method of successfully defending an argument by a proponent is to carry out a joint check to see if the premises are included in this starting point set. Such a check is called an *intersubjective identification procedure* (p. 166). This procedure functions as a way of drawing on shared background knowledge in a dispute.

As well as drawing on tacitly presupposed (old) knowledge, a proponent should be able to call in new knowledge to support an argument. According to van Eemeren and Grootendorst, the participants must have an *intersubjective testing procedure* (p. 167) by agreeing at the opening stage '*how they will determine* whether a proposition ought or ought not to be accepted.' Among the practical procedures used for this purpose are 'oral or written sources (encyclopedias, dictionaries and other works of reference) or it might include the joint conduct of observations or experiments' (p. 167). Often this procedure involves the citation of expert opinions, especially where specialized or scientific knowledge is involved.

An excellent example is the debate about the legalization of marijuana cited by Johnson and Blair (case 3.2). This particular example was as much a precedent type of slippery slope argument as a causal one. But the issue of the decriminalization of marijuana has provided other interesting case study materials of causal slippery slope argumentation.

During the 1960s, when smoking marijuana became fashionable among young people, the argument that use of marijuana could lead to the use of harder and more debilitating drugs, and thence to madness or dissolution of one's personality, was often ridiculed as a fallacious slippery slope argument. During that period, it could be taken for granted that a popular readership would not need much convincing to accept this argument as an instance of the fallacy of the slippery slope. At that time, serious discussions of the issue of whether marijuana should be legalized were also popular.

Subsequently, there have been numerous scientific studies that have documented the chemical effects of marijuana on the brain, and the resulting psychological consequences for an affected individual's personality. These empirical findings, as well as a shift in the tide of public opinion on the subject of drugs, have shifted the burden of proof significantly away from the presumption that the slippery slope argument in question can be taken for granted as fallacious. Now the presumption is likely to be, to the contrary, that the risks of serious consequences in taking any illegal drug could plausibly lead to addictive escalations.

What is interesting to note with respect to this particular instance of the causal type of slippery slope argument is how evaluations of it have changed, particularly through changes in public opinion and through the introduction of new empirical (scientific) evidence into the discussion.

3. Cases of Drug Addiction

Critical discussions about drug addiction often provide a fertile setting for the use of slippery slope arguments. One type of use of the slippery slope argument in this setting is to warn potential drug users not to take that first step of experimenting with drugs. A variation on this argument is to cite the progression from softer to harder drugs. Yet another type of discussion where the slippery slope comes in is the legalization issue. The opponents of legalizing drugs like marijuana often argue that an experiment in legalization would create wider use which, once set into effect, would be impossible to de-escalate.

When the causal type of slippery slope argument is used in an everyday discussion of a controversial topic like drug abuse by nonexperts in the field of the causal relationships at issue, it is interesting to see how the resolution of the slippery slope turns towards the appeal to expert opinion. That is, the evidence on which the slippery slope argument stands or falls generally turns out to be based on appeals to expert, scientific opinions. For generally, to resolve disputes about whether one thing causes another, scientific and statistical data are the relevant evidential considerations that carry most weight. In such cases, the causal slippery slope is revealed as a kind of argumentation that rests on empirical premises.

An excellent case study to illustrate this point was a debate in the House of Commons of Canada on December 11, 1981, which arose in response to a proposal to decriminalize cannabis offences (*Commons Debates,* December 11, 1981, pp. 13998–14005). The first speaker, Mr. Mel Gass (Member for Malpeque), spoke out strongly against the legalization of marijuana by citing 'grave consequences' in the form of 'a developing trend of evidence pointing to the harmful effects of marijuana' (p. 13998). Fighting fire with fire, Mr. Ian Waddell (Member for Vancouver-Kingsway), argued for decriminalization of marijuana by citing scientific and medical authoritative sources indicating that the known consequences of marijuana use are not as bad as Mr. Gass argued. Part of the dispute between these two arguers turned on the slippery slope question of whether the use of marijuana by young people leads on to heavier drug use and other serious problems which have a tendency to escalate.

Mr. Gass began his speech by citing several scientific experts on the damaging effects of marijuana, describing how the chemically active substances in the drug accumulate in the brain, and lead to long-term effects with persistent use. Between these appeals to expert opinion on the chemical effects of marijuana, Mr. Gass went on to advance a version of the causal slippery slope argument to support his case.

Case 3.7

The brain, reproductive process and the lungs are not the only body organs and functions that marijuana affects. Medical evidence points to damage to the entire cellular process, chromosome and genetic damage and mutation and suppression of the immune system owing to the use of cannabis. It has also been firmly established that tolerance to cannabis develops, providing a psychological basis for the necessity of the heavy chronic smoker to increase dosage, or to use more potent psychoactive drugs. While marijuana is not physically addictive, there develops a more subtle but no less real psychological dependence that is a formidable obstacle to discontinuance of its use.

So although we may believe that occasional smoking of marijuana is harmless in that we will not become addicted, it is very important to remember that cannabis is a habit-forming substance capable of producing dependence of a psychological nature.

One person who knows better than any of us the effects of marijuana is Dr. Ingrid L. Lantner of the Erinside Clinic in Willoughby, Ohio. She recently wrote that, in her observation as someone who regularly treats users: 'Marijuana is one of the most deteriorating drugs that youth and society has been exposed to!'

She explains that few of us or the users recognize the long range consequences. Individuals with symptoms such as fatigue, lack of motivation, depression, paranoia, changed sexual attitudes and forgetfulness do not realize the cause until after they are totally marijuana-free and have regained their original functions. (p. 13999)

Here the first two paragraphs express the basis of the slippery slope argumentation. This attack is then quickly supported by the appeal to expert opinion, citing the findings of Dr. Lantner as evidence. The nature of the alleged causal linkage cited is partly physical (chemical), but also partly a psychological dependence.

Mr. Gass then went on to cite many more effects of marijuana smoking, citing the problems Canadian youth will face if marijuana use becomes more common.

Case 3.7a

Studies have shown that those who smoke marijuana reflect an amotivational syndrome, a massive, chronic passivity, and experience symptoms such as mental confusion, inability to concentrate, diminished attention span, loss of will power, difficulties with concept formation and recent memory, serious loss of motivation, paranoid suspiciousness of others, especially young people of their parents, regression to a more infantile state, distortion of perception and reality, a tendency toward magical thinking, emotional disorders, and I could go on and on. It is quite a list. Is this what we want for our children? I certainly hope not. . . .

If the present trends continue, if adolescent marijuana use increases at its present rate, our society is on its way to acquiring an unmanageable number of emotionally and intellectually handicapped individuals. (p. 13999)

Finally, to place the keystone in his sequence of slippery slope argumentation, Mr. Gass followed up a further list of citation of expert sources on the bad effects of marijuana with an ultimate outcome predicted. According to these experts, decriminalization in British Columbia, Ontario, Oregon, and Maine has led to increased use and trafficking in drugs.

Case 3.7*b*

This prospect of increased cannabis use must force us also to face up to evidence that heavy users are likely to go on to the use of even more dangerous drugs. Mr. William Pollin of the National Institute on Drug Abuse through studies has concluded that: 'a significant causal relationship exists between the use of marijuana and the use of other drugs.'

He found a staggering 73 per cent of heavy users went on to use harder drugs. He also found that people who use marijuana had a thousand times greater chance of going on to heavier drugs than people who did not smoke marijuana.

A front page article in last Wednesday's *Globe and Mail* revealed that the use of LSD among Ontario high school students rose 67 per cent in the last four years. In light of Mr. Pollin's conclusions, this House must recognize that the outbreak of this mind-bending drug is largely the result of the casual acceptance and use of marijuana by our youth. Without a doubt, decriminalization will not just lead to higher marijuana acceptance but will unleash a drug abuse problem more severe than we have ever known. (p. 14000)

In this case, Mr. Gass has put the final elements of his slippery slope argument in place. His argument concludes that scientific evidence of the increased use of marijuana he has cited show 'that heavy users are likely to go on to the use of even more dangerous drugs,' but ultimately decriminalization would 'unleash,' through this escalation, 'a drug abuse problem more severe than we have ever known.' Mr. Gass concluded that 'extreme caution should be taken' when contemplating changes that could have such 'far-reaching effects' (p. 14001). This conservative argument concluded in a warning of the potentially horrible results that would ensue, once the first step of decriminalizing marijuana were to be taken.

Taking the opposed point of view, Mr. Waddell began his rebuttal by conceding that 'chronic use' of any drug, whether it be marijuana, alcohol, or tobacco, 'would bring one to a mindless stupor' (p. 14001). He then countered with an opposed appeal to expert opinion.

Case 3.7*c*

As a matter of fact, the problem that we have is that the medical evidence on marijuana is only suggestive and not conclusive. I think it stops far short of proving that heavy, regular use of marijuana may produce lung or heart disease, slow down or halt one's sex life, cause long lasting disturbances of behaviour and brain function, or lower one's resistance to infection.

An authoritative statement from the Addiction Research Foundation points out: '. . . what is not yet known is the frequency with which these health problems occur among cannabis users, the degree of use needed to produce them, and the percentage of users at risk . . . it is probable that any specific health problem due to cannabis will have a low incidence . . .'.

A Gallup poll indicated that about 15 per cent of the Canadian population, that is between 2.5 and 2.7 million people, have tried marijuana, and that among younger people between the ages of 18 to 24 the figure is over 25 per cent. Not being a scientist but based on common sense, that would indicate to me that if that many people had used marijuana for a period of time, we would in fact have a lot greater incidence of disease and ill-health than we have, if it caused all the things that the hon. member said it caused. It indicates to me that chronic users may have problems, but occasional users may not have those medical problems. (p. 14001)

Both by citing an expert opinion from the Addiction Research Foundation, and by citing statistics, Mr. Waddell argues that the scientific evidence on the harmful effects of marijuana is not conclusive. He takes the skeptical stance of trying to throw doubt on Mr. Gass's argument by disputing what is shown by the body of scientific evidence, claiming that the experts disagree, or at any rate that the available scientific evidence is open to differing interpretations.

The argument now turns on one expert opinion argument used to oppose the prior expert opinion argument.[2] But neither of these arguments is fallacious *per se*. Mr. Waddell is citing different expert sources of opinion in order to try to weaken the evidential basis of Mr. Gass's argument enough to make it unconvincing in relation to its burden of proof.

However, Mr. Waddell's argument then took a step further by suggesting that Mr. Gass was using scare tactics (*argumentum ad baculum*) by trying to exaggerate the bad effects of marijuana.

Case 3.7*d*

The hon. member spoke about young people. The problem we have with young people is that they believe what I have just said a minute ago. They

---

[2] See Walton (1987, ch. 7) and Walton (1989, ch. 7) for criteria for evaluating arguments based on appeals to expert opinion.

think we are trying to scare them. They do not think we are being straightforward with them. I do not think we are either. (p.14001)

Here Mr. Waddell tries to shift to a different audience in making a kind of *ad populum* appeal to the current preconceptions and attitudes of the young people at that time. But this rebuttal also functions as a way of dismissing the slippery slope argument of Mr. Gass. The suggestion is that all the evidence concerning the harmful effects of marijuana cited by Mr. Gass can be dismissed as a kind of ploy or tactic used by the conservative elements in society (authorities) to 'scare' young people into submission.

Mr. Waddell then went on to argue at length that marijuana is essentially different from harder drugs, and that the scientific evidence of its harm has been overrated (p. 14002). Addressing the question of progression to harder drugs, Mr. Waddell appealed to his own experience as a lawyer.

Case 3.7e

The final question which should be raised is whether decriminalization will lead to increased use of drugs. It is an important question. It seems to me that the evidence is that the number of cannabis users who progress to harder drugs is only a small proportion of the total number of cannabis users. Moreover, the prohibition against cannabis encourages the progression factor because it requires people to contact traffickers who deal in a variety of drugs. I have defended probably 400 to 500 cases of possession of marijuana. I used to know what happened to some of my clients in later years; I would follow them up. They never progressed to harder drugs. I knew many heroin addicts with whom I dealt. I have talked to them; they came into heroin for various reasons. (p. 14003)

Here, Mr. Waddell is citing the findings of his own experience, which are directly contrary to the scientific opinions cited by Mr. Gass. He is also arguing, contrary to the point of view represented by Mr. Gass, that the present criminal prohibition against marijuana 'encourages the progression factor' because it promotes associations between users and 'traffickers who deal in a variety of drugs.'

These arguments seem reasonable enough, at least insofar as they are attempts to cite empirical evidence against the slippery slope of Mr. Gass, which was in turn mainly based on empirical evidence, cited in the form of expert, scientifically based opinions.

What has been shown is that the causal slippery slope argument has a heavily empirical evidential basis—on both sides, *pro* and *contra*—which make it naturally lead to a 'battle of the experts.' This is especially evident in a case like the present issue, where the disputed causal relationships are directly relevant to statistical, scientific, and medical findings.

However, Mr. Waddell's argument should be open to more critical scrutiny when he veers towards the dismissal of the slippery slope argument as a scare tactic that will be ineffective in persuading young people who are already convinced otherwise. In his concluding remarks, Mr. Waddell cannot resist resorting to this argument once again.

Case 3.7f

My predecessor in Vancouver-Kingsway once made a speech about marijuana which was circulated. It was to the effect that marijuana was the devil's drug, and so on. I watched the reaction of the young people closely. They laughed at it, Mr. Speaker. (p. 14003)

Mr. Waddell is making the legitimate point here that laws are not effective in prohibiting behavior if the people affected do not believe in the laws. But his remark also suggests, wrongly, that the scientific evidence cited by Mr. Gass can be dismissed, because young people won't accept it anyway. This suggests, cleverly, that the opinions of the young people at risk are the opinions that really count in deciding this issue. This move is a species of *argumentum ad populum* (Walton 1989, ch. 4) that attempts to dismiss the prior slippery slope argument against the decriminalization of marijuana out of hand. This argument suggests that the deliberations of the Members of Parliament, or the question of who has the stronger arguments based on the evidence and reasoning given in the debate, are irrelevant, because those whose opinions really matter don't care about these things and aren't going to be moved by them. We return to a consideration of this type of argument in case 3.8.

Turning back to the arguments of Mr. Gass, it should be noted that by the standards of Walton (1989, ch. 7), several of his appeals to expert opinion are weak. He begins (case 3.7) by claiming that 'medical evidence points to' different kinds of physical damage caused by marijuana, and follows up by claiming 'it has been firmly established' that marijuana also has serious psychological effects. However, he does not cite any specific documents or experts to back up these claims.

When he does cite the name of an expert, Dr. Ingrid L. Lantner, his next appeal to expert opinion is much stronger, precisely for that reason. However, he does not indicate what field Dr. Lantner is an expert in, and although he quotes her, he does not give any information about the source or date of the quotation.

In case 3.7a, Mr. Gass cites a long list of psychological effects of marijuana use, evidently culled from sources of expert opinions, but does not document his claims at all, except to preface them by the phrase, 'Studies have shown that . . .' This evidence could be legitimate, but the argument, as presented by Mr. Gass, should be regarded as open to critical questioning until he does a much better job of documenting these studies, showing that they are genuine and authoritative sources.

Mr. Waddell's point in case 3.7f, that the use of the slippery slope argument can fail to be convincing to skeptical young people, has become an issue of concern in the 1990s, in connection with the increasing number of cocaine users. Especially worrisome was the sharp increase in the use of 'crack,' a form of cocaine inhaled by smoking. The worry here is that those who have used the slippery slope argument to warn young people about the dangers of these drugs may have been exaggerated, using the slope argument in a heavy-handed way to promote the false conception that everyone who tries crack becomes so severely addicted that it leads them to total ruin. An article in *Newsweek* (Martz: 1990) cited the dangers of this improper use of the slippery slope.

Case 3.8a

In their zeal to shield young people from the plague of drugs, the media and many drug educators have hyped the very real dangers of crack into a myth of instant and total addition. . . .

By the best estimate, at least 2.4 million Americans have tried crack, but contrary to the myth, less than half a million now use it once a month or more. And even among the current users, there are almost surely more occasional smokers than chronic abusers. As children in drug-using communities can see for themselves, the users show a wide range of drug symptoms, from total impairment to almost none. That doesn't mean it's safe to play with crack, or with most other drugs, legal or illegal.

Addiction is a slippery slope. But what worries a growing number of drug experts is that the cry of wolf about instant addiction may backfire. (p. 44)

The presumption here is that the use of the slippery slope argument to warn about the dangers of drugs like crack is basically reasonable. But the point made is that if the slippery slope argument is exaggerated, by being presented in a heavy-handed and overly strong way, that is not commensurate with the real data on addiction, it will not be convincing as an argument to those, i.e. young people, who are mainly at risk.

The astute observation here is that the slippery slope can become ineffective and clearly fallacious because it is used as a scare tactic when, in fact, the intended audience can see for themselves that the facts are otherwise. The *Newsweek* article goes on to cite the opinions of two experts that in fact the use of these scare tactics has led to a climate of skepticism.

Case 3.8b

'It's a dangerous myth,' says Herbert Kleber, the demand-reduction deputy to federal drug czar William Bennett. 'If the kids find out you're lying, they'll think you're lying about other things too.' The pattern is an old one. Exaggerated warnings about demon rum at the turn of the century sparked derision; the 1936 scare movie, 'Reefer Madness,' became a cult film for jeering potheads in the '60s and early '70s. And that in turn, as Kleber says, helped foster the delusion that cocaine itself was safe.

'We're seeing a whole lot of scare tactics,' says Sheigla Murphy, co-director of a National Institute on Drug Abuse study of cocaine use among San Francisco-area women. 'The truth is bad enough. We don't have to exaggerate it.' But the scare tactics have triggered a wider skepticism about the whole drug issue. (p. 44)

The article goes on to cite cases of users who have found crack easy to give up, but maintains (p. 45) that any addiction is hard to break, and that crack is highly addictive for some users. An expert (Kleber) is cited (p. 45) as saying that roughly one cocaine user out of five will become a 'chronic abuser' or addict. The article also stresses that addiction differs widely from one type of drug to another.

One conclusion we can draw from this case is that the strength of the slippery slope argument should be expected to vary from one instance of its use to another. Another conclusion is that in some instances, e.g. in the case of crack addiction, it is a somewhat weak kind of presumptive argument that admits of exceptions, but nonetheless is an argument that does carry a legitimate weight. The problem comes from attempting to exaggerate that weight through the unjustifiably aggressive use of scare tactics. The fallacy of the improper use of the slippery slope argument in such a case can be diagnosed as the tactic of pressing ahead too hard, using 'scare tactics' when the evidence does not justify loading the argument with this kind of weight. The danger is that the respondent can point out the weakness in your slippery slope argument and make it appear ridiculous, thereby refuting it totally in the view of a skeptical audience. By having exaggerated its claim, your slippery slope argument will destroy itself needlessly, or at least be open to such an easy and devastating refutation.

4. Practical Reasoning

The context of discussion of case 3.7 is that of a parliamentary debate. The two opposed parties are engaged in supporting opposed points of view on an issue of legislation. However, the slippery slope argumentation used by Mr. Gass to support his point of view presupposed a secondary context of discussion, that of advice-giving dialogue where a layperson consults a skilled expert for an opinion on how to solve a problem or carry out an action requiring technical expertise in a domain of specialized knowledge (Walton 1989, ch. 7).

The kind of argumentation involved in this type of case is not purely theoretical reasoning, directed towards drawing conclusions from premises that can be established as known truths. Instead, it is a practical problem of deciding what to do in a situation where even the experts do not clearly agree on what is established as true. Case 3.8 also concerned a practical problem of the same sort, where expert opinions were crucial.

The causal type of slippery slope argument is an adjunct to the argument from consequences, which is in turn a species of practical reasoning. *Practical reasoning* is a goal-directed type of argumentation which takes knowledge of an agent's situation into account in guiding the agent on how it is reasonable to act in a situation of incomplete knowledge. Practical reasoning is a sequence of practical inferences. The conclusion of a practical inference is an imperative to a course of action for a particular agent.

Based on two premises, one stating that an agent has a certain goal or intention in mind, and a second one stating that this agent knows that some particular action is a means to carry out that intention, practical reasoning draws the conclusion that the agent ought practically to carry out this particular action. In sequences of goal-directed argumentation, practical reasoning is a chaining together of the two basic schemes of practical inference represented below, where a is an agent, A is an action, and G is a goal.

Argumentation Schemes for Practical Reasoning

Necessary condition scheme　　　　G is a goal for a.

Doing A is necessary for a to carry out G.

Therefore, a ought to do A.

Sufficient condition scheme　　　　G is a goal for a.

Doing A is sufficient for a to carry out G.

Therefore, a ought to do A.

Practical reasoning is a goal-driven, knowledge-based, action-guiding kind of argumentation that concludes in a practical imperative of action in relation to the (usually imperfect) knowledge that an agent has of ways and means to proceed in a particular situation (Walton: 1990).

One context of argumentation where slippery slope arguments are often used is in planning. This can be government policy-making, it can be planning in other sorts of institutions like universities or corporations, or it could even be just a discussion of proposed social policies in an everyday conversation by parties not speaking as representatives of any institution. For example, slippery slope argumentation is a very common and central argument in discussions of medical ethics and policy discussions on the uses of medical technology and health care resources.

In this context, the use of the slippery slope argument is as a kind of warning or caution against possible abuses or bad effects of a proposed new policy. Thus it functions as a kind of conservative argument or safety brake on a proposed policy that may not have been tested very well.

This use of the slippery slope argument is a kind of argumentation that pertains to one aspect of the argumentation scheme for practical reasoning—namely the aspect that considers the possible negative side-effects of the proposed course of action that is the conclusion. The conclusion of an instance of practical reasoning is an imperative that directs a planner (or agent) to a specific course of action (or inaction) in a particular situation, as it is known to the planner. But every action has further consequences.

One important aspect of practical reasoning is the question of the possible side effects or consequences of a course of action being considered. This kind of reasoning has been called the argument from consequences (van Eemeren and Kruiger 1987; see also Windes and Hastings 1965: 223–36).

The *argument from consequences* has a *pro* and a *contra* argumentation scheme. Let A be an action. The *pro* scheme is the following: the consequences of A are, on balance, positive (as far as we know); therefore, you ought to do A. The *contra* scheme is the following: the consequences of A are, on balance, negative (as far as we know); therefore, you ought not to do A. In both schemes, the conclusion is a practical 'ought' (Diggs 1960). The conclusion contains a second-person 'you' where the context of discussion is advice-giving. In another context, that of deliberation (a species of planning), the conclusion contains the first-person 'I' in place of the second-person 'you.' Practical reasoning is argumentation because it always takes place in a context of discussion, dialogue, or deliberation. In critical discussion, one context, one party tries to persuade the other of the reasonableness of a particular line of action as the best way to proceed in a controversial or problematic situation.

In case 3.7, the context is a little more complicated still. Two parliamentarians are debating on who has the better argument—whether it is better to pass or defeat a proposed item of legislation. Their arguments are directed towards each other, but also, more generally, to the legislative body that will vote on the issue. Practical reasoning comes to be important in this type of debate especially when the key argument turns on an appeal to expert opinion. This kind of situation happens surprisingly often in parliamentary and congressional debates.

Practical reasoning is a pragmatic kind of argumentation, best judged in relation to a context of discussion or problem-solving situation. For each argumentation scheme, of either of the two kinds of scheme above, there is a matching set of critical questions of the following form.

Matching Critical Questions for Practical Reasoning
(1) Are there alternative means of realizing G, other than A?

(2) Is it possible for *a* to do A?

(3) Does *a* have goals other than G, which have the potential to conflict with *a*'s realizing G?

(4) Are there negative side effects of *a*'s bringing about A that ought to be considered?

Practical reasoning is essentially pragmatic because it is not the formal validity of the argument structure that is at issue in evaluating a particular case. Instead, if the premises of the argumentation scheme are satisfied in a situation, a burden of proof is thrown on the critic who rejects the conclusion to pose an appropriate critical question. If the question is relevant to one of the premises, the burden of proof is then shifted back to the agent to reply adequately to the question, in relation to the context of the situation at issue.

Planning characteristically involves discussing the pros and cons of a proposed course of action being discussed (Windes and Hastings 1965: 232). The planner tries to forecast or imagine the possible good consequences of the planned action, and also the possible bad consequences. The good or favorable consequences tend to support the action being considered, while the bad or negative consequences have the opposite effect (Windes and Hastings 1965: 227).

Generally, the slippery slope argument is used in this context as one way of counselling against the implementation of a proposed policy by citing its potentially bad side effects or negative consequences. But the slippery slope is a very special type of argument of this sort. Its hallmark is that it proceeds by small steps through a sequence of argumentation from the proposed policy to some bad, usually horrible or catastrophic consequence which is the ultimate outcome of the sequence.

Thus the slippery slope argument, as used in planning and policy-making, is a species of the argument from consequences.

But it is a special kind of subspecies that pertains to smaller degrees or steps in a bigger sequence of argumentation. Not all negative arguments from consequences are of this sort. Some are simply direct arguments that a bad outcome of some proposed line of action will occur. This negative argument from consequences has a general form of argument that can be identified with *modus tollens:* If A then B; not-B; therefore not-A. But A and B stand for proposed actions or outcomes of actions rather than propositions, and the conditional is not the material conditional of deductive logic. B is said to be unacceptable. But because B is a consequence of A, the conclusion is that A is unacceptable. The argument is not deductive in nature, however. For the conclusion is not that A is false *per se,* or totally unacceptable in any circumstances. The conclusion is only that A is unacceptable given that other known good consequences are not overriding.

A causal slippery slope argument can be said to be good or correct in the pragmatic sense of being correctly used to shift a burden of proof in a reasonable discussion. To be correct, in this sense, it must meet the requirements of its argumentation scheme. To be sustained as a correct, good, or reasonable argument in a context of discussion, it must reply adequately to appropriate critical questioning. This pragmatic structure is the basis of the evaluation of any causal slippery slope argument as weak or strong.

Thus although the causal slippery slope argument has, in its outer shell, a deductively valid structure as a sequence of *modus ponens* subarguments, its inner logic (the basis of whether it is a strong or weak argument in a particular case) is inherently pragmatic.

5. Argumentation Scheme for the Causal Slippery Slope

It is important to recognize the idea that a good causal slippery slope argument does not need to be perfect, or impeccable, beyond criticism, or good in every respect. It can be good—meaning that it is adequate to shift the burden of proof (reasonably) towards the respondent to whom it was directed in a discussion—yet still be open to specific criticisms. That is, it may still be quite possible for the respondent to reply effectively to it—

shifting the burden of proof back to the proponent—even though the proponent's original slippery slope argument was a good and reasonable argument.

A good slippery slope argument can have good arguments against it. Even though it is a reasonable argument (but weak, or not fully backed up in certain respects), there may also be good arguments to challenge it. Such critical questions or reasonable challenges to a causal slippery slope argument center on the premises in the characteristic argumentation scheme. Any of the supposed links in the causal chain can be questioned, and the badness of the final outcome can be questioned. Little, Groarke, and Tindale (1989: 241) express this point very well.

A good argument *against* slippery slope reasoning must establish that the claimed causal chain does not exist, or that the value of its ultimate consequence has been misjudged. The causal chain can be challenged by questioning one of the causal links, either by pointing out that it lacks support or that it is supported by poor causal reasoning. To avoid such criticisms we may have to construct a good causal argument supporting every link in the chain.

Govier's account stressed the undesirability of the whole series of events flowing from the initial action being contemplated, whereas Johnson and Blair (1983: 164) emphasized the 'weakest link' approach, where at least one of the steps is narrowed down to as the area of the argument open to challenge.

We can combine the best features of these analyses, and also broaden the scope of the analysis, by expressing the argumentation scheme for the causal slippery slope argument in the following way. Let the proponent and the respondent be two participants in a discussion. In the causal type of slippery slope argument, the proponent and the respondent can be typically thought of as two agents who are discussing policy, or contemplating possible courses of action in order to resolve a practical problem. One is advising the other on how to proceed, or they may be arguing about some controversial type of action like abortion or euthanasia. They need not be personally involved, they could be discussing the pros and cons of a proposed public policy that would affect a lot of people.

Next, let S_0, S_1, ..., S_n be a set of states of affairs or events that are possible outcomes of actions. The key characteristic of a state

S_i is that it can be causally connected to another state S_j. Another characteristic of any state S_i is that it is possible, in principle, for it to be brought about by an agent, who in this case is usually the proponent or the respondent. That is, agents can cause (or bring about) states of affairs.

To present the argumentation scheme, let it be part of the context of discussion that the one agent, the respondent, is considering bringing about a particular state of affairs S_o. The other agent, the proponent, is discussing the merits of this proposal with the respondent. The general direction of the interaction is that the proponent is advising or warning the respondent against this contemplated course of action by citing its negative consequences. In order to carry this out, the proponent can advance argumentation which follows the general scheme presented below, containing three distinctive premises.

Argumentation Scheme for Causal Slippery Slope

Initial action premise	S_o is up for consideration as a proposal that seems initially like something which should be brought about.
Causal sequence premise	Bringing about S_o would plausibly cause (in the given circumstances, as far as we know) S_1, which would in turn plausibly cause S_2, and so forth, through the sequence $S_2, \ldots, S_n$ (for some finite n).
Ultimate outcome premise	S_n is not something which should be brought about (because it is horrible, undesirable, etc.).
Conclusion	S_o should not be brought about.

The argumentation scheme above is used by the proponent of the slippery slope to try to dissuade the respondent from an action he is inclined to favor or is considering carrying out, or from thinking of this kind of action generally as a good policy in a given situation.

The function of this argumentation scheme is to shift the burden of proof against the side of the respondent to defend his proposed policy or contemplated course of action, if he can. The causal slippery slope argument should be judged reasonable, in a particular case, to the extent that it fulfills this function. This kind of argumentation is reasonable (correct, justified, strong, etc.) to the extent that it brings forward the right kind of evidence to meet the requirements of the three premises, thereby successfully putting forward a plausible argument. Reasonable requirements for burden of proof are determined by the context of the discussion.

According to the argumentation scheme proposed above, whether the causal slippery slope argument is used correctly or fallaciously depends on the context of dialogue. The fallacy, when (or if) it exists, is a pragmatic failure. But not all arguments identified as being of the causal slippery slope type are fallacious. This approach runs somewhat contrary to the analysis of Johnson and Blair, who think that slippery slope arguments are fallacious, even though they recognize argumentation from consequences as being non-fallacious in some instances. However, Johnson and Blair (1983: 164) rightly stress in their analysis of the slippery slope fallacy that one weak point which should be open to scrutiny in this kind of argumentation is the sequence of steps in the causal chain. As they put it, if at least one of these steps is unsupported or weak, the whole argument is open to challenge.

In particular cases that are instances of the causal slippery slope argumentation scheme, there can be varieties and different points of emphasis. For example, the sequence S_o, S_1, ..., S_n can go from better to worse in various ways, but it usually starts to get worse and worse towards the tail end. Typically, it is not just the ultimate outcome S_n that is judged to be bad. Most often, the first steps in the sequence seem acceptable, and it is towards the end of the sequence that things go from bad to worse. The thing about any slippery slope argument is that this sequence is gradual, and the exact cutoff point where things start to go bad tends to be elusive. But there is room for variety in particular cases. Sometimes it is the ultimate outcome that is most emphatically bad. In other cases, the neighboring states leading up to that ultimate bad outcome can seem to be highly undesirable as well.

How this argumentation scheme is used in a context of discussion is also important, and can vary. In the most straight-forward type of case, the respondent has advanced a proposal for action in the context of a plan. The proponent is an expert who has been consulted by the respondent, and the proponent is criticizing the plan by pointing out that the proposed action will have dangerous consequences.

In other cases, the context of the discussion can be more complex. In case 3.7, the two parties were engaged in a critical discussion about the issue of decriminalization of marijuana. The proponent of the slippery slope argument (Mr. Gass) was supporting the premises in his causal sequence of argumentation by appealing to expert opinions. This type of move presupposed a secondary context of dialogue whereby Mr. Gass had drawn conclusions based on his interpretation of expert opinions. In this type of case, there is a dual context of discussion. One context of discussion is being carried forward into another.

In this kind of case, the way to question the causal sequence premise set is to question the appeals to expert opinion that have been used as the evidence to support the causal links.

6. Critical Questions for the Causal Slippery Slope

Once all the individual steps in the causal sequence are filled in, there are basically three ways of critically questioning a causal slippery slope argument.

1. *Questioning the Initial Action Premise.* Does the proponent's description of the initial action rightly express the proposal being advocated by the respondent?
2. *Questioning the Causal Sequence.* Do any of the causal links in the sequence lack solid evidence to back it up as a plausible claim?
3. *Questioning the Outcome Premise.* Does this outcome plausibly follow from the sequence, and is it as bad as the proponent suggests?

However, because of the way the causal slippery slope argument is often presented, prior to asking these questions, there may be quite a bit of cleaning up to be done, by asking preliminary questions on how the argument is to be interpreted. These problems arise because the argument may be expressed in a condensed form.

Johnson and Blair recognize two typical forms of the slippery slope argument, a longer and a shorter form. In the longer form (Johnson and Blair 1983: 161), 'the whole series of causal steps is included.' (They are thinking primarily here of the causal type of slippery slope argument.) In the shorter form, 'just the first and last chapters of the causal story are included in the argument' (p. 161). This is a very important practical distinction in studying how the slippery slope argument is used as an argumentation tactic, because such an argument often works by innuendo or suggestion, as a kind of warning or threat. When it is used in this way, many of the intervening steps are left as unexpressed premises which may be implicitly known by the discussants, but are not filled in explicitly. This tacit dimension leads to some of the practical problems in trying to deal with slippery slope arguments.

An excellent example which shows how the short form works is quoted by Johnson and Blair (1983: 164) from a story in the *Windsor Star* (September 1972). In this case, the Canadian unions had been complaining that foreign visitors were taking jobs in Canada, contrary to immigration rules. In 1972, the Trudeau government proposed the possible remedy of issuing work permits to Canadian workers. Union leaders protested strongly to this, however, and Dennis McDermott, then Canadian director of the United Auto Workers, responded as follows.

Case 3.9

They would run counter to our traditional freedoms and would be *the first step* toward a police state.

The problem with this response, noted by Johnson and Blair (p. 164) is that the argument, as expressed above, gives us no idea what the intervening steps are supposed to be. We could imagine that work permits would make it easier for the government to keep track of who is working where. And the easy access to this information could, potentially, make it easier for the government to do other things, like make restrictions on where people can work, or something of this sort. But given that there would appear to be no reason to think that any restriction of this sort is likely, it's hard to see how the issuing of work permits, in and of itself, would lead to some sorts of restrictions that would in turn lead to a police state.

The argument in case 3.9 appears worrisome and even menacing partly because so much is unstated. The best way to respond to this kind of slippery slope argument is to request that the proponent fill in enough of the missing steps so that we can see how he is getting from work permits to the police state. Only then, when the argument is further filled out, can we begin to properly criticize it by questioning the weak links in the chain.

With the short form of slippery slope argument then, an antecedent critical question, or series of them, is needed in order to proceed to the next step of posing the regular set of critical questions that would be appropriate for the long form of the argument.

In other cases where the short form is used, however, it seems that just leaving out the specific sequence of the intervening steps in the argument is not the only thing that makes the argument weak or objectionable. The following excerpt from a letter written by Richard Nixon in the *New York Times* on October 29, 1965, was quoted as an example of a fallacious slippery slope argument by Hardin (1985: 63). His letter warned that the fall of Vietnam

Case 3.10

. . . would mean ultimately *the destruction of freedom of speech for all men for all time* not only in Asia but the United States as well . . . We must never forget that if the war in Vietnam is lost . . . the right of free speech will be extinguished throughout the world.

The argumentation in this case could, no doubt, be spelled out more specifically by indicating, after the manner of Kahane's version of the argument (Chapter 1.1), just how the spread of the presumptive extinction of free speech will proceed from one geographical area to the next. But would that make the argument any stronger? It is not clear that it would. The argument might seem just as weak even if specific geographical predictions of the sequence were to be filled in, after the manner of Kahane's version, for example. In fact, filling in the specific steps could even make the argument weaker, if done in a particularly unconvincing way. The basic problem with the argument in case 3.10 is simply that it appears to be a highly speculative prediction with little evidence (from hindsight, twenty years later) to back it up.

The conclusion to draw is that the short form of the slippery slope argument is not inherently fallacious, even though it is appropriate and reasonable generally (and in some cases, mandatory) to ask the arguer who has used it to spell out the steps in his reasoning in greater detail. This form of request, however, appears more like a point of order than a 'fallacy.' It is a request that the argument be made more explicit, prior to questioning or criticizing its weaker points.

Case 1.1, which concerned Susman's use of the thread and cloth analogy to argue against Fried's contention that the ruling of *Roe* v. *Wade* should be sustained, is also a short form of slippery slope argument. From this one step, Susman argued, the whole range of procreational rights in the U.S. will perish, just as when a thread is pulled, the sleeve falls off. This way of putting the argument is pungent, because it is so direct. But it leaves so much out that the argument cannot be properly evaluated unless the proponent gives us some idea of what the intervening steps are supposed to be.

To sum up, a causal slippery slope argument should be judged weak or lacking adequate support if either (*a*) it fails to supply enough evidence to meet the requirements of the three kinds of appropriate critical question, or (*b*) it is presented in an incomplete manner that fails to make the sequence of causal steps explicit enough to bear proper scrutiny.

7. Fallacy or Weak Argument?

A common problem with the textbook treatments of the causal slippery slope argument is that it is called a fallacy in cases where it would be more appropriate to call it a weak argument, or an argument that has not been adequately backed with the proper evidence. The problem here is that the term 'fallacy' is being used in too inclusive a manner. According to this overly broad usage, an argument which fails to give grounds or good reasons for the claim it makes is a fallacious argument.

According to Waller (1988: 179), '[t]he slippery slope fallacy occurs when one claims that an action will have bad consequences, but fails to give any grounds for the claim that such bad consequences will follow.' But this surely is too broad. Consider the following argument which claims that an action will have bad consequences.

Case 3.11

Marcia's young son Brad has eaten several chocolates from a box of these rich bonbons, and is about to take another one. Marcia says to Brad: 'If you keep on eating those things, you will be sick at your stomach!'

Now Marcia has failed to give any grounds for her claim that Brad will be sick. And she has claimed that the course of actions that Brad is apparently heading towards will have bad consequences. But has Marcia committed a fallacy? It is by no means clear that she has. Perhaps Brad will in fact eat all the candies and not get sick at his stomach. Marcia has not proved this, or even tried to give grounds for it. Yet she has warned Brad of the likely consequences of his actions, and it seems like it is, or could be a reasonable warning. She has also argued. She has presented a kind of practical or prudential argument to Brad which warns him of the bad consequences of a possible course of actions that Brad appears to be considering.

Whatever else we might want to say about Marcia's argument in case 3.11, I do not think we should say that it is an instance of the slippery slope fallacy, or any other fallacy. As an argument it may be weak, or perhaps lacking in supportive evidence—if evidence is really called for in this kind of case—but it would not be appropriate to say that it is fallacious.

Waller's own leading example (p. 178) of the slippery slope fallacy is part of a prosecutor's final speech to the jury in the Cunningham-Burdell murder trial of 1847, quoted from Henry Lauren Clinton, *Celebrated Trials*.

Case 3.12

If mawkish sympathy enters the jurybox—if ever mawkish sympathy takes control of the jurybox, if men surrender their feelings as men, then there is but one other step to take. Mawkish sympathy has then but to ascend to the judiciary, which, thank God, it has not yet reached! Then strike the scales away from the hands of Justice, pull the bandage away from one eye and place it on both, and let the community know that while it is true that juries

> 'When human life is in debate
> Can ne'er too long deliberate'

yet, that if they deliberate to such an extent as to give immunity to crime, by acquittal, when circumstances are damning, there will come into the world, and be inaugurated, that millennial triumph of the powers of darkness of which we all have read in Holy Writ. (Clinton 1897: 189)

This speech warned of the potential for the judicial system of giving in to too much sympathy and emotionalism in the jury box for criminals who really deserve tough penalties. It could lead to freedom for criminals to operate with impunity, to the kind of lawless and violent society where evil triumphs over good, as described in some of the prophetic warnings in the Bible.

Should we call this segment of this speech a fallacy? To the contrary, many today might well feel that this speech was highly accurate, and that the consequences of the kind of uncritical and emotional thinking in the law courts it condemned have in fact now materialized.

This argument is a slippery slope argument, to the effect that we should keep to strict legal standards when the circumstances are 'damning' and call for tough penalties. For once one exception is made, on purely emotional grounds not justified by the facts or by the rules of law, then unthinking leniency can become an accepted precedent which can be easily given in to. This may be a good argument, or it may not be. One can certainly appreciate that it could be a highly appropriate argument in some circumstances, however.

Waller (p. 178) is unfairly unsympathetic when he interprets the argument as saying, 'in other words, failure to convict will result in a millenium of Satanic rule.' The argument does not say this, and it is a very harsh interpretation of what it does say. The argument is a flowery and metaphorical way (perhaps appropriate for the rhetorical standards of the time) of warning the jury of the long-term danger of giving in to emotional reactions in a legal judgment where the circumstances do not merit such a response. In historical hindsight, this particular warning turned out to be highly prescient.

Johnson and Blair (1983: 164) give an analysis of the slippery slope fallacy that is similar to Waller's, but is more precise, and perhaps somewhat more narrow. According to them, there are three conditions for the fallacy, as given below. They do not say what the letters below stand for, but let us presume that M is an arguer, and that W, X, Y and Z stand for events.

Conditions for Slippery Slope (Johnson and Blair 1983)

(1) M claims that if W is permitted, it will lead to X, X will lead to Y, and so on to Z.

(2) M holds that Z is undesirable and therefore W should not be permitted.

(3) At least one of the steps in the causal chain is unsupported and open to challenge.

Johnson and Blair think that slippery slope argumentation is fallacious, but that such arguments need to be distinguished from (non-fallacious) appeals to precedent, a kind of legitimate argumentation.

Once again, however, the problem with this analysis is that it is too broad to capture the notion of slippery slope as a fallacy. If one of the steps in the sequence is unsupported and open to challenge, then the slippery slope argument can rightly be said to be weak, questionable, or open to challenge. But it goes too far to say that all causal slippery slope arguments have to be fallacious. Even if several of the steps in the chain are unsupported or open to challenge, the slippery slope argument could still be reasonable as an argument that shifts a burden of proof quite rightly, provided the questionable premises are plausible, or could be backed up in further discussion.

The solution here is to separate clause (3) in Johnson and Blair's set of conditions from the elements of the argumentation scheme for the causal slippery slope argument (conditions (1) and (2)). Condition (3) is not a part of the argumentation scheme *per se*. Rather, it represents one of the set of appropriate critical questions matching that argumentation scheme.

The general question now arises whether there are any real instances of the causal slippery slope fallacy at all. It is now clear that there are stronger and weaker causal slippery slope arguments. But are any of the weak ones so bad that they should properly be called causal slippery slope fallacies?

8. Does the Causal Slippery Slope Fallacy Exist?

The causal slippery slope argument consists of a series of causal steps that drive the respondent towards a conclusion that is horrible or unacceptable to him as a possible consequence of taking a first step that he is contemplating. At least, the proponent of the slippery slope argument is suggesting that this might be the outcome.

The proponent is warning the respondent that a dangerous outcome is a possible or plausible outcome of a plan that the respondent has advocated. The context of the discussion is based on the attempt to project the possible future consequences of a course of action being contemplated. Naturally this is always a chancy kind of guesswork, even though scientific evidence may exist that is highly relevant. Therefore the kind of reasoning that is involved is plausible argumentation.

Even so, there is an element of necessity involved in the presentation of a slippery slope argument, because the technique is to suggest that the respondent must be propelled down the slope, once he takes the first step.

It is this conflict between these two elements of plausibility and necessity that creates the kind of situation that leads to the charge of committing the causal slippery slope fallacy. Characteristically, the causal slippery slope is a weak kind of argument because it predicts future contingencies, and because causality is not a matter of necessity, especially where a long sequence of causation is concerned. But the causal slippery slope argument can sometimes use strong language to the effect that a dangerous outcome is *likely* to happen, or even that such an outcome is *inevitable*. Where this juxtaposition between a weakly presented argument and a strong claim of the unavoidability of the horrible outcome are marked, and where the proponent refuses to fill the gap by providing evidence or responding to appropriate critical questioning, it may be right to speak of a fallacy being committed. These are cases of the kind where, according to Schauer (1985: 382), the slippery slope claims are 'wildly exaggerated.' However, of all the cases we have examined of causal slippery slope arguments in this chapter, only two appear to have been this bad. Perhaps case 3.10 seemed pretty bad, because the conclusion appeared to be a radical prediction, and the evidence presented for it was minimal. And case 3.9 was equally bad, or perhaps even worse, for the same reasons. But even these two cases appeared ridiculous as arguments, at least in part, because they were severely condensed versions with no serious attempt made to spell out the steps of the causal sequence. Slippery slope fallacies seem to be much rarer than the texts and traditional treatments would have us believe.

Two logic textbooks, Barry (1976) and Hurley (1982), offer analyses of the slippery slope fallacy as an error of causal reasoning. Barry (p. 132) defines the *fallacy of slippery slope* (or *domino theory*) as 'the fallacy of assuming an action will inevitably lead to a consequence when, in fact, there is no such inevitability.' According to Barry (p. 102) someone who commits this fallacy does not understand what a *cause* is—if A causes B, it does not follow that one cannot prevent B from occurring once A occurs.

Hurley (p. 111) also sees the slippery slope fallacy as a variety of false cause fallacy, but defines it quite differently from Barry. According to Hurley (p. 111) the slippery slope fallacy 'occurs when the conclusion of an argument rests upon the claim that a certain event will set off a chain reaction, leading in the end to some undesirable consequence, yet there is not sufficient reason to think that the chain reaction will actually take place.' According to this account, the fallacy occurs where the first action *will* set off a sequence leading to the bad consequence. By contrast, according to Barry's account, the fallacy occurs where the first action *must* (i.e. will inevitably) lead to the bad consequence through the intervening sequence.

This is a significant difference in defining the requirements for an argument being an instance of the slippery slope fallacy. One analysis requires that such an argument claims that given the initial action, the bad consequence must occur. The other requires only that it claim that, given the initial action, the bad consequence will occur, without giving sufficient reasons to back up this claim.

The problem with Hurley's analysis is the same as that of many others already discussed. What it describes is a weak causal slippery slope argument that is not necessarily fallacious. Barry's analysis is on a somewhat better footing in this regard, because it only applies to cases where inevitability of the outcome is claimed by the proponent. It would not apply to many of the arguments usually cited in the textbooks as examples of the slippery slope fallacy, however. Indeed, it would not seem to include any of the cases studied in this chapter. Although some would see that as a liability of Barry's account, from the point of view of the direction our argument is taking here, it could be an advantage.

Our findings have tended to indicate that the causal slippery slope argument is not a fallacy, but an empirical argument that can be stronger or weaker in different instances, depending on the context of discussion and the evidence cited by the proponent. Both Hurley and Barry, as well as Johnson and Blair, Govier, Waller, and the other authorities cited, certainly seem to be on the right track generally in characterizing the bad causal slippery slope argument as occurring in the kind of case where the language in which the conclusion is expressed (whether it is that of 'will' or 'must') is too strong to be justified by the evidence given to back up the premises of the argument. But it remains to be seen whether any of these bad causal slippery slope arguments are so bad that they rightly deserve to be classified as special kinds of cases that merit the use of the term 'fallacy.' For they seem to involve no special, deceptive technique that sets them apart from the weak causal slippery slope arguments, except perhaps that they are extraordinarily weak. But this is a difference of degree, not of kind.

We could follow Barry and say that only the ones where the conclusion is claimed to follow *inevitably* from the premises are fallacious, as opposed to being merely weak. This proposal seems too narrow, however.

A broader approach would be to identify the fallacy of the causal slippery slope argument with the use of the tactic by the proponent of closing off any attempt by the respondent to bring forward critical questioning against the slippery slope argument. By this distinction, the weak argument is the failure to advance enough empirical evidence to support the argument. By contrast, the fallacy is the tactic of trying to cut off the possibility of introducing empirical evidence. For slippery slope argumentation is often used as a kind of scare tactic, to suggest that once a first step is taken, some horrifying outcome (which must be avoided at all costs) waits in the wings. This use of the argument often verges on the *argumentum ad baculum,* an appeal to fear or tactic of intimidation. What seems to make the argument plausible, for the respondent to whom it is directed, is the outcome that individual fears as a danger in a particular situation. Curiously then, the plausibility of a slippery slope argument often stems from an emotional pull to which a particular audience or respondent is susceptible.[3] It is therefore also often associated with the *argu-*

---

[3] For confirmation see Schauer (1985: 381).

mentum ad populum, or appeal to popular opinion (Walton 1989, ch. 7).

Another tactic that could be used to close off the introduction of new evidence by a respondent is the appeal to an authoritative source of expert opinion as the final word on the subject. And indeed, we saw, notably in cases 3.7 and 3.8, how the causal slippery slope argument is closely related to the *argumentum ad verecundiam.*

Could it be then, in many cases, that the causal slippery slope argument, when it is used fallaciously, is not fallacious because it commits some specially distinctive fallacy in its own right, but because it is associated with the use of other informal fallacies? Before finally commenting on this question, let us turn to one other problem—a problem of defining what sort of argument should count as a causal slippery slope argument.

9. Classification Problems

Little, Groarke, and Tindale (1989: 240) characterize slippery slope arguments as causal arguments that are 'used to show that certain actions should be performed or avoided because of their long-range consequences.' They see such arguments as stronger or weaker (good or fallacious) depending on 'whether the causal connections posited really hold and whether the final consequence has been properly judged to be desirable or undesirable' (p. 241). Thus they postulate that there can be two kinds of slippery slope argument, defining a *good slippery slope argument* as follows. 'An argument that shows either (i) that an action *should not* be performed or allowed because it will begin a causal chain leading to an undesirable consequence, or (ii) that an action *should* be performed or allowed because it will entail a chain of causes leading to a desirable end' (p. 241). Using upper-case letters to represent actions, Little, Groarke, and Tindale (p. 240) represent the form of the good slippery slope argument as follows.

A causes B, B causes C, and so on to X.

X is undesirable (or X is desirable).

Therefore, A is undesirable (or desirable).

This binary characterization runs contrary to the basic conception of the slippery slope argument advocated throughout this mono-graph and analyzed dialectically as a type of rebuttal in Chapter 6. For we have systematically argued here that a slippery slope is a type of rebuttal—a negative argument which attempts to show why an action should not be performed by citing an undesirable end it leads to.

This poses a puzzle. Are Little, Groarke, and Tindale right? Can slippery slope arguments also be positive arguments to show that an action should be performed because it leads by a causal sequence to a desirable end? We seem to have a borderline type of case at issue here.

Little, Groarke, and Tindale (1989) do cite two cases that they claim are instances of slippery slope reasoning leading to desirable consequences.

Case 3.13

. . . the argument that publicizing the 'greenhouse effect' will result in such sensitivity to the problem that people will put pressure on politicians and scientists to take the actions necessary to alleviate the anticipated danger. (pp. 240–1).

Case 3.14

That hard work in the early stages of your logic course will pay off on the final exam is another example of slippery slope reasoning toward a desirable consequence! (p. 241)

What should be said about these cases? Should they be treated as genuine slippery slope arguments or not? There seems to be room for argument on this question.

The second argument, in case 3.14, seems less plausible as a candidate to be a slippery slope argument. The term 'slippery slope' implies that once an individual takes a first step, things will then tend to run out of his control until he 'slides' towards the ultimate outcome in question. However, in case 3.14, the hard work in the initial stages of the logic course will, presumably, only pay off if it is continued later by the student. In other words, the hard work is a requirement of the later success, but it does not 'propel' the student towards the successful outcome at the end unless he keeps up that hard work later as well (something that is under his control, presumably). Thus the argument in case 3.14 intuitively does not seem like a real slippery slope argument, and the factor cited above is perhaps the reason why it does not.

But perhaps the argument in case 3.14 could be interpreted in a different way. Perhaps the claim could be that once the student does some hard work in the earlier stages of his logic course, the subject matter will become both easier and more interesting as he goes along. Thus there could be a kind of 'propellant' or 'escalating' effect as the course goes along, if those first steps are taken, painful as they seem.

But even under this interpretation, the argument in case 3.14 still does not seem like a real slippery slope argument, because the slippery slope argument is really an inherently negative kind of argumentation—it is a rebuttal or refutation where one participant in a dialogue has the role of attempting to convince another participant *not* to take a first step that the second participant is contemplating.

When this species of argumentation is presented in a positive guise, as in case 3.14, it is no longer a technique of refutation but a technique of positively convincing someone to take a first step in a sequence of actions. In this positive guise, it is really a different kind of argumentation directly opposed to slippery slope argumentation. This different kind of argumentation could be called the argument from gradualism.

The positive argument from gradualism will later—in Chapter 6.2—be shown to be of foundational importance in the analysis of slippery slope argumentation generally.

The argument in case 3.13 does seem to be more like what we have been considering to be the causal type of slippery slope argument. But it would seem that the reason this is so is that there is, in this case, what will presumably appear to the politicians and scientists in question as an undesirable consequence of a causal sequence. That ultimate, undesirable outcome (from the point of view of the politicians and scientists) is that people will 'exhibit sensitivity' to the 'problem' and 'put pressure' on these politicians and scientists. For these politicians and scientists, this is bad (presumably), or will be perceived by them as an undesirable consequence, even though we (as onlookers of the case, or third-party critics) are presuming that this consequence is good. We perceive this pressure as good, because (again, presumably) it will lead to positive steps to deal with a dangerous environmental problem.

So this case is on the borderline of being a slippery slope argument, or at least gives off appearances of being a causal slippery slope argument of the positive kind. But is it really? There is an ambiguity inherent in it.

If you reconstruct the context of the discussion in such a way that the politicians and scientists are the respondents, or play the role of the respondent in the dialogue, then the argument of case 3.13 can be said to be a slippery slope argument. Although this is one possible interpretation of the context of the argument, the more plausible interpretation is that you and I (the readers of the argument) are the real intended audience. But from this point of view, the argument of case 3.13 should not be classified as a slippery slope argument. Interpreted in this second way, it can be quite reasonably classified as an argument from consequences with the conclusion that publicizing the 'greenhouse effect' is a good course of action, one that ought to be undertaken by the respondent, because it will have positive effects on dealing with the problem.

Interpreted in this second way, case 3.13 is an argument from gradualism that advocates continuing efforts to publicize the 'greenhouse effect' so that gradually, public opinion will build up and put pressure on these third parties to take action.

There is another factor in case 3.13 that may also make it seem like a slippery slope argument—not a causal slippery slope argument but a full slippery slope argument of the sort that is analyzed in Chapter 5. This factor is a background presumption that an existing climate of public acceptance for a proposition will 'release a floodgate' once a sequence of actions has been carried along so far. But this is not a causal slippery slope argument. It is characteristic of the full slippery slope argument.

Moreover, the basic point remains that if case 3.13 is interpreted as a positive argument which advocates positive action to achieve a good result, it is an argument from gradualism, according to the classification proposed in this monograph, and not a slippery slope argument.

Regardless of how case 3.13 is to be interpreted, the binary characterization of the slippery slope argument advocated by Little, Groarke, and Tindale is rejected here as being too broad. What they call the 'good slippery slope argument' will be classified here as an argument from gradualism, a positive counterpart to the slippery slope argument which is not itself a slippery slope argument. This means that we are drawing a limit, or border, on what constitutes a slippery slope argument.

In other words, the following limitation is being advocated in relation to this type of case, expressed by the thesis below.

Limitation Thesis: *Just because an argument claims that a final outcome will ensure from a causal sequence that originates from an initial step, it need not follow that the argument must be classified as a (causal) slippery slope argument.*

Appealing to the limitation thesis, the arguments of cases 3.13 and 3.14 above can be classified as follows. Case 3.13 is an argument from consequences which involves a necessary condition which is an initial step towards a final (desirable) outcome in a complex sequence of actions, but it is not a (genuine) slippery slope argument. Case 3.14 is open to more than one pragmatic interpretation of its context of dialogue. According to one interpretation, it could be a type of causal slippery slope argument, but according to another more likely interpretation, it is not. Thus from the point of view of the analysis advocated here, the argument in case 3.14 should not be classified as a genuine slippery slope argument (at least under one interpretation), even though it does contain all of the required elements of a slippery slope argument (under both interpretations).

In other words, what we are requiring here is that a genuine slippery slope argument must have not only (1) an initial step, (2) a causal sequence, and (3) a final outcome, all put together in the right order. It must be an argument that utilizes such an outcome, cited as bad or undesirable for a respondent, in order to try to convince that respondent that he should not take the initial step. Arguments directed towards a respondent by a proponent, but not having all three of the elements used by the proponent in order to dissuade the respondent from embarking on the initial step, are pseudo slippery slope arguments. Or at any rate, they should not be classified as true slippery slope arguments.

Thus the problem of classifying slippery slope arguments requires a pragmatic approach. What defines a real slippery slope argument is how the argument is used by a proponent to persuade a respondent in a context of discussion.

10. Rethinking the Causal Slippery Slope

In case 3.6, some errors were found that could be identified with fallacies. In the description of the causal sequence of events in this case, many of the alleged consequences of women's suffrage were portrayed in picturesque and exaggerated language, e.g. 'break up the home,' and 'cause our forefathers . . . to turn in their graves.' This questionable use of language could involve fallacies, as we noted in Section 2 above. Also, the role of the cited cause, women's suffrage, was exaggerated by portraying it as the sole causal factor which would lead to the outcomes cited.

But is the argument of case 3.6 really an instance of the causal slippery slope fallacy? Putting aside the exaggerated and colorful language of the particular presentation in case 3.6, most of the predictions made have, in historical retrospect, turned out to be substantially accurate. Women do now behave with less 'feminine charm' to a substantial degree. They do 'wear trousers.' The birth rate has gone down considerably since 1920. There has now been a radical increase in divorces and 'broken homes.' Viewed as a prediction, implausible as the argument seemed, even in 1956, it now has turned out to be, in its main thrust, remarkably accurate. This striking observation should at least cause us to think twice before acquiescing in the judgment of Chase that the argument in case 3.6 is patently and obviously fallacious.[4] Generally, we need to rethink the whole idea of the causal slippery slope argument as a fallacy.

In order to approach the evaluation of the causal slippery slope argument in a more useful and adequate way, we need to stop seeing it as a fallacy, and place it in a broader pragmatic perspective as an argument that has two sides.[5] This kind of argumentation arises in a discussion at the following kind of juncture. One party is considering a course of action or inaction, based on his (and perhaps others') commitments to goals and the means to carry out those goals in light of present knowledge of a given situation. In this setting, a second party has focused on criticizing one aspect of the proposed course of action or omission, namely that it is likely to lead to serious, adverse consequences in

---

[4] Further discussion of this question can be found in Ch. 5.8.
[5] See Ch. 6 for an analysis of the dialectical framework of slippery slope argumentation.

the future, if carried out. One method of advancing this type of criticism is to use the causal slippery slope argument, citing an orderly chain of consequences as the route whereby a final, particularly serious adverse consequence will ensue.

Thus there are always two sides to this kind of argumentation. The proponent is using it to negatively criticize a prior argument of a respondent, based on practical reasoning. The respondent has his side of the argument to uphold, and he can react critically to the slippery slope critique in various ways. He could argue, for example, that, on the whole, the good consequences of his proposed course of action outweigh the bad. So not only can there be critical questions for a causal slippery slope argument, there are also ways of positively refuting it by posing counterarguments.[6]

Usually the respondent in a slippery slope argument is proposing that some action be taken. But in some cases—see cases 5.11 and 7.4, for example—the slippery slope argument is an attempt to persuade a respondent that something must be done, or otherwise the consequences of inaction will lead through successive stages of deterioration to a situation that is undesirable. Here, you are already set to slide down the slippery slope without having to do something to place yourself on the slope.

In Section 6 above, we saw that there are four basic ways of critically questioning a causal slippery slope argument. One is to request that any links missing in the presentation of the argument sequence be filled in by the proponent. This type of request for clarification applies especially to the short or condensed form of the argument. The other three ways given were to question the initial action premise, the causal sequence premises, or the outcome premise. Very often, critical questioning of a causal slippery slope argument is concerned with the evidence backing up the causal links in the sequence.

Taking a more positive approach, a critic can also attempt to strongly refute a causal slippery slope argument using counterarguments. One method, already noted in Chapter 2 in connection with the sorites, is for the respondent to mount another slippery slope argument which goes in the opposite direction from the proponent's original slippery slope argument. Another method is for the

---

[6] A more general account of tactics for countering all kinds of slippery slope argument—not restricted only to the causal type—is presented in Ch. 7.

respondent to modify his plan of action, or to propose a different plan that will not have the bad consequences cited by the proponent's slippery slope argument. There are many ways to proceed in attacking a causal slippery slope argument, for, after all, this type of argument is a species of argument from consequences based on practical reasoning. As such, it admits of many different kinds of counterattack. Some of these methods have already been studied in the literature on argumentation.

Suppose a critic attacks a proposed practical proposal for action by citing its allegedly dangerous or harmful consequences. How can the affirmative advocate of the proposal reply? According to Windes and Hastings (1965: 226), there are three ways.

(1) He can modify the proposal so that it will not have the harmful effect, either by eliminating or interfering with a causal factor in the action. (2) The advocate can refute the attack, contending that the harmful consequence will not result from his proposal. (3) He may overbalance with advantages any disadvantages of the action, demonstrating that the benefits are more important and extensive.

Windes and Hastings suggest (p. 226) that the advocate can choose among these three general methods, and pick the one that appears to be the strongest in the particular case at issue.

Attacks on causal slippery slope arguments most often turn on attacking the causal sequence premises, and the basic principle here is to focus on these links. This strategy would come under (2) in Windes and Hastings' classification.[7]

To evaluate a particular case in dispute, a critic needs to elucidate the nature of the linkages between each step of the sequence of connected stages. It is not too clear, in case 3.7 for example, how the usage of one drug is supposed to lead to the next, but presumably the basis of it is some sort of causal–behavioral link.

What could be meant by 'cause' here? To say that one action or event A causes another one, B, need not imply that B is an inevitable outcome of A (in every instance). Rather it can be interpreted to mean something weaker, along the following lines: where A occurs in a normal set of circumstances, (1) it is one factor that, taken together with other relevant factors, makes it more plausible or expectable that B will also occur, and (2) if A did not occur then, normally in the given circumstances, B would not occur either. This

[7] See n. 6.

type of account makes the causal relation between events or actions a loose relationship of what can normally be expected to occur relative to a *field*, or background horizon of presumed circumstances, held stable in a normal case of a given type of situation. This means that if there is a correlation between A and B, you can plausibly expect that A causes B unless the correlation can be explained by other means, e.g. a coincidence, or the intervention of a third factor, C, which causes both A and B. To argue from correlation to causation without taking into account these exceptive means (critical questions) is to commit the *post hoc, ergo propter hoc* fallacy.

Causal arguments that try to establish a causal connection between two events are generally empirical arguments that cite observations of the two kinds of event at issue, along with other observations. An analysis of causal argumentation is presented in Walton (1989, ch. 8), showing that in its more advanced forms, these arguments may be placed in a scientific context. Experiments may even be designed and run, in some cases, to test and verify suspected causal connections.

In general, however, the best strategy of criticism is to take the pragmatic approach of looking at the causal sequence of argument-ation as a whole.

Little, Groarke, and Tindale (1989: 241) indicated that the causal slippery slope argument can be challenged by questioning one of the causal links. Johnson and Blair (1983: 164), even more specifically, suggested attacking the weakest link in the chain. This advice is appropriate because the causal slippery slope argument is a *linked argument*, a kind of argument where each premise is dependent on the other premises—each premise is necessary to support the remaining premises in providing a basis for the conclusion. As Windes and Hastings (1965: 216) put it, 'If any issue is not proved, then the proposition is not proved.' They add that '[t]his process may go back several arguments, so that there is a chain of arguments leading to a conclusion.'

In a linked argument, the support of the conclusion depends on each individual premise. Hence the basic principle of plausible reasoning for all linked argumentation can be stated as follows, in the framework of Rescher (1976): the plausibility value of the conclusion should be raised to the value of the least plausible premise, in a deductively valid argument. This criterion for evaluating deductively valid arguments can be called the *least plausible premise rule*. When the requirement that the premises be mutually consistent is added, this rule amounts to the *consequence condition* of Rescher (1976: 15), which states that the conclusion of a deductively valid argument with consistent premises should be at least as plausible as the least plausible premise.

The causal slippery slope argument is a claim based on a projected causal sequence, which is in turn based on empirical evidence (to the extent that such evidence is, or will be available). In outline, it is a simple kind of argumentation to evaluate. There are different ways to criticize it, as we have seen. And sometimes, a critic is better off to focus on criticism of the earlier steps in the causal sequence, because these are less remote in the future. But generally, the causal slippery slope argument is a simple kind of argumentation which can best be attacked by questioning the plausibility of the individual causal links in the chain postulated by the proponent. Normally the best strategy here, following the least plausible premise rule, is to question the weakest link in the chain.

4

The Precedent Slippery Slope Argument

POLICIES and rules admit of exceptions in exceptional cases. They have an inherent vagueness of application similar to the vagueness of words and phrases. Slippery slope argumentation can arise in disputes about exceptions to rules, where an arguer presses for consistency between his own case and one that has already been conceded as an exception to the rule.

Case 4.1

A man is clocked at fifty-six miles per hour by a radar detection unit of the highway patrol in a fifty-five mile per hour speed limit zone. He argues to the patrolman that he should not get a ticket because the difference in speed of one mile per hour is insignificant: 'After all, it's really arbitrary that the agreed-upon speed limit is fifty-five rather than fifty-six isn't it? It's just because fifty-five is a round number that it is chosen as the limit.' (Walton 1989: 263)

Once the patrolman accepts this argument, the next speeder, clocked at 57 miles per hour, can argue that he must be let off too. Or otherwise, he might complain, the patrolman is not being fair. Since he has already conceded, by his previous ruling, that 1 mile per hour doesn't really make a significant difference, it would be inconsistent of him not to use the same criterion in judging this case too. Following the logic of this argumentation, eventually a speeder who is clocked at 100 miles per hour could insist that he too should not get a speeding ticket.

The patrolman could use the slippery slope argument to resist the very first argument of anyone who asks to be excepted. He could reply that if he makes one exception, in fairness and consistency he will have to make others. And once the word spreads, he will have to make so many exceptions that eventually the rule will be destroyed, or become impossible to enforce.

The kind of situation in which a slippery slope argument can arise is sometimes made more complex for the reason that some excuses for violating a rule can be legitimate exceptions to the rule.

Case 4.2

A patrolman stops a driver who has been speeding, and looks into the vehicle. He sees a passenger, evidently doubled over in agony, and the driver says: 'We've got to get him to the hospital immediately. He's having an acute appendicitis attack.'

Agreeing that this is a legitimate emergency, the patrolman escorts the car to the hospital at high speed, with his siren on.

The problem often posed by this kind of situation, however, is that not all excuses are equally legitimate.

Case 4.3

A patrolman stops a driver who has been speeding, and looks inside the vehicle. The driver points to the passenger, and says: 'He has a sprained wrist and I'm taking him to the hospital for treatment.' The patrolman replies: 'That is no reason for speeding.' The driver retorts: 'But the other day when I was taking my friend with appendicitis to the hospital, you allowed us to violate the speed limit.'

How is the patrolman to reply here? Presumably, he should say that although exceptions to the rule can be made in exceptional cases, not every case is exceptional. In case 4.3, presuming there was no potentially life-threatening emergency, as there was in case 4.2, the excuse is not comparable. Although the two cases are similar in some respects, what was a valid excuse in the one is not in the other.

This type of argumentation can lead to a kind of tug of war between a pleader for an excuse, and a resister who is responsible for upholding a rule. Presuming that the resister finds the first excuse legitimate, once having made this concession, he will find it harder to resist the second, and then the third and other comparable pleas. This difficulty of resistance arises where there is a parallel or analogy between each pair of cases—enough of a parallel to make a case that the similarity is relevant. Therefore, to resist this kind of slippery slope, the resister will have to go into each case on its merits, comparing relevant similarities and differences.

In Chapter 7, it will be shown generally how the slippery slope argument, as a distinctive type of argumentation, arises out of a particular type of initial situation, called a tactical basis in Section

3 of that chapter, which prompts the use of the slippery slope technique as an appropriate and effective move in a dialogue.

The precedent type of slippery slope arises as an appropriate response in precisely the kind of situation outlined in cases 4.2 and 4.3. There is a rule that has ostensibly been violated in a particular case, and the individual who has allegedly committed the violation cites an analogous case in his defence, as a precedent. Then there arises a tug of war between the pleader and the rule-enforcer on whether the instance at issue fits the rule or can be discounted on some grounds or other as an exceptional case.

Now in this situation, where precedents are concerned, there is always the logical possibility that there could be a continuum of cases as part of the issue, a chain of comparable cases where one analogous case leads to the consideration of another closely comparable case, and so forth, in a sequence. If the situation is right for this kind of sequential comparison of cases to arise, then it is the right sort of tactical basis for a precedent type of slippery slope argument to be advanced in the dialogue by one party.

It seems that this type of precedent-based slippery slope argumentation can be stronger or weaker, depending on the circumstances of a particular case. It could be the pleader for exceptions who has the stronger argument in some cases. But in other cases, the rule-enforcer who resists the plea might have the stronger argument. In this chapter it will be argued that it would be an error to classify a precedent slippery slope argument as fallacious simply because it is weak, or open to legitimate critical questioning.

1. Precedents in Argumentation

A *precedent* is a preceding case that can be used as an example or model instance which can lead towards the authorization of a new rule, practice, or way of proceeding with subsequent cases. Precedents can be used in argumentation for various purposes. Arguments based on precedents are often used to try to persuade someone to follow a particular course of action, or to plead one's case to be treated as an exception to a rule. They fit into the general framework of case-based reasoning, where a conclusion about a particular case is drawn from conclusions that have been arrived at in one or more similar, preceding cases.

A precedent need not necessarily lead to a new rule or practice, but is defined as a kind of case that might have a tendency to do so. This means that it is possible that the new case might lead to a new rule or practice, and also that there is some genuine likelihood or plausibility that it might do so. The idea is that there is some genuine threat of undermining or changing the old rule.

Problems about precedents, in the sense defined above, arise in a particular kind of context of argumentation in which case-based reasoning is used for a particular purpose. *Case-based reasoning* is a sequence that proceeds from one (or a series of) preceding case to one similar, subsequent case, and draws a conclusion about the subsequent case, based on similar, relevant features of the preceding cases. In arguments about precedents, the subsequent case needs to be judged in relation to some existing rule or practice, and the problem is whether it might lead to a new rule, or modification of the existing rule. The precedent type of slippery slope argument occurs in this context where there is a worry that, by the same sequence of reasoning, the new (subsequent) case might lead to still more new cases, where the sequence might lead to a case that threatens the rule.

Case 4.4

A rule printed in the academic calendar of a university states that all assignments must be carried out by the deadline set during the first week of term, unless the student is prevented from doing the assignment or is ill (as certified by a note from a physician). A student pleads that he could not write his test because his father died the day before.

In this case, the rule has two categories of recognized exceptions. The excuse offered might arguably fit the 'prevention' category. But the student was not literally 'prevented' from writing the examination. It is possible also that he could be exempted on compassionate grounds, even though the exception made does not fit one of the two recognized categories.

It is interesting to note that there is considerable scope for argumentation in this type of case in deciding exactly what counts as allowable under the rule. Anyone who has been on an appeals committee will recognize the problem. Judgment of the particulars of a case, in relation to a general rule or principle, is involved.

Suppose another student who has failed to complete an assignment by the deadline claims that she should be exempted because her grandmother died two weeks before the examination, citing the case of the other student (in case 4.4 above) as a precedent. She argues that since he was allowed to write a second test at a later time, she should be allowed to do this too. The instructor has to decide how to rule on this case, but if the student questions the ruling, she can request that it be taken before a committee.

Let's say that in case 4.4, the committee decided that the student should be permitted to write a second test on the compassionate grounds that it wasn't reasonable to make him write the test in these extraordinary and difficult circumstances, even though his situation did not fit either of the two categories of recognized exceptions in the rule. Now the second student can argue that her case is similar, in that she also had a member of the family die before the time of the test. The question then is whether her case is similar enough in the relevant respects to the precedent set in the previous case.

In a case like this, a problem arises where the case (*a*) fits the rule, and is allowable despite the rule, or (*b*) does not fit the rule, despite initial appearances, but appears to be allowable anyway. In such a situation, the problem case can lead towards the formulation of a new rule, or it can come to be recognized as an exception to the existing rule. These possibilities are outlined in Fig. 4.1. In this situation, it is important to realize that the rule may have explicitly stated exceptional clauses or qualifications built into it. Rules are characteristically defeasible, or open to possible exceptions. Second, we may often be dealing with a custom or practice rather than an explicitly stated rule. A custom or practice is a usual or normal way of doing something. Unlike a rule, it may not be stated in a rigorous or explicit way. As

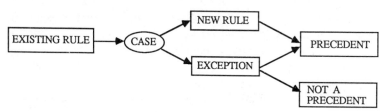

Fig. 4.1   How a case can lead to a precedent

illustrated in Fig. 4.1, in some instances an exception may have no implications for changing an existing rule. In such an instance, it is not a precedent.

When a precedent arises or is brought forward in the context of argument where it may challenge an existing rule, characteristically it leads to a kind of tug of war between the two participants involved, who could be called the *pleader*, the one who sees the rule as not applicable to his case, and the *resister*, who tries to uphold the rule, or its applicability, in the face of the new case.

This characteristic tug of war is actually the confrontation stage of a kind of adversarial dialogue between the two parties, who proceed to fight out their particular case. However, the type of dialogue involved is not simple, nor does it always take one context of dialogue as its specific format. Such cases can be fought out in the courts, according to the legal rules of dialogue. Often they partly involve practical reasoning, especially where responsibility for an action is concerned. And they can also involve critical discussion.

Whatever particular format of dialogue is involved, precedent-based disputes always involve the question of whether a particular case fits a general rule. A dispute arising out of this issue can take many forms. But whatever type of dialogue is involved subsequently, the evolution of the dialogue tends to follow a particular sequence. The pleader compares his case to some comparable case—possibly, for example, a previous case that has been exempted as an excuse already. The resister cites the need to enforce the rule fairly and impartially, and may also cite comparable cases to support his side of the issue.

When this typical confrontation situation sets in, it leads to an argumentation stage where each side pushes forward in order to resolve the dispute by marshalling evidence to support his side of the issue.

In case 4.4, for example, if the instructor accepts the excuse in the first case, once having made this concession, he may find it much harder to resist subsequent comparable pleas. The analogy between the cases tends to push towards allowing the comparable excuses. It may be very difficult for the instructor to resist this 'pushing forward' of argumentation, and eventually it may lead to a new rule, or to a reformulation of the old rule, perhaps with a new category of exception included in the rule. To resist this push of argumentation, the instructor may have to go into each individual case on its merits, comparing relevant similarities and differences. There are two main factors involved in this kind of argumentation: (1) the merits of each case in itself, and (2) the similarity of each new case to relevant features of the previous cases where a decision has been made and recorded.

In some cases, arguments using reasoning from precedent occur within an institutional framework of rules, policies, and mechanisms of resolution that are already established and codified explicitly. A university, for example, might have a structure of regulations and committees who meet to discuss problematic cases. The most outstanding example is legal reasoning, where careful records of important cases are kept that are important in deciding arguments.

It is well known that judicial decision-making is based on precedent. The legal principle is that of *stare decisis,* meaning (Rohde and Spaeth 1976: 35) that 'a court must abide by or adhere to previously decided cases.' According to Golding (1984: 98) this Latin term is an abbreviation of the phrase *stare decisis et non quieta movere* (to stand by what has been decided and not to disturb settled points).

Of course, in judicial decision-making, there can be many different good grounds for not adhering to precedent in a particular case. But the principle of *stare decisis* creates a presumption that needs to be overturned by argument. For example (Rohde and Spaeth 1976: 36), if a judge distinguishes a new precedent, he may do so by holding that the new case is 'sufficiently dissimilar' from the case that went before.

Precedents can also be limited by narrowing their scope (p. 37), or even overruled in some cases (p. 38), although direct overruling by the Supreme Court does not occur very often, according to Rohde and Spaeth (p. 38). Generally, in law, the precedent set by a higher court is more binding on a lower court.

Although reasoning from one case to another is more formally regulated by explicit rules of procedure in legal arguments, the same kind of case-rule argumentation can occur in less formalized contexts of argument, like ethical and public policy disputations. Whether the rules of a discussion are institutionalized or not, however, it will be seen in Section 4 below how, in evaluating such arguments, the 'language-game' or context of dialogue must be taken into account.

2. Varieties of Precedent Slopes

One important type of precedent slippery slope argument arises in the kind of case where the pleader presents a marginal excuse, i.e. an excuse that is not clearly in or out of the originally sanctioned class of excuses. This basic variant of the precedent slippery slope argument is used when the proponent argues that the case pleaded is closely similar to another case that clearly should not be allowed as a candidate for the originally sanctioned class of excuses. Or at any rate, the argument is that accepting the plea would set a bad precedent because it would lead to some clearly non-allowable case by a sequence of comparisons of similar cases.

This variant of the slippery slope argument can be reasonable in some cases, and weak, fallacious, or indefensible in other cases. For example, in case 4.3, if the patrolman were to reply, 'We can only use life-threatening, or very serious injuries as reasons for speeding. Speeding is itself very dangerous, and if we allowed everyone who has a non-threatening injury or other minor problem to violate the speed limit, it would be a very bad precedent.' While much depends on the individual case in this type of argumentation, it could well be that the patrolman's argument is quite reasonable and appropriate in this particular case.

Similarly, in case 4.4, if the student argued that he should be excused because his dog died, the instructor could reasonably argue that this excuse is not good enough because it would set a bad precedent. But if the instructor tried to use the same slippery slope argument from precedent where the student had pleaded that his mother had died the day before, the instructor's argument could be unreasonable.

Govier (1982: 309–10), however, emphasized the fallacious potential of this type of argumentation when she described the *simple dangerous precedent* argument type below as a 'transparently bad argument.'

Simple Dangerous Precedent Slippery Slope Argument (Govier)

(1) Case (*a*) is acceptable when considered solely on its own merits.

(2) Cases (*b*) and (*c*) and ... (*n*) are not acceptable.

(3) Feature F, in virtue of which (*a*) is acceptable, is also possessed by (*b*), (*c*), and (*n*).

(4) By permitting (*a*), we would bind ourselves in consistency to permitting (*b*) to (*n*). That is, (*a*), though acceptable on its own, is unacceptable overall, insofar as it sets a dangerous precedent.

(5) Therefore, (*a*) ought not to be accepted.

The example Govier gives (p. 309) illustrates how the defender of a policy can be overly dogmatic in digging in his heels to resist allowing even a reasonable exception.

Case 4.5

We know that your budget submission is late, due to the sudden death of your husband. Nevertheless we should not increase your budget as a result of this after-deadline submission. If we did, we would be bound in consistency to consider all the other late submissions as well, and we would have to accept late applications from others, some of whom are just lazy or disorganized. Your case is worthy, but cannot be allowed because it would set a bad precedent, binding us to take other applications from people who are late without the good excuse you have.

But clearly not all cases of resisting pleas for exceptions are as open to criticism or are bad arguments in the way that this one is, as case 4.3 above shows. According to Govier, the simple dangerous precedent argument represents a fallacious or sophistical variant of one kind of precedent argumentation which can be used by a proponent of a rule who is trying to defend the rule from a slippery slope attack. Certainly, however, the simple dangerous precedent argument shows one highly significant way in which this kind of argumentation can go wrong. But does it represent a distinctive kind of fallacy or characteristic sophistical technique of the slippery slope precedent argumentation?

To investigate this question we have to try to apply Govier's scheme for the simple dangerous precedent argument (above) to case 4.5. Presumably, case (*a*) relates to case of the death of the pleader's husband. And presumably, this case is meant to be 'acceptable, when considered solely on its own merits.' Hence we can presume that premise (1) is meant to be fulfilled by case 4.5. But cases (*b*), (*c*), ..., (*n*), the other late applications, are not acceptable, in case 4.5, corresponding to premise (2) of the scheme.

But what about premise (3) then? What is feature F? Govier does not tell us, but presumably there is some feature in virtue of which the death of one's husband is acceptable, and the other late applications also possess this feature.

But this does not seem right. The other late applications, 'some of whom are just lazy and disorganized' are presumably excludable precisely because they fail to have this special property F (whatever it is) that makes case (*a*) acceptable.

In short, it is hard to see what Govier is up to here. It looks as if the scheme for the simple dangerous precedent argument doesn't really fit case 4.5, as far as we can tell. It also seems as if case 4.5 is not really an instance of the slippery slope fallacy. It is just a very weak or erroneous use of the precedent slippery slope argument that is 'transparently bad' or unconvincing. Whether the simple dangerous precedent argument represents a fallacy is unclear. We return to this problem in Section 10 below.

Bernard Williams (1985) distinguished between two types of slippery slope arguments he called the *horrible results argument* and the *arbitrary results argument*. The first type is the more usual kind of slippery slope argument that ends in a horrible last step like the 'Nazi parade of horrors.' The second type of slippery slope could also be described as leading to a bad or undesirable result, but it is a more specific kind of undesirability that is involved. In the second kind of argument, the slippery slope leads to an arbitrary criterion.

Williams (1985: 127) gave the following example.

Case 4.6

Suppose that some tax relief or similar benefit be extended to couples who are not married. Someone might not object to the very idea of the relief going to unmarried couples, but nevertheless argue that the only non-arbitrary line that could be drawn was between the married couples and the unmarried, and that as soon as any unmarried couple was allowed the benefit, there would be too many arbitrary discriminations to be made.

In this case, it is not just that the result is horrible. The slippery slope leads to a more specific kind of problem, an arbitrary outcome that the argument would seem to inevitably lead to. The objection seems to be based on the initial premise that, in this case, the way of allocating the tax benefit was founded on a clear and nonarbitrary criterion. Once it is extended to include unmarried couples, however, there seems to be no way left to make any further clear distinction that would not lead to arbitrary discriminations.

The arbitrary results variant of the slippery slope argument seems to work by shifting a burden of proof onto the respondent by posing a question: 'How can you find any nonarbitrary, clear criterion, once we have abandoned the given criterion?' The presumption of this question is that the given criterion is clear and nonarbitrary.

In the arbitrary results argument, there is a suggestion that the respondent is in effect destroying the original workable criterion by attempting to move to a new criterion which will be unworkable, no matter how he tries to salvage it. This is in some respects similar to another kind of slippery slope variant which Govier (1982: 311) calls the *feasibility precedent* type of slippery slope argument.

Feasibility Precedent Slippery Slope Argument
   (1) Case (*a*) is acceptable, considered by itself.
   (2) Cases (*b*)–(*n*) are relevantly similar to (*a*) and are also acceptable, considered separately.
   (3) Allowing all of (*a*)–(*n*) is impossible.
   (4) Case (*a*), if allowed would be a precedent for (*b*)–(*n*).
   (5) Therefore, case (*a*) ought not to be allowed.

Govier (1982: 310–11) gives the following example.

Case 4.7

Allowing French parents to choose to send their children to French language schools which would have public support would be a precedent for allowing parents of Indian, Ukrainian, German and many other language groups to do the same thing. The public pocket could not support this. Even though the French language has a special place in the founding act of our country, and the French people are in a historical position which would justify their receiving schooling in French, we cannot permit French parents' public funding for French schools. To do this would be to commit ourselves to parental choice for parents of the other language groups here, but that is simply impractical. There is not sufficient funding for all deserving groups. And this being the case, we should not single out one group and give that group the privilege.

Is this a reasonable argument or not? It seems to depend on what is in fact feasible in a particular case. In this instance, it would also depend on the analogy between the situation of the French in Canada and the other language groups cited. Hence it seems that the feasibility precedent type of slippery slope argument could be reasonable in some cases, and fallacious, or at least incorrect, weak, or open to criticism in other cases.

Arbitrariness and nonfeasibility are different problems. The question of feasibility appears to be a practical matter of what the given resources can allow. Arbitrariness is a problem of applying a criterion in a fair way. Also, arbitrariness seems to be connected to linguistic matters of the clarity of a criterion. Thus the arbitrary results argument does seem to be somewhat reminiscent of the kind of problem posed in the sorites argument. Feasibility, however, seems to be a more purely practical matter.

Either could be applicable in many cases to support slippery slope arguments. Consider a variant of case 4.4, where a student tries to use a weak or inappropriate excuse for handing in a late essay. The instructor could try to counter with either the feasibility precedent or the arbitrary results variant of the slippery slope argument. One option could be for him to argue that if he allows this excuse, he will have to allow so many excuses that, in effect, anyone could hand in a late essay at any time, with impunity. The result then, presumably, would be that the whole system of having deadlines would effectively be destroyed.

But a second optional tactic is also open to the instructor. He could argue that as much as he likes this particular student, and would like to support him, the excuse that the student is distraught (because his dog died, or something of the sort) fits into no clear category of excuses. If the instructor accepted this excuse, he might argue, he would have no way of nonarbitrarily rejecting other students' excuses that they are distraught, not feeling very well psychologically that day, and so forth. The instructor could argue that if he has a doctor's note that the student has been too ill to complete the assignment, this is a recognized excuse based on expert judgment. But beyond that, he, the instructor, has no nonarbitrary way of judging malaise, or degrees of being upset over incidents in a student's personal life.

It seems then that the feasibility precedent variant and the arbitrary results variant are kinds of possible strategy that could be used optionally to back up many precedent slippery slope arguments. Neither of these variants is inherently fallacious. It would appear that in some cases the one variant might be more appropriate than the other.

Another variant of the precedent slippery slope argument arises where the proponent argues that if the respondent takes a first step this precedent will allow him so much power that he will inevitably be driven to decide other related cases in a like manner, eventually reaching some extreme point.

This form of the argument from dangerous precedent is a species of what Schauer (1985: 367) has labelled the *argument from added authority*. This argument is to the effect that allowing an initial precedent would grant additional authority to an institution or decision-maker, which would lead to a sequence of bad results, including some ultimate, horrible outcome. In this type of slippery slope argument, it is not the ultimate outcome that is cited as probable in itself, but it is the additional authority granted that would make it more probable as a future decision. Schauer (1985: 368) gives the following illustration.

Case 4.8

When it is feared, for example, that some future Supreme Court might interpret an equal rights amendment in such a way as to prohibit separate sex lavatories in public facilities, the argument is not based on any particular fear that this is likely to occur. Instead, the argument proceeds from the assumption that even the unlikely becomes more likely once jurisdiction is granted than it would have been without that jurisdiction.

The kind of danger cited in this variant of the argument is that given a background propensity to move in a certain direction, once authority is granted by conceding a first precedent, the floodgates will be opened to using that authority again and again.

Is this kind of precedent slippery slope argument always fallacious? It seems to be a weak or unreasonable argument in case 4.8, but that does not rule out the possibility that it could be a reasonable argument in some cases. For example, if one had argued prior to 1933 that if Hitler gained power horrible things would happen, it would seem in historical retrospect that the argument would have had some merit.

3. Fallacious or Not?

None of the kinds of precedent slippery slope argument examined in Section 2 appeared to be inherently fallacious. Instead, they seemed to be bad or weak arguments in some cases, but reasonable or strong arguments in other cases. A bad, weak, or erroneous argument is not necessarily a fallacious argument.

Those who are inclined to follow the tradition of thinking of slippery slope argument as fallacies, however, may be inclined to classify only the bad arguments as 'slippery slope arguments' and put the good arguments in some other category.

According to Johnson and Blair (1983: 165), slippery slope needs to be distinguished from appeal to precedent, a legitimate kind of argumentation. Johnson and Blair concede that appeal to precedent can go wrong, but when it does, the fault is different from that of the slippery slope fallacy. According to them, objecting to a policy on grounds of undesirable precedent is a type of argumentation of the following form (p. 165), where X and W are events.

(NP)
  (1) If you do/permit W, that will set a precedent which will justify doing/ permitting X.
  (2) X is undesirable.
  (3) Therefore you shouldn't do/permit W.

Johnson and Blair (p. 165) think that this form of argumentation for objecting to undesirable precedent is, in principle, reasonable. They add that it can go wrong, but when it does, the fallacy is not slippery slope but faulty analogy. The problem is not that a causal claim is unfounded, as in the slippery slope fallacy. Rather, these arguments from undesirable precedents can 'break down when two allegedly similar cases are not similar in the relevant respect' (p. 166).

Govier disagrees with Johnson and Blair, in that she sees these arguments from undesirable precedents as being species of slippery slope argument. But she agrees with them that such arguments are based on analogies. And she agrees with them that arguments from undesirable precedents can be reasonable in some cases. This means that the defender of an argument from dangerous precedents can, in some cases, back up his argument with good reasons.

What we should say about slippery slope arguments based on precedents is that they have two sides. The proponent of a policy or rule tries to resist pleas for exceptions by using techniques like the feasibility precedent argument and the simple argument from dangerous precedents, while the pleader for an exception cites the analogy, or lack of significant difference, between comparable cases. The arguments on either side can be reasonable, but can become unreasonable if pressed too hard with inadequate backing. Both sides of this kind of argumentation use techniques that involve analogy and consistency of concessions with a disputed case (or range of cases).

In consistency with the analyses of Chapters 2 and 3, it is appropriate to classify arguments of the form (NP) as *negative arguments from precedent*. The context of use of a negative argument from precedent is the following situation. A proponent is trying to dissuade a respondent from doing or permitting W. To this end, the proponent argues that doing W will set a precedent which will justify doing X. Therefore, by a kind of *modus tollens* argument which is similar in use to *reductio ad absurdum* in its dialectical use, the proponent advocates the conclusion: 'Respondent, you should not do X.'

The precedent slippery slope argument is not identical with (NP), but is a species or special case of (NP) where a sequence of precedents is involved, in the following scheme.

(PS)
   (1) If you do/permit W_0, that will set a precedent which will justify doing/permitting W_1.
   (2) W_1, by a sequence of precedents will lead to W_2, and so on to W_n, which will in turn lead to X.
   (3) X is undesirable.
   (4) Therefore, you shouldn't do/permit W.

The basic structure of the precedent type of slippery slope argument is reasonably well represented by the form (PS). Even so, we are still not very far along in understanding how this kind of argument is used, correctly or incorrectly, to rationally carry out or permit a course of action.

(PS) definitely fits the usual pattern of slippery slope argumentation, but does not appear to be a fallacious kind of argument. Judging from the cases surveyed in Section 2, it would seem that there can be different kinds of precedent slippery slope argument all of which fit the form of (PS) generally, but some of these arguments are strong and others are weak (or perhaps, even in some cases, fallacious). The problem before us is to identify and understand the underlying factors that account for the strength or weakness of this type of argument in a particular case. This is no inconsiderable problem, however, because as case 4.5 and the other cases in this chapter have shown, evaluation of (PS) in any instance involves comparing one particular case to another in judging whether an exception to a rule is legitimate or not. Traditionally, this method was called *casuistry* (from the Latin *casus,* meaning case). Although casuistry was practiced in ancient times and the Middle Ages as the art of applying moral and legal rules to particular cases, in the seventeenth century it came under severe attack (Hamel 1967: 196). As a result, 'casuistry' is now commonly used as a 'term of reproach directed against real or alleged abuses in the application of reason to legal or ethical problems' (Nelson 1973: 51).

The attacks on casuistry, led by Pascal's satirical treatment in his *Lettres Provinciales,* gave it an evil reputation that persists to the present day.

According to Jonsen and Toulmin (1988), Pascal's attack on casuistry was unfair, and had an impact far beyond its real merit, because of the literary brilliance of Pascal's satirical writing. Yet this attack had an enormous effect on the history of ethics, which subsequently turned into a highly theoretical subject that took little or no interest in the study of particular cases. This anti-case study attitude in ethics was dominant right up to the second half of the twentieth century when finally, through the advent of biomedical ethics as a primary area of concern for ethicists, the case study finally surfaced as an important methodological tool for moral philosophy.

The theological casuists did not attempt to set out an explicit methodology or show the intellectual steps used to analyze a case.

But Jonsen and Toulmin (1988: 251) have shown that they did have a kind of method. This method started with a paradigm case —for example, one showing that killing is clearly wrong. And then it proceeded by constructing analogous sample cases, similar to the paradigm case except for raising a question of a possible exception. For example, killing in self-defense against a direct unprovoked attack might be cited as a problematic case. Then in succession, a chain of cases was constructed, moving from the original clear case towards more complex and difficult cases that needed to be resolved (Jonsen and Toulmin 1988: 252). Thus it would seem that the practices of casuistry would have been a very natural setting for the slippery slope as a central type of argumentation.

It is quite strange that the use of the case study method has grown so much in other areas—such as legal and business studies —while it was excluded from ethics for so long. The current project of the revival of casuistry in a somewhat different form clearly depends on gaining a better understanding of case-based reasoning, the underlying intellectual structure of the case study method.

4. Case-Based Reasoning

Case-based reasoning proceeds by drawing inferences from one case (or a series of cases) to another case that is similar in certain respects. Of course, any two particular cases are always different in an unlimited number of respects, as well as being similar in an unlimited number of respects. Therefore, any conclusion drawn by case-based reasoning is inherently subject to exceptions. Such reasoning is therefore a form of plausible reasoning, a matter of how things may customarily be expected to go, as a matter of weight or burden of presumption.

Case-based reasoning is founded on analogy, which, in turn, according to the point of view advocated here, is founded on a basis of similarity of relevant characteristics between two cases. Similarity is a matter of degree. If case a is similar to case b, and case b is similar to case c, it does not necessarily follow that case a is similar to case c. It may be that case a is not similar enough *in a relevant respect* to case c to justify extending the analogy in question from *a* to *c*, even though *a* is analogous to *b*, and *b* is analogous to *c*. For example, an orange may be similar to a banana, and a banana may be similar to a cigar, but an orange may not be similar to a cigar. In judging such matters in any particular case of reasoning by analogy, however, much depends on what purpose the analogy is being used for. Moral and legal argumentation are two of the most prominent contexts of case-based reasoning by analogy.

According to Golding (1984: 98), the idea of adherence to precedent in legal and moral reasoning goes back, in its philosophical origins, to Aristotle's notion of justice or fairness, which required that like cases should be treated alike, and to Kant's categorical imperative, which required acting only on a maxim that can be willed as a universal law. One implication of these principles, in particular, is drawn out by Golding (p. 98): 'Unless some explanation can be provided, one tends to think that a person who makes exceptions in favor of himself or herself, or who makes inconsistent moral judgments, is morally unprincipled.' An example would be a socialist politician who has long decried the tax shelters of the wealthy, but argues that his own case, having made a lot of money from taking advantage of a legal loophole he admits is a quick-flip tax dodge, is different. The person who places himself in this situation is open to *ad hominem* attack, a particularly powerful form of argument in the political arena (see Walton 1985*a*). If you have personally advocated a rule or principle, but then show by your actions that you do not appear to be applying the rule to yourself, such an evident conflict of commitments would place your integrity in question.

In conflicts of commitments of this kind, the consistency that is apparently violated is not logical consistency. It is a kind of consistency of commitments that has to do with treating like cases differently. Once a particular case is decided in a certain way, consistency of this type requires that when a similar case comes along, it should be decided in the same way (unless there are relevant differences in the cases, or other good reasons why they need not be treated alike).

The making of any normative rule that applies to human conduct creates precedents because the commitment to the rule, once incurred, places limits on subsequent commitments that may be incurred or retracted. An apparent conflict of commitments places a burden of proof or explanation on the individual whose commitment to a rule of conduct has been called into question. What is involved is not a logical but a practical inconsistency. As Stoljar (1980: 110) succinctly put it, moral rules, once agreed to or put in place, provide a basis of precedent for treating like cases alike and unlike cases differently: 'For it is in the nature of a moral rule that it commits us to a decision once it is made simply because we cannot decide a like case differently, although the question to what precise extent we are so committed may still need to be settled by further argument.' Stoljar adds that this same characteristic is true of legal rules and precedents, and that the legal technique of using precedent is an application of the principle of universalizability advocated by moral philosophers (p. 110). In both contexts, however, the rules admit of exceptions, and therefore the consistency in treating like cases alike yields only a kind of presumptive, practical universalizability that is defeasible.

Except for explicitly legal treatments, there appears to be no literature on the evaluation of appeals to precedent cases in argumentation, despite the writings on the case study method generally—see Klein (1988)—and the enormous literature on the subject of reasoning by analogy. The latter subject comprises a recent flood of literature in philosophy, literature, and the social sciences, and especially in computer science.

One work that seems most likely to be relevant to the topic of reasoning from precedent is a recent Ph.D. thesis in computer science (Simpson 1985), where a model of case-based problem-solving was used to aid in dispute mediation. According to Simpson's model (p. 3) case-based problem-solving involves the recognition of similarity between a current case and a preceding set of cases in memory, so that the most appropriate case can be selected from the potentially applicable ones. Simpson's method is essentially one of trial and error, using feedback. If the solution to the previous case provides a solution to the current case, the latter is then used to update memory. If not, an attempt is made to understand the failure, to test a remedy, and to use this information to achieve a better understanding of the problem (p. 5).

The objective of Simpson's research is to extend the capabilities of automated problem-solvers by allowing the use of analogies to similar cases in previous experience. The reasoning involved is a kind of learning from or exploiting previous experiences by either successfully using previous solutions that applied to a similar case, or steering the problem-solver away from faulty decisions that won't work.

How case-based reasoning can be used to aid problem-solving in dispute mediation is illustrated by the Sinai Dispute Case (Simpson 1985: 2).

Case 4.9

A mother reads in the paper about the Sinai dispute (before the Camp David Accords). She is reminded of the Korean War since both are disputes over land, both are competitive situations in which the conflict cannot be resolved completely for both sides, and in both, military force had been used previous to negotiations. Based on this reminding, she predicts that Israel and Egypt will divide the Sinai equally, since that is what happened in the Korean War.

She later reads that the U.S.A. had suggested this solution and it had been rejected by both sides. She is reminded of her daughters' quarrel over an orange. She had suggested that they divide it equally, and they had rejected that, since one wanted to use the entire peel for a cake. Realizing that she hadn't taken their real goals into account, she then suggested that they 'divide it into different parts'—one taking the peel, the other the fruit. This reminding provides the suggestion that failures may occur because the goals of the disputants are misunderstood. She therefore attempts a reinterpretation of Israel's and Egypt's goals. By reading more closely, she learns that Israel wants the Sinai as a military buffer zone in support of national security, and Egypt wants the land back for national integrity.

She is reminded of the Panama Canal dispute since the disputants, disputed object, and goals are similar to those in the newly understood Sinai dispute. In that case, the U.S.A. returned economic and political control of the Canal to Panama, but retained military control for national security reasons. Analogy to that incident leads the mother to decide that a similar division of the Sinai would be reasonable and guides the refinement of the 'divide into different parts' plan. Replacing the U.S.A. by Israel (the party currently in control of the object) and Panama by Egypt (the party who used to own it and wants it back), she predicts that Egypt will get economic and political control of the Sinai, while its normal right of military control will be denied.

In this case, the mother compared three different cases, the Korean War, the orange dispute, and the Panama Canal dispute, and then applied these to the case of the Sinai dispute. According to Simpson (p. 3), the analogy allowed the mother to make a quick estimate of a plausible outcome of the Sinai dispute without a 'lengthy and static investigation of possible alternatives.'

In the Sinai Dispute Case, the orange dispute and the Korean War are only 'precedents' for the Panama Canal dispute in the derivative, non-literal sense that they are preceding cases used by the mother as models which suggest a possible solution to the Panama Canal case. They are not precedents in the sense defined above, because they are not being used by the mother to authorize a new rule or practice. The important distinction is that the context of argumentation is different—the reasoning, in both instances, is based on analogy, but the analogy is used for different purposes. In the Sinai Dispute Case, the mother uses the analogy to solve a problem by comparing previous similar cases which she remembers to a new case where knowledge of the previous solutions can be transferred. Arguments about precedents (as the term is defined above) arise in a context where a new case arises and there is a question of whether it can be dealt with by an existing rule (custom, practice) or whether it leads towards creation of a new rule (or modification of the existing rule).

The precedent slippery slope argument arises within this second context of argumentation, functioning as a kind of conservative argument warning of the possibility (or plausibility) of a chain effect of future precedents leading to some undesirable outcome. Like the kind of argumentation involved in Simpson's Sinai Dispute Case, it is also case-based reasoning. But the case-based reasoning is set within a different context of argumentation. The purpose and structure of the problem, and the kinds of stage of discussion used in order to try to resolve the problem, are different.

The use of the precedent slippery slope argument involves a context of dialogue where a pleader or respondent has made a request to a proponent who is in the position of an authority or judge who must uphold a rule in some kind of institutional or authoritative framework of argumentative discussion. The pleader claims that his case should be treated as some sort of special exception to the rule, and that therefore, in this particular case, he should be exempted from a requirement of the rule. The proponent must make a decision on the issue, but generally his obligation is to uphold the rule, and it is incumbent upon him not to make exceptions unless there are sufficiently strong reasons to do so. Typically, the pleader says: 'My case is similar to this other one, which was previously granted the status of an exception. If you are to be consistent in your judgments, you will grant my case the same status.' One way the proponent can use to resist the pleader's argument is to reply: 'Yes, the other case you cite is similar (in some significant respects) to your own case. But your own case is likewise similar to another case, which is in turn similar to another case, and so forth, until we are confronted with this final 'danger case' or 'horrible outcome,' which is clearly not acceptable. Therefore, on these grounds, we cannot take the initial step of granting your case as an exception to the rule.' This form of reply is the use of the precedent slippery slope argument to rebut the respondent's plea.

Now such a reply can be reasonable in some cases, unreasonable in others. But what factors, in general, make it reasonable or unreasonable? The answer is that there is no single, isolated factor. You have to look at the context of the dialogue as a whole, including the following factors. Does the case fit the rule or not? Does it fall under a class of exceptions recognized in the rule? Or if not, is it a reasonable exception anyway? On what grounds is it an exception? Is it similar in relevant respects to the previous case cited by the pleader? Was the previous case rightly granted status as an exception? Even though the two cases are similar, is that outweighed by special features of the new case that make it objectionable to treat it as an exception? Are there comparable cases to be brought into consideration? The last question then leads on, in some cases, to the question of whether precedent slippery slope argumentation is appropriate, through asking the general question of whether there are possible future cases that are likely to arise as precedents, once this case is granted the status of an exception. It may even be asked whether this granting will lead to a new rule being formed.

Wittgenstein puzzled long and hard over the problem of how we can decide whether a rule is being followed correctly. In his later philosophy, he came to the conclusion that the only criterion we can use to decide whether a rule is rightly being followed or not is 'ultimately the entire language-game to which the rule belongs' (Hintikka 1989: 284). Wittgenstein posed the following question in the *Blue Book*: 'Let me ask this: what has the expression of a rule—say a sign-post—got to do with my actions? What sort of connection is there? Well, perhaps this one: I have been trained to react to this sign in a particular way, and now I do so react to it'. (*Blue Book*, sect. 198), quoted by Hintikka (1989: 294). The final reply that Wittgenstein settled on to answer this puzzling question emphasized that any such judgment must be made in a holistic fashion, in the context of the 'language-game,' as Wittgenstein called it, in which the rule and the particular case in question are situated: 'a person goes by a sign-post only insofar as there exists a regular use of sign-posts, a custom.' In short, there is no easy answer, no single factor that can be cited, in judging whether a rule is being followed correctly or not in a particular case.

Even so, there are a number of key factors to be considered, notably including those cited in the list of questions just above in this section. Of primary importance in connection with judging the precedent slippery slope argument is the factor of case-to-case consistency. As noted at the beginning of Section 4, this factor is closely connected to *ad hominem* argumentation.

5. *Ad Hominem* Circumstantial Inconsistency

Both slippery slope arguments and circumstantial *ad hominem* arguments are based on a proponent's allegation that there has been a failure of case-to-case consistency on the part of a respondent. Many of the most serious and subtle cases of personal attack in argument cite an ostensible inconsistency between what the arguer professes and his personal actions or circumstances. Such an allegation of inconsistency may undermine an arguer's credibility by suggesting that he is a liar, a hypocrite, or a person who does not stick to his own principles. This type of attack can be very dangerous, and needs to be handled with great care (see Walton 1985a and 1989, ch.6).

Circumstantial inconsistencies are often much harder to pin down than logical inconsistencies. When a criticism of circumstantial inconsistency is advanced in an argument against a person, a good deal of further dialogue and argument may be required to settle whether or not the criticism is reasonable or fallacious. In fact, most arguments against the person are neither fallacies nor knock-down refutations. In most cases they are more fairly treated as challenges, queries, or criticisms of an argument (Walton 1985*a*). As such, they may be either knocked down or backed up by further reasonable dialogue. Such criticisms can often be replied to with varying degrees of effectiveness.

Case 4.10

You have just argued for better state benefits for the elderly in need of medical care. But you yourself have been a longstanding and dedicated member of the Conservative Party. The basic position of your party is to cut back on government bureaucracy and bring more control to the private sector. You are being inconsistent!

Here the cited inconsistency is between the arguer's special circumstances or position as being a member of the Conservative Party and his contention on a specific issue that is alleged to be contrary to that position. This kind of criticism could be rejected as unwarranted because the original argument for better medical benefits for the elderly could have been based on good evidence and sound reasoning. To discount or exclude that possibility by attempting to force the arguer to yield to his own special circumstances may be to ignore or to attempt to suppress the possibility that his conclusion on this specific issue may be true, or at least based on reasonable evidence and argument.

The problem with case 4.10 is to know from the text and context of dialogue what the critic's conclusion is supposed to be. Is he concluding that the arguer's position on medical care for the elderly is wrong or strongly refuted by his personal attack? Or is he only suggesting that the arguer's position is open to question, and that the arguer owes us an explanation of the alleged inconsistency? This latter interpretation does not require total rejection of the argument, but only a shift in the burden of proof for the arguer to defend his position if he can.

If the arguer criticized by the argument against the person in case 4.10 has taken up a position on the issue of health care for the elderly that goes strongly against his Conservative principles, elsewhere expounded and strongly advocated, his position may be open to reasonable questioning and challenge. To criticize him for being inconsistent might not be unreasonable. It seems that when such a circumstantial criticism is pressed too far or mounted unfairly it becomes fallacious. So just as with the previous cases of the argument against the person, there is a general problem of distinguishing, in a particular case, whether the argument should justifiably be discounted as unreasonable or not. An argument against the person should not always be peremptorily dismissed as worthless.

The 'poisoning the well' and circumstantial variants of the argument against the person are similar in outline and strategy, except that the circumstantial variety essentially involves an allegation of inconsistency. According to Engel (1976: 109), the term 'poisoning the well' arose from a dispute between the nineteenth-century churchman John Henry Cardinal Newman and the novelist and clergyman Charles Kingsley. Kingsley suggested that Newman, as a Catholic priest, did not place the highest value on truth. Newman protested that by 'poisoning the well' Kingsley had made it impossible for him (Newman), or any other Catholic for that matter, to prove anything, or take any further serious part in the discussion. Although Cardinal Newman was attacked for being a Catholic, the allegation was not that his religious commitment involved his argument in an inconsistency. The accusation was a simple claim that Newman, as a Catholic, had an inescapable personal bias. But in case 4.10, and also in case 4.11, the argument against the person turns on an allegation of circumstantial inconsistency.

Both the circumstantial and poisoning the well varieties attack the trustworthiness of an arguer by raising questions about his impartiality or integrity as a reasonable arguer who should be taken seriously. In still other cases, the argument can be classified as a direct personal attack because the arguer is directly alleged to be of bad character, or in particular, to have a bad character for veracity. But in this kind of *direct* or *abusive ad hominem* argument, there is no allegation of inconsistency. However, in case 4.10, the argument was classified as a circumstantial attack because of the claim of the arguer's special circumstances as a member of the Conservative Party. The question raised there was the consistency between Conservative principles and the arguer's call for better medical benefits for the elderly. By questioning the arguer's consistency, the critic suggests that the arguer may lack integrity. Perhaps he is dishonest or has not thought out his personal position on the issue with any depth or thoughtful insight.

Thus both the direct and circumstantial personal arguments attack the personal credibility or trustworthiness of an arguer. The special difference between the two cases is that the inconsistency alleged in case 4.10 is between the arguer's statement and the special circumstances of his position, the policies he is committed to. There is no allegation of inconsistency necessarily alleged as an important part of what makes the abusive *ad hominem* an argument against the person. In that type of case, it is simply a direct attempt to discredit the argument by appeal to a personal characteristic which, it is hoped, the audience to whom the argument is directed would find distasteful and repugnant. Hence there is an important difference between the two varieties of argument against the person. Yet both arguments are a rejection of the personal trustworthiness or impartiality of the arguer who is criticized.

Another typical example of the circumstantial *ad hominem* argument reveals more about the thread of continuity between the two basic types of argument against the person.

Case 4.11

You of all people should agree that abortion is wrong. After all, you're a Catholic. Yet you personally had an abortion!

This type of argument against the person is classified as an instance of circumstantial attack. And one can see why. If the person to whom the argument is directed really is a Catholic and accepts that position, she seems caught in a circumstantial inconsistency. For if she has had an abortion in her own case, and admits to it, this seems to suggest that she is personally committed to an acceptance of abortion as a practice. After all, would not the critic here allege that actions speak louder than words? The person criticized may not be logically inconsistent. But the problem alleged is that there could be some indication of a personal or circumstantial inconsistency. The allegation is that the woman has not 'practiced what she preaches.' Clearly then, case 4.11 is rightly seen as an instance of the circumstantial type of argument against the person.

On the other hand, the argument of 'poisoning the well' used against Cardinal Newman is a direct personal attack because it attacked him for his affiliation to the Catholic Church. Here the allegation is that Newman cannot be an impartial or reliable arguer because he is biased to one point of view. However, notice that both attacks have to do with the arguer being a Catholic. The difference is that in case 4.11 there is a circumstantial inconsistency alleged, whereas in the Newman case no particular inconsistency is alleged.

Whether it be the direct, poisoning the well, or circumstantial variety, the argument against the person shares the general identifying feature that it attempts to refute a person's argument by appealing to allegations about the personal background, ethics, affiliations, or special circumstances of that person, in order to discredit their credibility or impartiality as an arguer. While not always fallacious, this form of attempted refutation is extremely powerful and dangerous in argument. It must always be handled with care.

What is characteristic of this personal style of criticism of someone's argument is that the criticism goes beyond a concentration on the premises and conclusions, the propositions that made up the person's argument. It goes beyond by bringing in consideration of the arguer's position as based on his or her commitments. These commitments may be derived from personal facts about the arguer being criticized, or they may derive from previous statements, affiliations, or circumstances of the arguer.

6. Personal Circumstances and Actions

Very often it is characteristic of circumstantial arguments against the person that the special circumstances cited are actions alleged to have been carried out or consented to by that person. The suggestion conveyed by such arguments is that a person's actions often reveal their true convictions and principles more accurately than what the person says. Indeed, case 4.11 concerned the allegation that the woman in question had personally had an abortion. But does this action necessarily mean that in her case there is a circumstantial inconsistency between her convictions or position on the one hand, and her actions on the other? It is a good exercise here to ask how someone criticized by 4.11 might possibly respond in dialogue.

It is of course well known that the Catholic theological position is based on a Thomistic philosophy that has as a fundamental principle the goal of the flourishing of the human species. Great stress is laid in this philosophy in respect for the potential of human life. Consequently, the Catholic position generally is to only allow abortion as morally permissible in exceptional cases. However, such exceptions have been occasionally recognized by Catholic practitioners—for example, cases where the life of the mother is at risk, or where the fetus could survive birth only under a cruel burden of deformity or mortal illness. Now no information given so far rules out the possibility that the woman against whom the argument in case 4.11 is directed might be able to respond by arguing that her abortion should come under the heading of one of these exceptions. Whether such a response could be reasonable would depend on what the Catholic position on abortion truly is— if it could be spelled out—and on what the particulars of this individual case are. As far as case 4.11 has developed, information on these two factors has not yet been clearly specified as part of the argument.

Now there appears to be little reason to doubt that pointing out a logical inconsistency in someone's position or argument is a legitimate criticism, in general. It is legitimate, because an inconsistency implies a contradiction. And any collection of propositions that contain a contradiction cannot all be true. At least one proposition in the collection must be false. Therefore, a logically inconsistent position, as a totality, cannot be consistently maintained.

However, let us return to case 4.11. Does the Catholic woman's position contain a logical inconsistency? No, it does not, at least as far as the criticism in case 4.11 has been developed by the person who had advanced this argument. If the Catholic position is committed to the proposition that abortion is never permissible in any case, then if that woman had consented to her abortion, she could fairly be accused of being inconsistent. But such an interpretation would not be a fair or correct account of the Catholic position. If the woman intentionally had the abortion while she was a practicing Catholic, and could give no reason for arguing that the case was an exceptional one, then it would be plausible to maintain that her position may be open to a charge of circumstantial inconsistency. But in evaluating such a charge, much would have to depend on what assertions of her knowledge, intentions, and actions the woman would commit herself to in further dialogue. Although she may have seemed inconsistent, it remains possible that she may have had some credible reason why she acted as she did. A reasonable approach to argument would at least seem to require that she be given some benefit of the doubt, and a chance to respond to the argument against her personal position and conduct.

One main lesson of this example is that there is an important difference between a logical inconsistency and a circumstantial (case-to-case) inconsistency. A logical inconsistency is a well-defined set of propositions containing a contradiction. A circumstantial inconsistency depends on the presumption that certain personal actions or other personal circumstances suggest or make plausible that there may be a logical inconsistency inherent in an arguer's position. But the problem is that an arguer's position in realistic practices of argument is rarely spelled out or specified as a well-articulated set of propositions. Not only am I unlikely to be able to spell out precisely someone else's position on a controversial issue like abortion, I may not even be able to articulate or know my own position until it further emerges in dialogue and discussion.

It follows then that in judging claims of circumstantial consistency or inconsistency of two or more cases that are alleged to be comparable, the judgment must be made in the context of dialogue (or 'language-game,' in Wittgenstein's sense) as a whole.

In case 4.11, we saw that there is a plausible appearance of inconsistency if someone who claims to be a Catholic has an abortion. But that appearance of inconsistency could be refuted if the person might give evidence that her case is a legitimate exception. Because the critic does not spell out the Catholic position on abortion well enough so that it can be clearly applied to the specific case at issue, his attack leaves plenty of room for a reasonable reply. His attack in this case is not erroneous as it stands. But it should be recognized that it is a very weak shift of the burden of proof that, if challenged, must be backed up more deeply. Such a failure to back up the attack, therefore, should come under the heading of case-based argumentation.

7. Rebutting Arguments from Case-to-Case Inconsistency

In practical terms what this new dimension of case-based reasoning means is that we have learned a proper defense against a circumstantial personal attack. This defense, as in case 4.12, is to claim that one's personal situation is different from the alleged parallel in some relevant respect.

Case 4.12

Defense by Citing Different Circumstances

BOB. Professor X, I notice that you just refused to spend more time with that student to give him some extra help with his essay. But I remember you saying once that when you were an undergraduate, you really appreciated the individual help and personal contact you had with your professors. You thought that this personal approach was the most valuable aspect of your undergraduate education. Are you being consistent here?

PROFESSOR X. Well, Bob, I appreciate your point. I still do feel that personal one-on-one instruction is the ideal for excellence in undergraduate teaching. But times have changed. When I was an undergraduate, we had small classes, and a professor could spend time with each student individually. Now, however, classes are overcrowded, teaching loads have increased enormously, and it is no longer possible to give extra help to every student by personal discussion of their individual problems. I still try to maintain my educational ideals of excellence in teaching, but the changing economic conditions and enrolment patterns—things over which I have very little if any control—do not permit the same level of individual instruction.

In the dialogue in case 4.12, Professor X's reply to Bob's reasonable questioning of X's circumstantial consistency is to claim that X's personal circumstances are different, in an important respect, from the situation of professors when he was a student. Is it a reasonable reply? Well, of course, it depends on whether the two cases, the two sets of circumstances, really are different in the respect he cites, or whether they can be shown to be different enough to substantiate his claim that they are. But if his claim is a plausible one, from what he and Bob know of the changing times in education, then his reply successfully shifts the burden of proof back onto Bob's side. If it does this, it is to be judged a successful and reasonable reply to Bob's personal criticism. The judgment clearly depends on the two sets of circumstances and their comparative similarity to each other, or what is known of them at the stage of the dialogue where the criticism was advanced. Such criticisms are generally best regarded as defeasible, because subsequent dialogue may turn up new and relevant information about these circumstances.

In many case-to-case disputes, however, it is not so much the actual circumstances that are at issue, as the question of how those circumstances may be described. In such cases, the dispute between an arguer and his critic may be, to a great extent, a linguistic dispute about the terminology which is appropriate or justifiable to describe a situation in which the arguer is involved personally. The following case will illustrate this type of dispute.

Case 4.13

SOVIET DIPLOMAT (SD). The American intervention in Central America shows how the U.S. uses force to violently suppress the rights of peoples to run their own countries. This superpower intervention is imperial domination of neighbor states.

AMERICAN DIPLOMAT (AD). How do you deal with these facts? East Central European nations have been enslaved by Soviet armed forces for forty years. The invasion of Afghanistan has been in force for six years. Your country is guilty of blatant acts of suppression of rights by force. If the shoe fits, wear it!

SD. The Soviet Union's police actions in these instances have been carried out on the basis of strict respect for the rights of people to determine their own development, and have been carried out to help these people solve their own internal problems by peaceful means. This is not imperialism.

What we know of the facts in these disputed situations might suggest that the Soviet military interventions have been the more forceful take-overs. However, a good deal of the dispute is about the language which can justifiably be used to describe the situations. SD uses argumentative terms like 'imperialism,' 'force,' 'violently suppress the rights of peoples,' and so forth. But he refuses to use the same terms to describe Soviet actions that plausibly appear to be parallel or similar in the relevant respects.

In this type of argument, the burden of proof is on the defender, SD, to reply to AD's circumstantial argument against the person. Since the two types of circumstance do appear to be basically similar, the circumstantial challenge of SD's argument by AD is a plausible argument. SD's attempt to repel the challenge by linguistic retrenchment indicates that it is reasonable to question whether he is being consistent in his use of language in the two disputed sets of circumstances. He has replied: 'Our case is not similar to yours.' But instead of giving good reasons, he has simply retreated into a dogmatic refusal to apply the same terms to the two parallel sets of circumstances. This failure to respond to the challenge is not an acceptable reply in reasonable dialogue.

Criticisms and disputes that turn on controversies about the uses of argumentative language in dialogue are extensively studied in Walton (1989, ch. 9). But here it is worth while observing that evaluation of many case-to-case arguments also have a linguistic element. They are not so much disputes about the facts, but about the kinds of word that can be reasonably used to describe these relevant facts or circumstances. In short, some circumstantial arguments against the person are based on the criticism that an arguer is not using his terms in a consistent manner, and is using them to serve his own interests in a biased manner.

The many arguments based on case-to-case claims of inconsistency we have looked at in this chapter can be criticized, questioned, or evaluated as reasonable or unreasonable though they are neither deductively valid, nor inductively confirmable, nor susceptible to evaluation completely by deductive or inductive standards. They are cases of plausible argument. Even so, we have recognized some criteria for evaluating them as strong or weak in different cases.

8. Exceptions to the Rule

Whether a slippery slope argument of the *ad hominem* type is reasonable or fallacious depends on the context of dialogue. As noted in Section 5 above, the judgment depends on what Wittgenstein called the 'language-game,' or 'form of life.' Most rules, whether they be rules of conduct, rules of language, or rules of a game, have exceptions. But there are no explicit rules for judging whether or not something is a legitimate exception, or whether the context is one that should rightly admit of exceptions.

An interesting example comes from Black (1970: 12–13).

Case 4.14

When I play chess with a child, we may allow one another to 'take back' bad moves. If we used the privilege too often, the game would be impossible to play; but if we retract a move only occasionally, the whole affair is quite feasible.

The problem posed here is that takebacks can be allowed for pedagogical purposes, but if they are allowed too freely, the game ceases to be like a 'real' game of chess any more. It would destroy the purpose of the game. Thus to promote the right context of orderly interaction appropriate to teach the beginner, takebacks should be allowed only in exceptional circumstances, and not in every or too many instances. But whether or not a takeback should rightly be allowed seems to depend on the particular situation—on the beginner's state of knowledge of the game, on how disastrous the move would be, and so forth. There seems to be no rule (certainly no rule of chess) to determine when a takeback should be allowed or not.

Lamb (1988: 8) compares Black's example of the takebacks in chess with the slippery slope objections to euthanasia, in an instructive way. Just as takebacks are sometimes acceptable in chess, certain ways of 'accelerating the dying process' might be acceptable, in exceptional circumstances, in good medical practice. But it would be a different question or context if one were to try to offer precise rules for performing euthanasia as regular medical procedures, as has now happened in the Netherlands, where euthanasia is regularly permitted according to definite rules.

The precedent type of slippery slope argument is feasible as a kind of argumentation because the argument turns on a set of rules and an exceptional series of situations not covered by the rules. Typically, the reasoning from one proposed exception to the other is based on analogy, a kind of argumentation that does not appear to be rule-governed. Certainly, at any rate, the proposed exceptions cannot be decided by the original rules in a particular case of slippery slope argument based on precedents.

In this regard, the precedent type of slippery slope appears similar to the sorites type in an important respect. Both work because the argument starts in a clear area and proceeds towards and into a grey area, where issues are not cleanly resolved by the existing set of definitions or rules.

In this respect, the precedent type of slippery slope argument is also markedly similar to the traditional fallacy of *secundum quid.*

According to Hamblin (1970: 28) *secundum quid,* which in Greek, παρὰ τὸ πῆ, means 'in a certain respect,' is the name for a traditional fallacy which refers to errors that involve 'neglect of necessary qualifications.' As Hamblin shows, however, there is considerable uncertainty and difference of opinion in the traditional accounts of the logic texts on what sort of error or logical failure is supposed to be covered by this term. It has often been associated with, or mixed in with other alleged fallacies like 'hasty generalization' and 'accident,' according to Hamblin (p. 29).

The existence of these traditional categories of fallacies indicates that we can run into problems of faulty reasoning when dealing with arguments, policies, rules, or generalizations that can properly admit of exceptions in special circumstances. The same kind of problem has arisen in recent research on artificial intelligence, where in expert systems, reasoning for example, there can be 'rules of thumb' of the form, 'Most cases of A are (normally, we can reasonably expect) cases of B (except in special or non-normal circumstances).' These kinds of rule are designed to admit of exceptions, so their logic is based on 'confidence factors' or plausible reasoning. In this respect, the logic of inferences based on such exception-prone generalization is inherently different from the logic appropriate for deductive or inductive reasoning. See Rescher (1976) for a formalistic account of some of these inherent differences.

Practical reasoning is essentially defeasible, and hence the slippery slope argument is defeasible. Slippery slope arguments are always held together by a sequence of *modus ponens* steps linked together.[1] The link in each step is normally a presumptive conditional that is inherently defeasible, meaning that it makes a claim that if an event occurs in a particular situation in normal circumstances, then another event might plausibly occur, all things

---

[1] Defeasibility is defined in Ch. 1.8.

being equal.[2] But such an inference is always qualified. If new information comes into the premises, the conclusion can change.

According to Levinson (1983: 114), an inference is defeasible if it is possible to cancel it by adding additional premises to the original ones.[3] Deductive logical inferences are not defeasible.

But the kind of inference characteristic of each link in the sequence premise of a slippery slope argument is defeasible. The glue that holds slippery slope argumentation together is therefore a kind of Gricean implicature, not a deductive logical inference. The slippery slope argument is a kind of warning that some horrible outcome might happen through a sequence of linked developments from some first step. Properly construed, however, this type of argumentation has at its core a kind of practical reasoning which is relativized to routine ways of doing things in a situation where, all else being equal, outcomes of a particular sort can reasonably be expected.

According to Golding (1984), legal arguments are normative arguments (p. 42) that are species of practical reasoning (p. 55): 'it is a characteristic of this context of practical normative reasoning that when a judge has a good reason for accepting a certain normative conclusion, he is *committed* to accepting and acting on the conclusion, unless there is (another) good reason for not doing so' (p. 107). The form of arguments from analogy, as represented by Golding (p. 107, quoted below) shows how they represent practical reasoning. In this argumentation scheme, x, y, ... stand for individuals.

Form of Argument from Analogy (Golding: 1984)
  (1) x has characteristics F, G, ...

  (2) y has characteristics F, G, ...

  (3) x also has characteristic H.

  (4) F, G, ... are H-relevant characteristics.

  (5) Therefore, unless there are countervailing considerations, y has characteristic H.

Because the conclusion contains qualifications, referring to

---

[2] See Walton (1989, Ch. 9) on the defeasible nature of arguments from analogy.
[3] The analysis of this structure is presented in Chapter 6.4 and 6.5.

possible 'countervailing considerations,' the premises do not deductively imply (entail) the conclusion. Rather, the argument from analogy commits one to accepting its conclusion only on the presumption that such countervailing considerations—which could be in the form of other arguments, e.g. counteranalogies— are not known. Golding adds (p. 111) that one is justified in drawing an unqualified conclusion only if there are no counter- vailing considerations.

Thus the correctness or incorrectness of a precedent slippery slope argument should be sought in the notion of reasonable commitment to a conclusion (on the basis of a plausible presump- tion that can be retracted under certain conditions or exceptions) in a context of dialogue. Reasoned dialogue should be allowed to include the retraction as well as the incurring of a commitment, according to the rules of dialogue.

In evaluating slippery slope arguments four factors regarding exceptions to rules or concepts are especially important. One is that there can be legitimate exceptions to a set of precise rules which is appropriate for a given, initial context of argument. The second is that there can be a shift to a different context of argument which concerns the issue of the legitimacy of proposed exceptions. The third is that the original rules no longer govern this secondary issue, or provide a means for resolving it. The fourth is that the shift from the one context to the other may be itself impossible to define, quantify, or exactly specify, using the original set of rules or concepts.

It should be noted here as well that it should be regarded as perfectly legitimate in some cases to argue about whether a situation is an exception to a rule or not. Legal argumentation, for example, is legitimately precedent-based. When a new case arises that challenges a previous ruling, participants in a court case can dispute the pros and cons of changing the old rule, or of admitting or denying the claimed exception. This kind of argumentation is, in the proper context, perfectly legitimate, and there need be nothing inherently fallacious about it.

Another thing worth noting about precedent arguments is that whether a case is to be decided in accord with a rule, or as an exceptional case which falls outside any rule, depends on the social or institutional context in the particular case. Euthanasia argu- ments are a good example of this context-sensitive feature. In the

Netherlands, according to Rigter (1989: 31), doctors practicing euthanasia will not be prosecuted if they follow a set of strict guidelines handed down by the Supreme Court and elaborated upon by the Royal Dutch Medical Association. According to these rules, Dutch physicians are allowed to actively terminate the life of a patient on the patient's request, if the patient is suffering severely with no prospect of relief.

In North America, by contrast, such acts of euthanasia by a physician are sometimes tolerated by the courts by being treated as exceptional cases, even if they technically amount to murder, according to the letter of the law.

The outcome of the ruling may be the same, in both cases, but the basis of reasoning by which that outcome is arrived at is quite different. In the Dutch case, such an act is judged permissible because it meets the requirements of the rule. In the North American case, the act is judged permissible because it is treated as an exception to the rule.

A rule of this sort, then, is not mechanically applicable to all cases. It sets a burden of proof which a putative exception has to overcome. But whether a case is judged by the rule, or as an exception to it, depends on the background pragmatic, e.g. institutional, context of the system of rules in that particular case. Slippery slope arguments, therefore should be evaluated in relation to a particular, given case.

9. Antecedent Climate of Opinion

In some cases of the precedent type of slippery slope argument, the initial step triggers the further developments which follow by a kind of releasing effect. This can occur, for example, in a context where there is a horizon of public opinion in favor of a certain kind of action, but some inertia, blockage, or prohibition against this kind of action which could be overcome or destroyed by a single precedent. The slippery slope argument does not lead directly to the final outcome, nor does it deductively imply the conclusion which is that outcome. Instead, it facilitates that conclusion by removing an obstacle to a tide of opinion that is already pressing toward that conclusion.

An example is given by Lamb (1988: 1).

Case 4.15

In 1967, a black murderer, Aaron Mitchell, was denied an appeal for clemency by Ronald Reagan, who was at that time the Governor of California. Following Mitchell's execution there was a moratorium on state executions until 1977, when the convicted murderer, Gary Gilmore, won the right to be executed by a firing squad in the State of Utah. Since Gilmore's death there have been scores of other executions and, given the public appetite for capital punishment (72 per cent in the U.S.A. in favour according to a recent opinion poll), it is plausible to predict that, all things being equal, the number of state executions will continue to increase.

As Lamb (p. 1) puts it, the first step in this kind of case does not determine further developments, 'but it can be said that it facilitates such developments when there is a social situation in which they are likely to achieve approval.' Gilmore's case was unusual in that he voluntarily demanded his own execution. But its exceptional nature appears to have been passed over, and it seems to have functioned as a kind of precedent which led to many subsequent executions for murder where no demand to die was expressed. It seems quite plausible then, as Lamb suggests, that the Gilmore case functioned as the initial step of a slippery slope argument that led to many other subsequent cases of capital punishment in the U.S.A. by a kind of precedent that redefined the boundaries of a kind of action that became more acceptable on a wider scale.

But there is more to this case. In this case we can see in retrospect how Gilmore's execution led to other executions for capital crimes. That is the way things happened, evidently. But where the slippery slope argument could have been used would be prior to any of these events, where an arguer might be trying to warn others of the possible consequences of the proposed Gilmore execution. If someone were to have argued in this way, then it seems that their slippery slope argument would have been justified as a good one by subsequent events. In such a case then, the slippery slope argument could have been a reasonable argument, and subsequent evidence could have shown that it was reasonable, i.e. it was performing its legitimate function as a kind of warning that subsequent capital executions would increase, because of the Gilmore decision.

What made the slippery slope argument strong or reasonable, in this case? It did not seem to be, at least exclusively, formal considerations that one step was linked to the next by some sort of conditional, or bridging principle. What seemed most significant was a pragmatic factor—namely that there existed in this case a strong antecedent climate of opinion in the U.S.A. in favor of the death penalty at that time. Thus the predicted developments by the slippery slope proponent in this case were not 'merely possible.' Because of this existing climate of opinion, good reasons were there to support the claim that these developments were highly plausible as outcomes of the precedent set by this one case.

In this case, there is evidence that can be cited by the proponent of the slippery slope argument, and questioned by its critics. The evidence here is contextual—it concerns a given climate of opinion which formed a plausible presumption in relation to the future developments which could be plausibly predicted to ensue in the case in question.

What is needed then, to give a proper framework for the critical evaluation of precedent slippery slope arguments, is an argumentation scheme for this type of argument that can help us to determine on which side a burden of proof should lie in a particular case, relative to the background presumptions and context of dialogue for that case. This argumentation scheme should have premises which can be supported by a proponent who is using the argument. These premises, along with the appropriate conclusion, should indicate key critical questions that can be asked by a reasonable critic (respondent) who has the role of shifting the burden of proof against the side of the proponent in the dialogue. Fulfillment of this burden by backing the premises and replying adequately to these critical questions has the function of supporting the precedent slippery slope argument as plausible, relative to the discussion.

10. Argumentation Scheme for the Precedent Slippery Slope

Arguments based on precedents are quite common in everyday reasoning, but it appears to be very uncommon to recognize them in logic as a distinctive kind of argumentation. Not much appears to be known about them, from a logical point of view. However, they do have three general characteristics that stand out immediately. First, they are species of the argument from analogy which compare one particular situation with another. Second, they involve case-based reasoning which proceeds by comparing key features of one particular case with key features of another particular case. Thus they have a kind of open-ended quality, where the conclusion depends on what is known about the characteristics or facts of a particular case. Third, they are based on plausible reasoning, resting on presumptions about certain features of a case held to be significant, all other things being equal. The presumption is that a field or background context of a particular situation can be held constant, or taken for granted, assuming the situation is normal, relative to our usual expectations about this kind of case.

Precedent slippery slope arguments characteristically occur in a context where one party is appealing to another party, in order to argue that his special case is an exception to the rule that the other party is obliged to uphold. The proponent of the slippery slope argument is the party who is obliged to uphold the rule. We will designate as respondent the party who pleads that his case can be excused as an exception to the rule.

This terminology may seem to be backwards at first. But it is correct, once we see that the slippery slope argument is similar in use to a *reductio ad absurdum* argument (indirect proof), where the one party is trying to refute the thesis of the other by assuming it (for the sake of argument), and then showing it is untenable because of its unacceptable consequences. It is the proponent that is the one who has the role of carrying out this procedure of reducing to absurdity, or at any rate to unacceptability. Although the respondent seems to act first, because he is the one who brings forward the plea to be excused, the one who carries out the slippery slope technique is really the one who 'responds' secondly. In one sense then, he is the 'responder.' But from the viewpoint of the use of the slippery slope argument, he is really the proponent, because he is the one who is using this negative technique to refute the argument of the other party.

The precedent slippery slope argument typically arises out of the following initial situation (tactical basis). There is a rule R, and normally a given class of allowed excuses or exceptional cases which may already be recognized in relation to inferring from R. A new case arises, and the respondent pleads it as an exception. Should it be allowed (included in the given class) or not? That is the problem, or question to be resolved.

One possible response by the one who must uphold or enforce the rule, in this kind of problem situation, is to try to make it harder for the pleader to get his way by advancing a slippery slope argument. It is a kind of preserving or conservative tactic to try to maintain or uphold the rule against the move to get around it. The argumentation scheme has three premises.

Argumentation Scheme for the Precedent Slippery Slope

Claim to exceptional status premise:	Case C_0 is claimed to be an exception to the rule R (an excusable or exceptional case).
Related cases premise:	Case C_0 is similar to case C_1, i.e. if C_0 is held to be an exception, then C_1 must be held to be an exception too (in order to be consistent in treating equal cases alike). A sequence of similar pairs of cases $\{C_i, C_j\}$ binds us by case-to-case consistency to the series, $C_0, C_1, ...,C_n$.
Intolerable outcome premise:	Treating case C_n as an exception to the rule R would be intolerable (for the various kinds of reasons which could be relevant, as indicated in the summary of varieties of precedent slippery slope arguments below).
Conclusion:	Case C_0 cannot be judged to be an exception to the rule (an excusable or exceptional case).

This argumentation scheme can be implemented in different ways, producing different varieties of the precedent slippery slope argument.

The basic type of precedent slippery slope argument, illustrated by case 4.3, is the simplest kind of case where a plea for an excuse or exception to a rule is not allowed on the grounds that it would (or might plausibly) lead to a chain of precedents which would end in some intolerable outcome. As case 4.3 illustrates, this kind of slippery slope argumentation can be used reasonably to uphold a rule in some cases.

On the other hand, case 4.5 (Govier's budget submission case) shows how this very same kind of precedent slippery slope can be weak, erroneous or unreasonable in other cases. Govier, describing the form of this argument as the *simple dangerous precedent* type of slippery slope argument, called it a fallacy. But in her description of the alleged fallacy (just above case 4.5) much depends on how the phrase 'acceptable when considered solely on its own merits' is construed. If this phrase is interpreted in a strong sense, it could even be implied that the schema for the simple dangerous precedent argument (as described by Govier) contains an inconsistency, implying that the case in question is both acceptable and unacceptable in the same respect. But does that mean that the precedent type of slippery slope argument is a fallacy? No, it does not. It only means that Govier's schema is not a good analysis of the fault or weakness in case 4.5.

The real failure in case 4.5 is that the related cases premise of the argumentation scheme for the precedent slippery slope simply fails to hold. The woman in case 4.5 in fact had an acceptable excuse—her husband had just died. The argument in case 4.5 does not show (and presumably cannot show) that such a precedent would lead by a sequence of properly comparable cases to the bad outcome of accepting applications from 'people who are late' who are 'lazy and disorganized' and who do not have a 'good excuse.'

Therefore, we propose rewriting clause (1) of Govier's simple dangerous precedent form of slippery slope argument to replace 'is acceptable' with 'might be acceptable.' So rewritten, it is no longer a fallacy, and instead represents the basic type of precedent slippery slope argument. So reconstructed, it becomes an instance of the form of argument (PS) in Section 3, which is in turn a simplified version of the argumentation scheme for the precedent slippery slope, just above. According to our new and revised version of it then, the simple dangerous precedent slippery slope argument is the basic type of precedent slippery slope argument. This basic type can now be seen to have several variants. Each of these variants, like the basic type, is inherently reasonable as a plausible argument type in a context of dialogue, but can become weak, erroneous, or fallacious in some cases, when not used properly. These abuses mainly occur when one of the premises is not adequately supported by the evidence given in a particular case. However, just because one of the premises is not adequately supported, this failure to meet burden of proof is not necessarily a fallacy. The cases studied in this chapter show that very often a precedent slippery slope argument can be open to critical questioning without being fallacious.

The simple dangerous precedent argument, as described above, can now be taken to be equivalent to what Williams (1985: 127) called the horrible results argument. The arbitrary results argument warns against the bad sequence of outcomes that would result from granting jurisdiction to a decision-maker or institution —see case 4.8. The third variant (see case 4.5) is the arbitrary results argument. This variant too can be reasonable in some cases, weak or even fallacious in others. The fourth variety is the feasibility precedent slippery slope argument, illustrated by case 4.7. It too is a reasonable kind of argument that can sometimes go wrong, or be inadequately supported in dialogue.

The fifth variety recognized here is the short form of the precedent slippery slope argument illustrated by case 1.1 (the case where a court precedent was said to be the 'thread that would unravel the whole cloth' and lead to disaster). Like the causal and sorites slippery slope arguments, the precedent type also admits of shorter and longer forms of presentation. The short form version, while incomplete, and therefore generally open to critical questioning, is not inherently fallacious.

These varieties of the precedent type of slippery slope argument are summarized below.

Varieties of Precedent Slippery Slope Arguments

Simple dangerous precedent argument	The intolerable outcome is a non-allowable excuse or exception
Argument from added authority	Additional authority granted to decision-maker would lead to a sequence of bad results
Arbitrary results argument	The intolerable outcome is a series of unclear or arbitrary decisions about what to include

| Feasibility precedent argument | The intolerable outcome is an unworkable or impractical rule |
| Short form | Any one of the above with steps in the related case premise omitted |

Each of these variants on the precedent slippery slope argument is inherently reasonable, if used properly, according to the requirements of the argumentation scheme for precedent slippery slope arguments. To see how they can become open to criticism in some cases, we need to turn to an examination of the set of critical questions for this argumentation scheme.

The arbitrary results argument is typified by Williams's example of case 4.6. The slippery slope argument in this case was to the effect that extending a tax benefit from married couples to unmarried couples would lead to too many arbitrary discriminations being made. Presumably, this would be bad both in itself and because it would lead to difficulties in implementing the tax relief scheme which could eventually undermine or even destroy the whole basis of the original proposal. What started out as a clearly defined proposal has become unclear by leading to all kinds of borderline cases which would be very difficult to judge without simply extending the benefit to virtually everyone. The slippery slope argument functions here as a legitimate tool for shifting the burden of proof onto the advocate of the original proposal to show how it can be clarified or revised to eliminate these bad effects.

The feasibility precedent type of slippery slope argument is typified by Govier's example of the French language schools funding (case 4.7). The problem here was that if the funding were to be extended to all the language groups, it would be impractical, because there is not sufficient funding for all deserving groups. The intolerable outcome cited in this type of case is that of impracticality. That is, the original proposal would allegedly be destroyed not because of its arbitrariness or lack of clarity, etc., but simply because it would become impractical to implement it for all the claims that would be judged as deserving, once the initial exception was granted.

This argument could quite possibly be making a good point. How good it is depends on the particulars of the case. But the point made by the slippery slope argument is good enough to call for a response. Like the other slippery slope arguments of this chapter, it is a defeasible argument, but not a fallacious argument.

Generally, the argumentation scheme for the precedent slippery slope argument shows you how you can go about criticizing an argument of this type in a particular case. Judging by the text and context of dialogue in the given case, you need to see whether the appropriate premises have been put forward, and if they have been backed up by sufficient relevant evidence to meet the requirements of burden of proof for the dialogue in relation to the initial presumptions in the case. If not, you should ask specific critical questions to pinpoint the missing items.

In none of the cases in this chapter was the precedent slippery slope argument so bad or systematically erroneous, unfair, or misleading that it could be properly said to be fallacious. That does not mean, however, that precedent slippery slope arguments are never fallacious. Like the other three basic kinds of slippery slope argument, this type can be used in a fallacious way if it is pressed forward too hard as a tactic to try to win a cheap victory by violating any specific rules of a reasonable dialogue.

What is impressive, however, is how often it is used as a basically reasonable kind of argumentation. In Chapter 7.7–9, a case study of its use in a Supreme Court will show how powerful an argument it can be.

5

The Full Slippery Slope Argument

THE full or combined slippery slope argument, introduced in Chapter 1. 2, is similar in many points of comparison to the three other kinds of slippery slope argument. Indeed, it combines all three. But in so doing, it is typically a much more complex kind of argumentation which requires a good deal of evidence to properly support. It has been used with notable frequency in recent ethical controversies, particularly on subjects in medical ethics like euthanasia, as indicated in cases 1.3, 1.4, and 1.5.

The full slippery slope argument is a complex network of argumentation that involves eight component types of argument: (1) argument from gradualism, (2) argument from consequences, (3) practical reasoning, (4) argument from analogy, (5) argument from popular opinion, (6) argument from precedent, (7) causal argumentation, and (8) the sorites type of argumentation, which exploits vagueness. The context of all cases of slippery slope argument is that of practical reasoning, where an agent's goals are being evaluated in relation to the available means of carrying out these goals in light of what is known about a particular situation. Often, however, slippery slope arguments involve planning for a whole population or group of individuals in order to set institutionalized standards of acceptable behavior. Hence it is a kind of argumentation that can be highly appropriate in a context where controversial ethical issues concerning the possible long-term consequences of contemplated social policies are being discussed.

As indicated in case 2.5, the use of the full slippery slope argument against euthanasia has often exploited comparisons between current worries about euthanasia as an increasing practice and the coming-to-be of the mass killings of the concentration camps in the Nazi era. The utilization of this alarming argument raises the historical question of whether in fact there was a kind of slippery slope sequential sliding in the Nazi era from public acceptance of the initial programs of sterilization and euthanasia—evidently supported and largely approved by the medical profession, in particular—towards more and more widespread policies of killing the 'socially unfit,' until the eventual outcome was the implantation of the program of mass murder in the death camps. Findings of Lifton (1986) indicate that there was a sequence of roughly this sort in the historical coming-to-be of the death camps.[1]

However, this historical question is not the basic problem of analysis of the full slippery slope argument. The basic problem is to understand how some previous horrible outcome like the Nazi death camps can be used as part of a technique of argument by a proponent to refute an argument (like the argument for euthanasia) he rejects.

1. Two Classic Cases of Euthanasia

The full type of slippery slope argument incorporates the leading elements of all three of the previously identified types of slippery slope argument. It also adds an element of the *argumentum ad populum* (see Walton 1980, 1987: 33) to the effect that once each new step in the sequence is activated as a permissible policy, people will become accustomed to it, and move on towards acceptance of the next step.

A classic example of the full slippery slope argument is the following argument against euthanasia, cited in Walton (1987: 209).

Case 5.1

If we allow non-utilization of aggressive therapies in intensive care units, we have to allow other waiving of treatments that might shorten life. For example, we should allow patients to decide not to take chemical treatments for cancer. But if we allow that, it is a short step to allowing patients to take medications that might have the effect of shortening life, even if the treatment is not aggressive or painful. And if we allow that, it is just another short step to allowing patients to alleviate any uncomfortable or undesirable situation by committing suicide. Once we reach that stage, it becomes very easy to recommend euthanasia for mentally retarded persons, or anyone who requires inconvenient or costly treatment or support. Now we all know from the experience of Nazi Germany, it is a short step from there to elimination of any 'socially undesirable,' i.e.

---

[1] See the discussion in Chapter 1.2.

politically dissident persons. So once you start in with euthanasia at all, you are on a slippery slope to disaster.

As noted in Walton (1987: 209), this argument is partly causal in nature, and partly linguistic because of the vagueness of a term (like the sorites argument). Because of the vagueness of the term 'euthanasia,' it is difficult to resist the pressure to assimilate each step to the next step in the series. But there is also a causal sequence. For once a given step becomes policy, it becomes a causal factor in leading towards the acceptance of the next step (according to the argument).

This causal sequence, however, has an important element of the *argumentum ad populum* in it. Once people become comfortable with one stage of the development, the argument suggests that this climate of acceptance will be a factor in easing the transition to the next step as a new policy. This *ad populum* element is clearly brought out in Govier's account of the structure of this type of argument, which she calls the full slippery slope argument.

The Full Slippery Slope Argument (Govier 1982: 315)

(1) Case (*a*) is prima facie acceptable.

(2) Cases (*b*), (*c*), ..., (n) are unacceptable.

(3) Cases (*a*), ..., (*n*) are assimilable, as they differ from each other only by degrees, and are arrangeable as a spectrum of cases.

(4) As a matter of psychological fact, people are likely to assimilate cases (*a*)–(*n*).

(5) Case (*a*), if permitted, will be taken as a precedent for the others, (*b*)–(*n*).

(6) Permitting (*a*) will cause the permission of (*b*)–(*n*).

(7) Case (*a*) should therefore not be permitted.

The *ad populum* element is clearly identifiable in premise (4), and also to some extent in premise (5). The causal element is evident in premise (6). Otherwise the full slippery slope argument has the structure of the sorites argument. Thus it combines all three of the simple slippery slope arguments in one complex structure.

It is interesting to notice that the full slippery slope argument can be presented in many different ways. In some presentations, it can be a weak kind of argumentation that functions more as a warning or caution by citing how it is 'easy' or 'natural' to go from one step to the next step in the sequence. In other presentations, the sequence from each step to the next may be portrayed in much stronger terms as 'necessary' or 'inevitable.' There are all kinds of mixtures possible in how the argument is presented, even if the basic sequence and subject matter of the slippery slope argument are the same.

For example, consider the following more extreme form of the slippery slope argument against euthanasia enunciated by Bishop Joseph V. Sullivan.

Case 5.2

If voluntary euthanasia were legalized, there is good reason to believe that at a later date another bill for compulsory euthanasia would be legalized. Once the respect for human life is so low that an innocent person may be killed directly even at his own request, compulsory euthanasia will necessarily be very near. This could lead easily to killing all incurable cancer patients, the aged who are a public care, wounded soldiers, all deformed children, the mentally afflicted, and so on. Before long the danger would be at the door of every citizen.

Once a man is permitted on his own authority to kill an innocent person directly, there is no way of stopping the advancement of that wedge. There exists no longer any rational grounds for saying that the wedge can advance so far and no further. Once the exception has been made it is too late; hence the grave reason why no exception may be allowed. That is why euthanasia under any circumstances must be condemned. (Cited by Rachels 1986: 171)

In this case, several of the links are phrased in such a strong fashion that there seems no room for escape. The phrases used include 'compulsory euthanasia,' 'necessarily be very near,' 'no way of stopping the advancement,' and 'no longer any rational grounds' for resisting 'the wedge.' By contrast, the transitions in the similar case 5.1 are milder, using terms like 'short step' and 'easy to recommend' (even though the phrase 'have to allow' is also used once).

Although the two cases do appear similar in subject matter and in the general line of the argumentation, closer inspection reveals significant differences. Many of the individual steps cited in the one case are different from those cited in the other. In general, the mode of presentation of the slippery slope attack is markedly stronger in the second case, because of the language used to describe the linkages of the steps of the sequence. In the second case, once the initial step is made, the argument indicates, the transition to the 'danger' or intolerable conclusion is inevitable. The argument even states that there 'exists no longer any rational grounds for saying that the wedge can advance so far and no further.' This is an extreme version of the slippery slope argument. The conclusion is that we don't dare take that first step at all or the game is over. This argument is so strong that one can easily appreciate why many commentators have classified the slippery slope argument as a fallacy.

It has already been shown in Chapter 1.7, how slippery slope is an inherently defeasible type of argumentation that does not lend itself well to supporting strongly phrased conclusions about something that will happen 'necessarily' or 'inevitably.' In Chapters 6 and 7, defeasibility will be brought out even more generally as an important characteristic of the use of slippery slope arguments in deliberation.

Basically, it is for this reason that the argument in case 5.2 should properly be classified as an instance of the slippery slope fallacy. The argument in case 5.2 advances the claim that, in this instance, there is 'no way of stopping' the slippery slope once you are on it. But given the inherent problematicity, vagueness, and controversy-susceptible nature of the term 'euthanasia,' and the difficulty of predicting the future with anything like 'necessity,' this claim is impossible to support. The use of such strong language is really therefore best interpreted as an inappropriate tactic to try to shut off the flow of questioning in the discussion on euthanasia. It is a tactic to try to prevent any speaker for the pro-euthanasia side of the argument from asking further appropriate critical questions about the issue. In effect, that is the way the argument functions, whether the proponent actually intended it or not. Thus his use of the slippery slope argument is a misuse of the technique which hinders, or in this case even blocks, the legitimate sequence of the dialogue.

The previous case, however, is much milder. None of the steps outlined appear to be portrayed as inevitable, except perhaps the first one. Each step after that is described as a natural, short, or easy transition. Thus the argument suggests or warns that taking the first step is embarking on a road that ultimately leads to 'disaster.'

That is not to say, however, that the steps in the first argument are not open to critical questioning. The last part of the slippery slope argument is based on an analogy or comparison between the situation of the current era and the situation of the Nazi euthanasia. Is this a good enough analogy to sustain the argument?

One point in its favor, noted in the discussion of case 1.5, is the evidence cited there showing a connection between the killing of 'impaired' persons (called euthanasia by the Nazis) and the subsequent mass killings of the concentration camps. However, exactly how the one practice led to the other in Nazi Germany is a controversial question for historians.

Whatever the exact sequence of events that took place in the Nazi case was, could there be the real danger of a comparable sequence of events occurring in the context of the present era? This is quite a difficult socio-historical question because there are so many different factors that could be taken into account in attempting to draw a broad comparison of this sort between two historical epochs. The situation of the current era in North America, for example, would appear to be quite different in many respects from that of Nazi Germany between 1933 and 1945. Hence such a comparison has to be highly questionable.

Whatever arguments *pro* and *contra* can be advanced or refuted, the analogy behind the last phase of the slippery slope argument in case 5.1 can be challenged on many grounds, and is therefore not easy to support. It can be challenged by critical questions concerning the alleged similarity between the two periods. The second argument (in case 5.2) does not depend on such a specific analogy, and is therefore easier to defend (at least in this respect), even if it lacks the additional punch contributed by the Nazi analogy.

The first argument generally seems to be open to criticism for different reasons from the second. It is the extreme language of 'inevitability' that makes the second argument most objectionable, whereas it seems that one of the most objectionable aspects of the first argument is that it questionably describes the first few stages —like 'non-utilization of aggressive therapies in intensive care'— as 'euthanasia,' when many physicians and other commentators would object to this strong language (Walton 1983, ch. 9). For in some cases of non-utilization of aggressive therapy in intensive care, it could be highly misleading and prejudicial to label these decisions not to use therapy as 'euthanasia.' Much depends on how this controversial term is to be defined, in the context of a discussion.

Thus both slippery slope arguments are open to critical questions for reasons of the kind of language used. But the leading objections to the one argument appear to be different from those appropriate for the other. And the one argument is more extreme and more objectionable than the other because it is not phrased in a way that leaves it open to critical reply or rebuttal. The second argument phrases its conclusions in a much stronger manner, thereby making it impossible to give enough convincing evidence to come anywhere near giving the required support to that argument.

Generally, the slippery slope argument is fallacious where it is used as a tactic to hinder or block a reasonable dialogue, in violation of the rules for the proper conduct of that type of dialogue. The slippery slope is a defeasible type of argument, based on presumptions at a particular point in the progress of a dialogue. Because it is defeasible, it is always open to possible rebuttal, and in general, the party in the dialogue who the slippery slope argument has been used against has a right to reply to the argument, and to ask critical questions, or put forward rebuttals in open discussion, if he so wishes. Fallacies come in when the argument is used to block this right, in a particular case.

The most common type of fallacy in using the full slippery slope argument is to phrase the argument in an unjustifiably strong manner—in terms of 'inevitability' or 'necessity' of the outcome— as a tactic to block any possibility of subsequent rebuttal or questioning. Thus van Eemeren and Grootendorst (1987) are generally right when they categorize the slippery slope fallacy as a fault of inappropriately applying a scheme of argumentation (p. 289). What that argumentation scheme is, in the case of the full slippery slope, is shown in Section 8 below.

But van Eemeren and Grootendorst are not specifically right, in several respects, when they explain slippery slope as a fallacy:

rejecting a course of action because it is supposed to lead us from bad to worse, whereas it is not necessary for the alleged

'Tolerating euthanasia leads to genocide. That's why I'm opposed to it.'

consequences to occur at all (*slippery slope*)
(causal argumentation)

(1987: 290)

This account of the fallacy is precisely backwards. The fault in the fallacy is not that it is 'not necessary for the alleged consequences to occur.' Indeed, it is *never* necessary, at least in the normal range of cases, for the alleged consequences to occur. The fault is one of trying to force someone else to reject a course of action by *claiming* that alleged bad consequences are necessary.

What van Eemeren and Grootendorst describe is all right—it could be a reasonable kind of slippery slope argument, for example—namely 'rejecting a course of action because it is supposed to lead us from bad to worse, whereas it is not necessary for the consequences to occur . . . ' It is perfectly all right to reject a course of action because it is supposed to lead from bad to worse, even if it is not necessary for the consequences to occur. What is fallacious is using this kind of argumentation to block all possible further reasonable discussion by a tactic of making it *appear* to be the case that it is necessary for the supposed consequences to occur. This tactic is virtually always fallacious in slippery slope arguments, because the future consequences of proposed human actions are always projected by means of argumentation relying on defeasible presumptions.

Another point is that the example van Eemeren and Grootendorst use is not a good one to illustrate their analysis. It is not a case of (purely) causal argumentation. It is a very weak (short form) version of the slope argument against euthanasia. But it is not a fallacious argument, according to the analysis of the slippery slope argument in Chapter 6.

It seems then that the full slippery slope argument can come in various gradations. In some cases, it seems worse off critically than in others. And in some cases, we can even say that it is a fallacious argument. But in many cases, it would not be justified to say this.

2. A Case of Pornography and Censorship

The following passage occurs in the context of an argument entitled 'The Real Issue Is Repression' (Sullivan 1982). The article concerned a protest by an Action Committee on the Status of Women who were protesting the showing of a film they considered pornographic. Mr. Sullivan argued against the feminist campaign against pornography on the grounds that it has a 'censorious streak' that runs against freedom of expression.

Case 5.3

It's . . . unfortunate that freedom of expression has a cost, and the cost is license. People are always prepared to abuse their privileges, for fun or profit. A lot of gentle and fair-minded people are menaced by that abuse.

But repression is never the answer. The repression of sexual issues in Victorian England bred a banquet of perversions unequalled even in today's snake-pit era of abandon.

The main problem with repression is who does the repressing? Who defines pornography? Who sets the limits?

The local school board? The town council? The court? The federal government? The provincial government? Invariably, repression is contagious, and it's not long before they all get in the act.

In no time (it happened recently), somebody decides to ban Huckleberry Finn because it harbors racist sentiments. And the Minot, North Dakota School Board bans *Newsweek* because it is too liberal.

And as the pall of censorship descends, people become afraid of their own thoughts.

This argument uses the slippery slope strategy. It is claimed that once 'repression' sets in by somebody defining pornography, then the repression is contagious and we must go all the way down the slippery slope until even decent literature must be condemned. Notice, however, that there is also a use of the loaded definition in the claim that anybody's definition of pornography can fairly be described as 'repression.' The term 'repression' is a loaded word that refers to unjustified restriction of freedom of speech or expression. Describing all restriction of pornography as 'repression' is therefore a loaded use of the word to support one side of the argument. The use of loaded terms in argumentation is not necessarily fallacious, but it is worth being aware of it in evaluating an argument.

Thus this argument combines the loaded use of terms and the slippery slope. Instead of supporting his slippery slope argument by showing why each step must lead to the next, why repression must be 'contagious,' the author uses the loaded language as main support for the argument.

Another thing to notice is that repression is said to be 'invariably' contagious, meaning that there is no way to avoid the slippery slope to the final outcome, once the first step has been taken. Putting the conclusion in this extreme form makes the argument open to a charge of fallacious use of the slippery slope technique.

The article does, however, present some evidence to support the slippery slope argument. By asking who defines pornography, the article suggests that there is no single authority to define pornography, thereby giving some evidence that the slippery slope may take place.

Another piece of evidence offered are two of the steps in the alleged slippery slope sequence—the Huckleberry Finn case and the Minot, North Dakota case. These cases are analogies, but do at least illustrate the kinds of step that could take part in the slippery slope argument advocated by the article.

Another item of evidence advanced by the article is the reference to the social climate of acceptance. Using extremely colorful language, the article draws an analogy between the repression which bred a 'banquet of perversions' in Victorian England and 'today's snake-pit era of abandon.' Here however, the analogy is weak, because there is no evidence given that the 'snake-pit era of abandon' of today is due to repression. In fact, the argument seems to go against itself somewhat by referring to the tolerance of 'abandon' of the present social climate of opinion, because this would not be a very favorable climate to support repression.

The slippery slope argument in case 5.3 should therefore be judged as quite weak, and the article tries to make up for this failure to present convincing evidence by the use of colorful and heavily loaded, emotional language. For all we know, the article may be right that the feminist campaign criticized has a 'censorious streak,' but the use of the slippery slope argument to support this criticism is, in this case, neither effective nor convincing.

Case 5.3 is an instance of the full slippery slope argument because it combines several elements. As mentioned above, there is a reference to the social climate of acceptance. There are also several analogies used in the argument. But a key part of the argument is the use of the sorites technique of suggesting that the slippery slope will occur because nobody can give a definition of the term 'pornography' that everybody can agree to.

The slippery slope sequence is not explicitly spelled out in case 5.3 in much detail. It seems likely that precedent, and also causal sequences, may be involved. But the two aspects explicitly mentioned are the social climate of acceptance and the vagueness of the term 'pornography.'

The main problem with case 5.3 as an argument is that it began with considering a particular objective of criticizing a protest of an Action Committee, but then rose to a higher level of generality by criticizing censorship generally: 'repression is never the answer.' But the larger question of whether censorship (generally) can be criticized by the slippery technique of arguing that it leads to repression or other bad outcomes is quite a difficult argument to support. It is full of controversial premises that can be subject to interpretation and dispute.

Inevitably then, the short argument in case 5.3 is very weak. The author's tactic is to try to prop it up with loaded terms and aggressive use of language, which produces a colorful but weak argument.

But should we conclude that the argument in case 5.3 is so weak and one-sided that it may be categorized as a fallacious slippery slope? In this interesting borderline case, on balance, the best approach is not to go so far as to call it fallacious. As noted above, the argument used the term 'invariably,' and this does make it open to a charge of fallacious use of the slippery slope technique. But on the other hand, the argument does leave some room for rebuttal, even if it uses overly strong language in relation to the evidence it puts forward. In this case, in line with the concept of fallacy put forward in Chapter 1, it is best to conclude that the argument is not so bad that it should be called fallacious, even though, to be sure, the argument is open to all kinds of critical question. It is a weak and poorly presented argument, but not a fallacious one.

3. The Short Form

In many cases where the short form of the slippery slope argument is used, it just isn't clear whether the supposed links in the sequence are meant to be causal, precedents, or sorites connections of similar cases. Yet often, in such cases, it is fairly clear that a background of the social climate of acceptance is a required factor in making the argument work.

For example, case 5.4 occurred in the context of a report on the debate over parental leave. According to a Family and Medical Leave Act before Congress, time off work would be guaranteed for parents with newborn infants, people with very ill children or elderly parents, and newly adoptive parents. Opponents of the bill argued that it is a first step towards forcing companies to pay employees for time off, to a much greater extent than they can afford to offer voluntarily.

Case 5.4

Opponents of mandated parental leave say that, in time, most companies will offer it voluntarily—as a means to lure skilled workers. They're worried that the current bill is just the first step down a long road that will end with mandated paid leaves—a benefit that they say companies simply can't afford. (Kantrowitz and Wingert 1989)

In this case there are clearly elements of precedent and popular acceptance involved in the projected slippery slope to mandated paid leave. But we are given so little information about the alleged steps of the projected sequence that, for all we know, it is quite possible that causal and sorites links are involved as well. Hence the slippery slope in this argument, like case 5.3, appears to be very weak.

But there is an important difference between case 5.4 and case 5.3. In case 5.4, the authors who reported on the slippery slope argument were not adopting the role of the proponent of the argument. Instead, the article in which case 5.4 appeared was reporting on the question of parental leave, and presenting both points of view on the issue. One of the arguments reportedly used by the opponents of mandated parental leave is the slippery slope argument quoted in case 5.4. But it is no straightforward matter to criticize this argument as erroneous or fallacious, because we are getting a secondhand report of what the argument is.

As presented, the argument is short and incomplete—a mere sketch of a slippery slope argument. But whose fault is that? Or is it even a fault? The proponents of the argument are reported as being 'worried' about the possible consequences of mandated parental leave as a policy. They are not reported as saying that the undesirable outcomes cited are 'inevitable,' or anything of that sort. While we do need to know more about the specifics of this slippery slope argument to evaluate it properly, there appears to be nothing fallacious about reporting the gist of the argument briefly by citing only the main essentials of it. Even if nobody knows all the steps down the 'long road' cited in case 5.4, it can be quite legitimate to cite it as a report that some participants in an argument are 'worried' about the possibility that the future may set us on this road.

In evaluating cases of the short form of the slippery slope argument, it may often be most appropriate to begin by asking questions of analysis, to try to determine the missing steps in the sequence of argumentation that constitutes the slippery slope.

In many of the examples of slippery slope arguments we have examined, especially in the short form arguments like case 1.1 and case 5.4, the text of discourse given for the argument omitted many of the intervening steps which would be needed to bring the argument anywhere near meeting the requirements of a proper fulfillment of the sequential premise in the argumentation scheme. However, according to the viewpoint proposed here, it would be incorrect and misleading to classify such a case automatically as an instance of the slippery slope fallacy.

Consider case 5.4, for example. In this case, opponents of a policy of mandated leave for parents are said to be 'worried' that a current bill for this policy is the 'first step down a long road' that will end in something that is impractical and undesirable. In the text of case 5.4, however, none of the steps in this 'long road' are specifically spelled out. Should we say then that the argument in case 5.4 is an instance of the slippery slope fallacy?

The best answer is to say that this argument is not fallacious, as the text for 5.4 stands, but is merely incomplete. For, according to the analysis of slippery slope argumentation advanced here, this type of argument can be quite reasonable as a way of challenging an action or policy that is being considered by warning that it might possibly or plausibly lead to a particularly worrisome, dangerous, or important goal-defeating outcome.

A short form slippery slope argument like the one in case 5.4 then might make a good point, and be a reasonable argument, even if it is quite weak, as it stands, because the sequential premise leaves many significant steps inexplicitly stated. What an ideally rational critic should do in such a case is to reply by asking the proponent for more information, or if this is not possible in the context of the discussion, to declare the argument incomplete until the appropriate steps can be filled in, to accord with the requirements of the sequential premise of the argumentation scheme applicable to that case.

4. Techniques of Attack

In principle, the full slippery slope argument is a reasonable kind of argumentation, as we hope to show in this chapter. But it is not an easy argument to support adequately, because it combines the previous types of slippery slope argument, making it more complex. And it normally has a very broad sweep, by relying on a popular acceptance premise (premise (4) in Govier's scheme above). This makes it not an easy argument to support, because attempting to predict public opinion, in the long term especially, is a hazardous undertaking.

Problems occur when the job of marshalling the evidence necessary to support this kind of argumentation as a basis for planning, and acting on reasoned presumptions about the future, is not fulfilled. Instead, in some cases, an attempt is made to trade on a respondent's fears or other emotions about the dangerous outcome cited in the slippery slope argument. There are all kinds of ways of trying to do this.

One way is to turn the warning into an *ad baculum* argument by threatening the respondent with the outcome he fears (see Woods 1987). Another way is to attribute hidden motives or to suggest that there is a conspiracy to carry out a plot to set the wheels in motion towards the intolerable outcome cited.

The problem with full slippery slopes is that because they concern events in the future, they have to be based on plausible presumptions—an inherently weak form of reasoning. Hence they can be subject to suggestions and imputations concerning what might happen. Suggestions of this kind can easily be turned into sophistical techniques of attack in argumentation.

The context of the speech below was a debate on the government's proposal to introduce a plastic social insurance card to be used by the public in connection with government benefits.

The government spokesman also noted that the card would be redesigned to have a maple leaf superimposed by the word 'Canada' in place of the traditional Federal coat of arms. The response of an opposition member is given below.

Case 5.5

HON. GORDON CHURCHILL (WINNIPEG SOUTH CENTRE). Mr. Speaker, this is a rather interesting disclosure finally forced out of the Minister of Labour by questions on orders of the day by the Leader of the Opposition over the last week. He has now given us a very weak excuse for removing from the social security card the coat of arms—

SOME HON. MEMBERS: Shame.

MR. CHURCHILL.—which of all symbols is surely the most distinctive of the national unity of this country. For the Minister to tell us shamefacedly that this is not suitable because of Provincial attitudes will not go down with the public at all. I think it is a disgrace that this government should continue its whittling away of our history and traditions. We now see a continuation of their program of destruction of our history and traditions. The removal of the coat of arms from the social security card is the first step, I suppose, in the removal of the coat of arms from all other places where it is displayed in Canada. Will the next step be the removal of the coat of arms from this building? This is a disgraceful announcement by the Minister of Labour. (*Hansard, Canada: House of Commons Debates*, June 11, 1972, p. 2250)

Mr. Churchill is using a slippery slope argument to raise questions about the intentions of the opposing party, accusing them of 'whittling away' the country's history and traditions. He sees the removal of the coat of arms from the social security card as a first step to its removal from all other places where it is displayed in Canada. Since each step is alleged to lead to succeeding steps, this case is an instance of the slippery slope argument. Mr. Churchill does not back up his slippery slope attack with any real evidence or justification, so it should be regarded as a weak argument at best. However, he does pose the second step of the argument in the form of a question to the opposing party: 'Will the next step be the removal of the coat of arms from this building?' As a form of questioning the position of the opposing party, Mr. Churchill's use of the slippery slope argument is not fallacious in the way that case 5.2 was open to criticism. He does not conclude that these next consequences *will* happen. He is only questioning whether they *might* happen.

On the other hand, in place of appealing to a climate of social acceptance as a factor in the alleged slippery slope, Mr. Churchill is imputing a malevolent 'program of destruction' of 'history and traditions' to the governing party. The imputation is that the intentions of the governing party are so bad that, given any excuse —like removing the coat of arms from the social security card— they will use that as a lever to pry further, 'whittling away' the people's history and traditions. This imputation may be accurate or it may not be. But what should be said is that it is a kind of *ad hominem* attack which reads dark motives into the government's action of proposing to remove the coat of arms from the card.

In this case, the slippery slope argument is used as a kind of warning, but it is an ominous or threatening warning about alleged government policies or intentions that most of the audience of the speech would be likely to view with alarm. Here the use of the slippery slope technique is allied with the use of an *ad hominem* argument that imputes sinister motives to the government. The claim is that the government is trying to secure public acceptance of changes by 'whittling away' at accepted traditions by small degrees.

This case should not be evaluated as an instance of the slippery slope fallacy, even though it is a highly questionable slippery slope argument, and it is associated with another kind of fallacy. What is especially interesting in this case is that the short form of the slippery slope argument is used as a tactic of innuendo. As such, it does appear to be a highly effective and scary argument that would be successful in shifting presumption onto the government side. It is the kind of argument that would raise doubts unless an effective reply was made to it immediately.

However, it would not be effective to reply simply, 'Your argument is a slippery slope fallacy!' in this case. What is needed is the use of an equally effective tactic to reply that shows in detail why the fears Mr. Churchill has raised are groundless, or if they are not, what is being done about it. Such a response would require specific knowledge of the case at issue.

In general then, there is a practical problem of advising a respondent how to counter the use of clever tactics associated with the use of slippery slope argumentation. The problem is essentially practical because any general tactical advice will need to be tailored to the specifics of a case. This will be the job of Chapter 7.

For the moment, note that it is one thing to spot the weak

premises in a slippery slope argument. It may be another thing to counter or rebut the argument effectively.

The interesting twist in case 5.5 is that the proponent is claiming the government proposal to remove the coat of arms from the card is actually *against* public opinion. Instead of popular acceptance, the thrust of the slippery slope argument is provided by the government's alleged intent to 'whittle away' at traditions.

Thus the respondent in this argument is not the Minister of Labour. It is the public that Mr. Churchill is trying to persuade. Hence the dialogue is somewhat more complex than it may seem —there are three positions involved.

In this case, the *ad hominem* attack against the opposing party is used as a sophistical device to try to back up the slippery slope argument by arguing that the governing party is a group that has a continuing tendency to 'whittle away' at traditions, always trying to destroy the history and traditions of the country.

It would be incorrect to conclude, however, that the argument in this case falls short of a full slippery slope argument because it does not involve a claim about a progressive series of changes in public attitude. The change in attitude required for a full slippery slope argument does not have to be that of any particular social group, like the general public, at any particular time or place. For the full slippery slope argument can be used in relation to various different social groups or populations. It could be that the attitude of one group propels the argument forward while that of another group resists this forward momentum.

5. The Public Acceptance Premise

The full slippery slope argument depends on a premise postulating that a certain type of action is contagious in leading to related actions because the populace, or the group who will carry out these acts, is inclined to move from one step to the next. This seems like a psychological or empirical requirement which predicts how people will act.

However, from a point of view of studying the kind of reasoning involved in slippery slope argumentation, it is not necessary to construe this premise in a psychological way. It need not be a description of the beliefs of some group or populace. Instead, it could be judged to represent the commitment of the group to a particular policy or kind of action, within the context of a given social climate.

According to Hamblin (1970: 257), a participant in an argumentative dialogue (dialectical game) has a *commitment-store,* a set which collects a tally of that participant's commitments as incurred through the moves he makes in the dialogue exchanges. Hamblin thinks that this set represents a kind of profile or persona of a participant's beliefs, but it need not correspond with his real beliefs. Commitment-stores operate according to rules. For example, one rule of a dialogue might be that if a participant asserts a proposition, then that proposition is immediately added to his commitment-store. Thus the commitment-store is defined in a particular case by the rules of discussion that are appropriate. It is partly a function of rules for rational discussion.

A pragmatic approach to the slippery slope argument should present its analysis in terms of the commitments of the proponent and respondent, in a context of reasoned discussion, as far as these things can be judged from the given text and context of the particular case.

This approach does involve a kind of empirical causality, but one mediated through the feedback of social expectations and changing horizons of what is considered acceptable and non-exceptional. The factor of social context turns out to be important, because it is what often gives the slippery slope argument its thrust to push forward towards the horrible outcome cited in the conclusion. It is this background of social transfer or 'contagiousness' that makes the full slippery slope so often an effective scare tactic and device for counseling a conservative policy of sticking to established guidelines. For it makes the descent down the slope more than a matter of mere logical possibility, giving the argument power as a vehicle of reasoned persuasion.

What about the so-called psychological (or sociological) premise then? How should it fit in to our assessment of the full slippery slope argument in a particular case?

The premise in question states that some third-party group or populace is inclined to accept a policy or is posed to go ahead with a particular line of action. As Lamb (1988: 53) puts it, the slope argument judges the significance of an action not in terms of its logically possible consequences, but in terms of 'plausible probabilities' in the 'context of a social climate.' The slope argument requires the drawing of plausible inferences about how a social group is likely to act, based on a reading of the commitments of the group in the context of a social climate.

What these remarks suggest is that a full slippery slope argument should be judged as reasonable or not in a context of discussion where some particular propositions can be presumed to be plausible, reflecting a given horizon or climate of public opinion. These propositions may be presumed to be initially plausible (subject to subsequent modification or correction during the course of the argument) by both participants as part of their common starting points, established during the opening stages of the discussion. These are plausible presumptions that set a burden of proof.

How the slippery slope argument functions as a rational way of shifting the initial presumptions of a case in discussion through the use of a connected sequence of presumptive conditionals is brought out explicitly in the analysis presented in Chapter 6.

6. Feedback and Circular Reasoning

What characteristically propels the full slippery slope argument along is a feedback cycle. Once an individual begins to engage in a new practice, the practice may become more acceptable or popular to other parties who observe it. But then as more people begin to engage in this practice, it tends to become popular or acceptable as a customary or standard way of doing things. However, success in this acceptance as a popular custom, in turn, leads to more and more people engaging in the practice. Thus the growth cycle of a popular trend continually goes back and forth between the actions of a group and the expectations of what is considered normal or acceptable to that population.

The full slippery slope is therefore related to two other kinds of argumentation traditionally labelled as informal fallacies: *petitio principii* (circular reasoning) and *argumentum ad populum* (appeal to popular pieties). But neither of these kinds of argumentation is necessarily fallacious. Circular argumentation is inherent in plausible reasoning based on popular opinions and accepted presumptions about standard practices and normal expectations.

But it does not follow that all such argumentation is fallacious (Walton 1985*a*).[2] Circular reasoning is fallacious in a context of dialogue that has a requirement of evidential priority. For example, in an inquiry, the premises have to be better established (evidentially prior to) the conclusion that is to be derived. But not all contexts of reasonable dialogue have a requirement of evidential priority.

Practical reasoning is circular because it uses feedback to test out how an untried practice is working in particular circumstances. By this kind of process of testing and feedback, practical reasoning arrives at a provisional conclusion that a new practice is acceptable because it is working out in a new situation (Walton 1990; see also Walton 1991).

The following exchange took place during a panel discussion (Crighton 1990) on research on human embryos which was televised on BBC–1 in the program *Family Matters* on February 21, 1990. During *in vitro* fertilization, embryos are created in the laboratory from the fertilized eggs of the mother. Normally, some of these 'clusters of fused cells,' as an embryo could be described, are left over once the implantation has been carried out. These remaining embryos can be used for scientific and medical research. During the discussion, the audience was informed that embryo research is important not only for infertility practice, but also for trying to find the causes of genetic diseases, like muscular dystrophy and cystic fibrosis (Crighton 1990: 3). Such research could also be important to learning about causes of congenital deformities in babies, according to a physician interviewed during the panel discussion (p. 4). Thus it became evident during the discussion that the scientists believed that there are important benefits from continuing research on human embryos. They put forward the point of view that this research should be supported and expanded.

A conflicting point of view was advanced by two parents of disabled children, who argued that 'all research with human embryos must immediately be stopped' (p. 4). The basic premise

[2] The connection between *petitio principii* and slippery slope is not a universal one, however, for circularity in an argument should be distinguished from an argument about circularity. It is not circular reasoning to assert that a process of circular feedback will develop. See Walton (1990) on feedback in practical reasoning.

behind this argument was that an embryo is a human being, a person who has a right to life. The various arguments put forward by the participants in the *Family Matters* discussion centered around this basic conflict of opinions. One side argued that research on human embryos must be stopped, the other side argued that it should be continued, and even expanded.

The current ruling in Britain is that research on embryos was permitted for up to the first fourteen days of development. The slippery slope question arose when the possibility of keeping these cells alive for a longer period as a 'bank for spare parts' was addressed to Dr Virginia Bolton. Her reply was the following argument.

Case 5.6a

I think it's fair to say that scientists would actually work within the framework of the legislation which is laid down, and scientists have agreed and have been working for the last few years within the framework of voluntary licensing, the Voluntary Licensing Authority (which is now called the Interim Licensing Authority), pending, hopefully, the intro-duction of a statutory licensing authority. Scientists and doctors have been working well within the guidelines laid down by that authority and we would abide by the recommendations that may be statutory. So fourteen days is perfectly acceptable to us, and, in fact, we are unable to culture human embryos further than about six or seven days at the moment—so it's hypothetical, the fourteen days, anyway. (Crighton 1990: 7–8)

Speaking on behalf of scientists who are working in the area, Dr Bolton predicted that the fourteen-day limit would be 'perfectly acceptable,' adding that it is also 'hypothetical.' This reply minimizes or plays down the possible danger posed by expansions of the fourteen-day limit in the future, thus serving as a reply to slippery slope worries.

However, the response of the other side to these reassurances directly rebutted Dr Bolton's claim. Anne Widdecombe pointed out that during recent discussions in Parliament, there had already been talk of a limit of twenty-one days, a 'jump' of seven days. In opposition to Dr Bolton's argument, she posed a slippery slope.

Case 5.6b

Now, we know that research was going on for things like Parkinson's Disease, on quite advanced foetuses—as they're called, I would call them unborn children—so I don't think there's any question that the scientists would be happy with fourteen days. Once they got to the point where they could go further, and I take what Virginia Bolton says, they can't at the moment so of course they're happy— but, once they get to the point where they can, they'll be back and I think if anybody wants to look at the slippery slope argument, all you've got to do is to look at all the promises that were made. For example—and this is just an example—when the abortion laws were passed, it wasn't going to lead to a lot of abortions, just in a few extreme cases. Now we've got a hundred and eighty-four thousand a year so it's not going to lead to scientists going over the fourteen mark—no, no, no, they wouldn't do that. You tell me that in six years' time, if we pass this Bill, it simply is a terrible slippery slope. Today, the Embryo Research Bill, tomorrow the Foetus Research Bill. (Crighton 1990: 8)

By drawing an analogy to the case of abortion legislation, Ms. Widdecombe fuels the slippery slope against human embryo research. She argues that once the scientists have time and resources to build up their research efforts, as allowed by the fourteen-day guideline, they are going to push ahead 'over the fourteen mark.' The parallel alleged is to the case of the abortion law where, despite initial reassurances to the contrary, it led to a large number of abortions. The argument is that, similarly, the Embryo Research Bill will lead to more and more research of this kind until the ultimate outcome of research on human fetuses will eventuate.

What is especially interesting in this case is that you would think that Dr Bolton's reply would be adequate to stop the slippery slope argument in virtue of the precise cutoff point of fourteen days having been established. And so it would, if this were purely a sorites type of slippery slope challenge.

But, on the contrary, Anne Widdecombe's reply is quite a strong slippery slope rejoinder. Taking a longer time frame for the argument, she maintains that, in the future, once things get rolling, the bad outcome will (eventually) occur. The reason she gives for this claim is the following. If we give them (scientists and doctors) this much of a concession (as a first step), it won't stop there. They will carry it further—'they'll be back.' This premise makes it clear that the argument in this case is a full slippery slope —the mechanism fueling the slippery slope is the research initiative taken by the doctors which will inevitably be 'successful' in leading to new techniques that will be useful, and thereby win powerful support for its continued use. The appeal to the force of public opinion, which is part of the feedback cycle of the advancement of new technology, makes it clear that this is a full type of slippery slope argument. Although there is a precise guideline, the full slope alleges it will be pushed back as time goes on.

In slippery slope reasoning, a new practice appears reasonable as a next step because it is similar to precedents that have already been put into practice. Once the new practice is tried, and it seems to work out, or become acceptable, then it achieves the status of being a precedent for a next step. The sequence is linear, because it proceeds from one step to the next. But it also has a circular structure, because new practices are always being refined and modified once it is seen how they are functioning in particular circumstances. As exceptions to general rules and practices are found by experience, the rules and practices can be codified in a more careful way, in order to deal with these problematic cases. As such difficulties are successfully dealt with, the new practice becomes more widely acceptable as standard procedure.

Thus the slippery slope is not purely linear, as it may seem to be on the surface. It does have a circular aspect. Such circular goal-directed knowledge-based reasoning is, however, characteristic of practical reasoning generally, and is not, in itself, evidence that this kind of reasoning is erroneous or fallacious.

The slippery slope appears primarily to be an argument about the projected consequences of an action. As such, it appears to consist mainly of a chain of presumptive conditionals. And from a semantically oriented point of view, the evaluation of the argument would seem to center around the question of whether these conditionals are in fact true or false. Although, this aspect is an important part of the picture for slippery slope arguments, it is not the whole story.

From a pragmatic point of view, the slippery slope argument has a two-participant structure. One participant in a critical discussion has the role of advising or warning the other participant not to embark on a first step in a course of action the second person is deliberating about. Why not? Because the contemplated course of action is said, by the first participant, to have bad consequences. But in what respect are these consequences supposedly 'bad'? Presumably, they are being claimed to be 'bad' in the sense that they contravene some values, goals, or principles that the second participant is committed to. That is the basis on which the first participant is advising against the course of action at issue.

Thus the dialectic of how the respondent should critically react to a slippery slope argument, and how the proponent should rationally support it when challenged, should take into account this dual aspect of slippery slope. Any principle, value, or general goal is always in the process of being tested out and modified in particular situations. One reasonable way to respond to a slippery slope argument, therefore, might be to reformulate your general principle on what you consider to be 'bad' in relation to the specifics of a situation at issue. Or you might argue that, in this particular situation, another goal is more important, and should be accorded priority.

For example, in case 5.5 Mr Churchill objected to the proposed removal of the coat of arms from the social security card because it was a 'whittling away' of traditions, and a removal of a distinctive symbol of national unity. It is presumed by Mr Churchill that preserving tradition and national unity are important and valuable goals for all concerned in the discussion.

But it is not above challenge that this can be taken for granted, in connection with the slippery slope argument. A respondent could argue that while tradition is important, the new logo of the maple leaf is a symbol of freedom and equality, and in this instance it is more important to stress Canada as a place of freedom and equality in a world full of oppression and the use of force to suppress human rights. Thus the respondent could concede that tradition and national unity are important goals for Canada, but that in this particular situation, the equally important goals of freedom and equality should be given priority. That is, the social security card is an appropriate place to have a symbol that represents these values.

With the slippery slope then, it is always a question of how general goals are implemented in a specific situation. This often requires a circular process of adjustment.

7. *Ad Populum* and *Ad Baculum* Arguments

The *argumentum ad populum* is also often taken to be a fallacy (Hamblin 1970; Walton 1987). One of the main reasons for this presumption is that it is perceived to be a kind of argumentation that appeals to emotions (mass or popular enthusiasm) instead of appealing to legitimate reasons for a conclusion. The presumption here that it can never arrive at a reasonable conclusion on the basis of an emotional assessment of a situation, however, is highly questionable.

There is nothing wrong, in principle, with appealing to emotions in argumentation. However, this type of appeal can become a problem for several reasons. First, it can indicate a dialectical shift from a persuasion dialogue to a quarrel. Second, it can be an irrelevant move in an argument which moves the line of argumentation away from the issue of the dialogue. Third, in some cases what can happen is that the speech act containing the emotional appeal may not be an argument, or part of an argument, at all. This may indicate that some nonargument type of move is being made by one party to a discussion that has the purpose of distracting or confusing the other party. The offender in this type of case may have opted out of the argument altogether. But this can be a problem if the other party does not see this kind of move for what it really is.

While it is true that there are many different techniques of argumentation that can exploit appeals to emotions in highly effective ways, the mere presence of an appeal to emotion should not (by itself) trigger an accusation that a fallacy has been committed.

When Aristotle discusses the use of appeals to emotion in sophistical reasoning, the tenor of his discussion is quite different from what our familiarity with the standard treatment of this subject in modern logic textbooks would lead us to expect. Aristotle gives out candid and remarkably interesting advice to a reader who would like to learn how to cheat in argumentation, and get the best of an adversary or persuade an audience unfairly. For example, he suggests that one device is to go for a long argument, because it is hard to keep many things in mind at once (*De Sophisticis Elenchis* 174^{a}18). Another device is speed, which makes people lag behind, so they can't see what is coming

(174^{a}19–23). A third device is to appeal purposely to anger or contentiousness, in order to discombobulate your opponent: 'Further, there are anger and contentiousness; for when people are agitated they are always less capable of being on their guard. Elementary rules for rousing anger are to make it plain that one wishes to act unfairly and to behave in an altogether shameless manner.' (174^a 19–23). Note that the appeal here is not necessarily or specifically to pity, fear (force), or popular sentiments. Nonetheless, the technique of sophistical refutation described by Aristotle is one of exploiting such appeals to emotion in order to get the best of an adversary in argument unfairly. What he describes is a sophistical tactic, in the sense of a technique of sophistical refutation which has the potential to be used unfairly to defeat an opponent in argument. It is a use of appeal to emotion, a use that can be subject to clever misuse.

Although the use of emotional appeals in argument is generally held to be out of place in a scientific inquiry, it can have a proper place in a critical discussion, negotiation, or other type of dialogue, if it is not abused or used as a sophistical tactic of attack.

The problem with some slippery slope arguments is that because this type of argument is a species of warning, based on citing negative consequences of a contemplated course of action, it comes close to or suggests that a threat is being made. Clearly then, in these cases, there is a close and interesting relationship between the slippery slope fallacy and the *ad baculum* fallacy. The classic case exhibiting this connection is case 3.8. Here the criticism of the use of the slippery slope argument to persuade young people not to experiment with the drug crack was that this argument would backfire because the intended audience perceive it (with some justification of evidence) as a scare tactic. Hence they dismiss it as a sophistical tactic of intimidation, a fallacious *ad baculum* appeal.

A key problem with this type of slippery slope case, and indeed with many negative arguments from consequences, is how to interpret the speech act in the argument—is it a warning or a threat? For example, the following argument is an example of the argument from consequences.

Case 5.7

Two politicians are discussing the issue of the right to have an abortion. The one advances the point of view that a woman does not have the right to have an abortion, on the grounds that the fetus has a right to life. The other, a pro-choice advocate, replies: 'If you argue for that point of view, you will not be elected, and mobs of angry women will hold demonstrations on your front lawn.'

If the second politician is simply warning the first politician, giving him practical advice about the likely consequences of going public with the argument he proposes to advocate, there would be no fallacy in his argument. But this is not the only way his speech act could possibly be interpreted.

If the second politician's argument is interpreted as an attempted refutation of the argument of the first politician, it is a fallacious argument from consequences. Why? Because the shift to practical reasoning by citing the consequences of enunciating such an anti-abortion argument is a move which is not a legitimate criticism of the first politician's argument *per se*. It does not address or consider the merits of the first politician's arguments against abortion. By shifting to considering the practical consequences of advancing the argument, instead of considering the merits of the argument in itself, this argument from consequences is an irrelevant and illegitimate move, a sophistical tactic, and not a real or legitimate refutation of the original argument.

Even worse would be the case where the second politician makes it clear that she is making a threat, i.e. where she makes it clear to the first politician that she intends to bring about such an angry demonstration if she can. This would add an additional dimension to the argument, making it a fallacious *argumentum ad baculum*.

The problem with many of the most subtle and effective cases of the fallacious *argumentum ad baculum* is that they are put forward in the guise of an indirect speech act—the utterance is ostensibly put forward as a warning, whereas, in reality, it is clearly meant to express a threat. This use of the negative argument from consequences is clearly evident in the classic *ad baculum* case cited by Copi (1986: 106).

Case 5.8

According to R. Grunberger, author of *A Social History of the Third Reich,* published in Britain, the Nazis used to send the following notice to German readers who let their subscriptions lapse: 'Our paper certainly deserves the support of every German. We shall continue to forward copies of it to you, and hope that you will not want to expose yourself to unfortunate consequences in the case of cancellation.'

On the surface, this is an argument from consequences, used as a warning to the subscriber. Quite clearly, however, it is really meant as a threat to take action should the subscriber cancel. From what is known about the Nazis, it would be clear that they would be quite capable and willing to carry out the threat. The subscriber had better not cancel. Such a threat is, of course, rightly thought not to be a good reason for continuing to subscribe to a newspaper. Hence the use of argument from consequences in this type of case is judged to be an *ad baculum* fallacy.

However, in all cases of this type, it all depends on whether you interpret the speech act as a warning or a threat. The slippery slope argument, or any argument from consequences, can be quite legitimate if it is conveying a warning to a respondent not to carry out a contemplated action because it is too risky. But we should be quite wary if the warning is being used as a threat. A threat is an emotional appeal, with all the dangers of abuse that emotional appeals can have in argumentation. It could be used to try to shut off the proper flow of the discussion, or to twist it to irrelevant considerations of the possibly painful consequences of holding a particular view by expressing it in argument.

A warning is a speech act by a hearer to inform a speaker about negative consequences of some act being contemplated by the speaker (see Searle 1969: 67–8). By contrast, however, a threat is an attempt to get the hearer to refrain from such an action by conveying the message that you (the respondent) will take steps actually to bring about these bad consequences unless the hearer complies. The difference is that in making a threat, the respondent expresses a willingness to intervene to ensure that the negative consequences will come about.

However, we have to be careful here. Not all threats are fallacious, or even arguments. A threat only becomes fallacious where it is used in argument to block the legitimate goals of dialogue for that argument. But where a slippery slope argument expresses a threat by indirectly using the citing of negative consequences, one must be careful to examine whether tactics of intimidation are being used fallaciously to subvert the legitimate goals of dialogue.

It should be added here, as well, that an argument doesn't have to be a threat to be an *ad baculum* argument. It could also be an appeal to fear, or a use of 'scare tactics,' which is not a threat. Granted, there is ambivalence on this subject in the textbook treatments, some defining *ad baculum* as appeal to force, others as the appeal to a threat, and still others as an appeal to fear (or intimidation). A broad conception of the *ad baculum* argument could encompass all these notions. While the central or paradigm idea of the *ad baculum* is that of a threat which appeals to fear, other appeals to fear or uses of tactics of intimidation can quite properly be included under the *ad baculum* heading as well.

In some cases, however, the use of 'scare tactics' could be a legitimate form of warning or practical reasoning for various purposes. Only where arguments of this kind which appeal to emotions of fear are used as sophistical tactics to get the best of a partner in dialogue by deceptively or unfairly blocking or thwarting the proper goals of the dialogue should we judge that a fallacy has been committed.

Thesis: *the* ad baculum, ad misericordiam, *and* ad populum *arguments are not fallacies in every instance of their use, but in many cases they are warning signals that indicate dangers in an argument. There are various kinds of danger involved, e.g. dialectical shifts, or premature closure of argument, or shifts in the burden of proof. Sometimes the danger is posed by an adversary who is cleverly exploiting emotion for deceptive tactical reasons.*

These argument appeals should not always be treated as fallacies, but on the other hand, they should not be treated as pseudofallacies either. They are often indications that a fallacy might occur, or be occurring. So it is often better to speak of an *ad baculum warning* or an *ad populum warning,* etc., broadly speaking.[3] Even so, in some cases, it will turn out that a fallacy has occurred. However, the fallacy is not simply the appeal to a specific emotion

---

[3] See Walton (1980) and Woods (1987) for supporting views.

(like fear, pity, or whatever) *per se*. The fallacy can be one of several kinds of failure. It could be a failure of relevance, for example. It could be the use of an emotion for tactical and deceptive ends in argumentation functioning as a cover-up for the failure to fulfill properly the requirements of burden of proof.

When an appeal to pity, fear, or popular pieties occurs in an argument setting, it is appropriate to mark the place in the discourse where the appeal was made, and study it further. Through analysis of the text, a diagnosis of the argumentative import of the appeal to emotion can be made. But this analysis, in different cases, can lead to different kinds of conclusion. It could conclude that the appeal to emotion is appropriate, or that it is open to questioning, or, in some cases, that it is fallacious.

8. The Argument from Popularity

The conventional accounts of *argumentum ad populum* see emotional appeal as part of the fallacy. But *argumentum ad populum* also contains another kind of argumentation which is implicit in the following forms. These two forms could be called the basic forms of the *argument from popularity* (Walton 1989: 89; see also Johnson and Blair 1983: 156–60).

(P1) Everybody accepts that A is true.

Therefore, A is true.

(P2) Nobody accepts that A is true.

Therefore, A is false.

In the context of an inquiry, neither of these forms of argument is generally valid, for, in such a context, popular acceptance does not establish the truth or falsity of a proposition. However, as plausible inferences, arguments of the form (P1) and (P2) could function as reasonable arguments, in some cases, in persuasion dialogue. They could be reasonable in such cases in the sense that the conclusion could be a plausible (but defeasible) presumption, where the premise is warranted. This does not mean that they establish the truth of their conclusions, but only that they can make the conclusion a reasonable presumption to accept in the absence of evidence to the contrary.

Thus (P1) and (P2) are weak arguments generally, but they are arguments that can have a legitimate function, in some contexts of dialogue, of directing a respondent towards a particular course of action when objective knowledge of the facts is lacking and a practical decision must be made in a given situation.

Consider the following case. Karen and Doug are riding their bicycles along a bicycle path in the Netherlands. They are recent arrivals in the Netherlands, and are not sure about the rules and conventions for riding bicycles on bicycle routes. Doug is following behind Karen.

Case 5.9:

KAREN. Ride beside me.
DOUG.   I'm not sure it is OK to do that.
KAREN. Everybody does it.
DOUG.   But what if somebody needs to pass?
KAREN. They will ring their bell.

Karen's statement that 'Everybody does it,' is an argument from popularity, yet it seems like a reasonable one in the context. What she is suggesting is that it seems like a plausible indicator that it is acceptable to ride side by side, judging from the observation that lots of other pairs of cyclists are doing it with no sign of disapproval from anyone. Since Karen and Doug do not have any direct knowledge of what is allowed in this regard, a plausible presumption is that it seems to be OK. At any rate, this presumptive conclusion does appear to have some reasonable grounding on a basis of plausibility. It could turn out to be wrong, but it can also be a presumptive basis for action, in the absence of more definite knowledge.

A subtle problem with this argument, however, is that it is not purely an *ad populum* appeal. Because Karen and Doug are new arrivals in Holland, and unsure about the rule for riding bicycles, they are appealing to 'what everybody does' based on a presumption that the others they observe do have a knowledge of these rules. Thus the standard of what everybody else is doing, in this case, constitutes a kind of knowledge or expertise that Karen and Doug do not presently have. Thus the argument in this case could possibly be categorized as an *ad verecundiam* appeal.

This case is one of those interesting ones that lie on the borderline between two of the traditional fallacy classifications. It is both an *ad populum* and *ad verecundiam* argument. It is initially obvious that it is an argument from popularity, but the *ad verecundiam* aspect of it is more subtle.

As well, it is a curious kind of *ad verecundiam* argument that is involved, because it is not exclusively expertise that seems to be appealed to, but perhaps customs, or the notion that the other bicycle riders are likely to be in a better position or a special position to know the rules.

Moreover, it should be noted that although the argument from popularity in reasonable in some instances, it is often a very bad argument in other cases. We are all familiar with the ubiquitous use of this argument by children to justify unacceptable behavior by retorting: 'Everybody else is doing it.' Such an argument may not adequately address the question of whether the behavior at issue is acceptable, in some cases.

To make an argument of form (P1) or (P2) reasonable in a discussion, there has to be some reason to think, or at least some reasonable presumption, that the population cited in the premise has some genuine knowledge about what is acceptable, or that they generally behave in a manner that meets the customs or expectations in question. And, as noted above, even if the premise is warranted, the argument can still be open to challenge in some instances. For popularly accepted customs and practices, like rules, can be subject to exceptions in exceptional cases.

It is not hard to appreciate how the *argumentum ad populum* has gained a reputation as an informal fallacy. An emotional appeal to popular opinion is often accorded much more weight in argumentation than it should really have, when many other relevant factors should also be considered in arriving at a conclusion. The reasons are not hard to find. Often, the wish or need to belong to a dominant or trendy group is almost irresistible.

But in other cases, the *argumentum ad populum* can be a reasonable argument, even if it is often a fairly weak argument, based on plausible reasoning, given the lack of firmer, more objective evidence on which to arrive at a decision.

Also, the *argumentum ad populum* has turned out to be much more complex than the simple fallacy it initially seemed. Often, the heart of it is the argument from popularity, a kind of argument which can be erroneous, and is inherently weak, but can be a reasonable argument in some contexts of dialogue. Each case should be studied on its own merits, in its proper pragmatic context of discussion.

How much attention should be paid to popular opinion can be a very tricky question in some cases of argumentation. In political debate (in democratic countries), it can be disastrous in argument to pay too little attention to popular opinion. However, if a politician is perceived as following popular opinion too closely— for example, by paying too much attention to public opinion polls —this can be interpreted by critics as evidence that he is lacking in principles or reasoned convictions. Popular opinion is certainly one important factor in any political decision. But to defer too heavily to popular opinion, while overlooking other important factors, can be a bad error in some cases.

Many lessons have been drawn from the case of Munich, where Neville Chamberlain appeased the Nazis when Hitler threatened to invade Czechoslovakia in 1938. Chamberlain undoubtedly made a tragic error, and in hindsight, many misperceptions of the situation have been cited as the source of his misjudgment. But one error, in particular, may have been an overestimation of popular opinion favoring appeasement.

Case 5.10

Another Chamberlain mistake, history has decreed, was to pay too much attention to public opinion, particularly the British people's fear of war and their desire to spend scarce resources on social reforms. The lesson drawn there, as John F. Kennedy put it in an Inaugural Address haunted by Munich, was that a great nation must 'pay any price' to defend its values on foreign shores. (McGrath 1988)

In hindsight, Chamberlain's misjudgment can be identified as an error of weighing popular opinion too highly in a decision. But at the time, it would have been very difficult to say with any confidence that Chamberlain's attention to public opinion was an error, given the number of factors involved, and the controversial nature of the situation at the time.

The slippery slope argument depends on initial presumptions about the climate of public opinion. But many slippery slope arguments involve long-term predictions, or even predictions about what might come about after an indefinite period of time. But that does not always mean that slippery slope arguments are fallacious. It does mean that slippery slope arguments are best treated as defeasible arguments that are based on presumptions, and are subject to correction as more information comes in, or as a situation changes.

It is helpful here to look at two contrasting cases below. In case 5.11, the slippery slope argument is properly used to press for action and is nonfallacious. In case 5.12, the slope is used fallaciously. The following case involves a sequence of dialogue where the slippery slope argument is used at one point as a move made to carry practical reasoning forward.

Case 5.11

Bob and Charlene have offices in a newly renovated university building. The hallways have been completely redecorated. The stairwell has been repainted in white, and looks very neat except for a green sticker fixed permanently to the glass on the door, reading 'Mulroney Trade Deal—No Thanks! (Canadian Labour Congress).' The sticker shows evidence of someone's having tried unsucessfully to scrape it off.

BOB. The hallway looks very nice now. The decorators have done a beautiful job. I hope it stays this way.
Often, university property is not treated very well, and you get graffiti in the halls.

CHARLENE. Yes, it looks beautiful, except for this ugly sticker.

BOB. I'll call maintenance. Perhaps they could try to scrape it off with a razor.

CHARLENE. According to studies of this subject, if you can keep an area free of graffiti or defacements like these stickers you are OK. But once you get one, the whole area will become filled with them.

Charlene's argument is an all-in (full) type of slippery slope. The purpose of it is to press for action. Bob proposes to undertake the action of calling maintenance to get the sticker removed. Charlene uses the slope argument to give a reason why he should go ahead and do so (quickly).

It is an all-in slope because a version of the popular opinion premise is involved—presumably, the slope works because the existence of even one sticker or graffiti encourages people to go ahead and add more. In this case, however, it is not an opinion that is contagious but an object or action (the sticker, or the act of putting it there) that leads to further acts of defacement.

The initial premise is the nonremoval of the sticker. The induction premise is the leading of the placement of one sticker or graffiti to the act of someone producing another in the same area. The dangerous outcome is 'The whole area will become filled with them.' The conclusion is the advisability of going ahead with action to have this sticker removed.

One especially interesting feature of this slope argument is that it is an argument for positive action, i.e. it counsels *against* nonremoval. More usually, the slope is a conservative argument for inaction.

Is Charlene's argument fallacious or not? It seems to be quite a reasonable argument, as far as it goes. Bob does not respond to it (as far as we know, in the given case). So we have no evidence whether he raises critical questions concerning the argument, or how Charlene might reply to such questioning. So Charlene's argument is an opening move in an action-oriented type of practical discussion of a problem which shifts a burden of proof towards a particular course of action. As far as one can tell from the dialogue, Bob is also in favor of the action of calling maintenance. Charlene's argument merely adds more weight to the course of action Bob has already proposed. Hence the use of the slippery slope argument in this case appears to be quite reasonable, and there is no evidence of either party having committed a fallacy.

Note that Charlene backs up her slope argument using an appeal to expert opinion or *ad verecundiam* type of argumentation. The appeal is vague, because specific sources or studies are not cited. But that, in itself, is not evidence that Charlene has committed an *ad verecundiam* fallacy. Charlene's argument is weak. She could give more evidence. But it is not so bad that we should call it fallacious.

Indeed, in case 5.11, we could say that the slippery slope argument has been used in a reasonable and proper way, in its given context of dialogue. By contrast, let us consider another case where the slippery slope argument has been used as a fallacy, meaning that it has been used in such a way that it blocks the legitimate goals of the type of dialogue the speakers are supposed to be engaged in.

Two countries that bordered on each other, Borakia and Karobia, had often had wars with each other, in the past, that had pushed their border one way or the other. Several years ago, an area called Fulfillment Mountain fell into the hands of the Boraks after the Lightning War. This hill, on the border of the two countries, contained areas held to be sacred by both groups. In particular, one area on the hill, called the Holy Sanctuary of Light by the Karobs, was regarded by them as their most important religious shrine. It was thought by the Karobs to be the place where their deity had ascended to heaven. After the Lightning War, the Boraks had wisely ceded administration of Fulfillment Mountain to the Karobs, giving them permanent access to worship there and to conduct pilgrimages to the Holy Sanctuary of Light.

However, a small group of religious conservatives among the Boraks, called the Beards, claimed that the Karobs should have to move their shrine from the Holy Sanctuary to somewhere else, off Fulfillment Mountain. An ultranational group, the Beards claimed that Fulfillment Mountain was the religious and spiritual center of Borakian culture, and that the Karobs should not have exclusive rights to it. The majority of the Boraks, however, rejected this point of view, reviling the Beards as dangerous extremists who lacked tolerance and a balanced point of view.

The Karobs often discussed among themselves how to deal with this apparent threat posed by these developments. The leaders of one ultranationalist religious group among the Karobs, called the Moustaches, teach their followers that those who die defending the Holy Sanctuary of Light go immediately to heaven. In the following case, the leader of the Moustaches, Karaz, discussed national policy with a moderate Karob political leader called Zarak.

Case 5.12

ZARAK. I think it was wise and generous of the Boraks to cede the administration of the Mountain to us. Although it was not right for them to take over this whole area from us in war, nevertheless the Mountain is now in Borakian territory. We should not push the issue too much at this time, and it might not hurt us to let some of them worship there occasionally, as long as it does not interfere with our worship in our holy places on the Mountain. After all, they have some holy places on the Mountain too, and the majority of them appear to be open to reasonable discussion.

KARAZ. Those Boraks plan to take over the Mountain of Fulfillment, as shown by recent Beardish agitations. If we give the Boraks even one centimeter, if we let them place even one toe on the Mountain, it will be the end of our holy places.

ZARAK. Now wait a minute. The Boraks have indicated that they are willing to discuss the issue. As difficult as it is for us, I think we should talk with their leaders to see if we can reach a negotiated settlement that will let us preserve our right to the Mountain, even if it means some compromises.

KARAZ. It will be easier for us to die first. I am telling our young people now to ward off the Borak attack on our holy place by dying a glorious death. Take up sticks, rocks, or whatever weapons you have at hand. Kill the infidel Boraks!

In this case, Karaz used the slippery slope argument when he said, 'If we give the Boraks even one centimeter, if we let them place even one toe on the Mountain, it will be the end of our holy places.' This conditional statement is a prediction, using the all-in type of slippery slope argument which presumes that, given Borak public opinion and attitudes, inevitably a small concession will lead, step by step, to a concession of the whole Mountain. Yet judging from what Zarak said, such a presumptive inference is not based on an accurate reading of Borak public opinion. Instead, Karaz has based his assumption on the kinds of opinion and attitude which could be attributed to the Beards. But according to the information given in the initial situation described in the case, the Beard point of view is not the same as, or representative of a point of view attributable to the Borak public generally.

In this case, the slippery slope argument is used to press for action, but in a precipitous and overly aggressive way that fails to respond appropriately to the practical argumentation put forward by Zarak. The slippery slope argument is used as a device to attempt to force a polarized and quarrelsome attitude into place that is consistent with the negotiation type of dialogue advocated by Zarak. The slippery slope argument is used to appeal to emotions of fear and hostility and to shut off avenues for open discussion of the problem or negotiations that might lead to a verbal solution of the conflict.

The key to whether the slippery slope argument is a fallacy in this case is the question of how Karaz responds to Zarak's practical argumentation. The more he tries to suppress critical questioning of his own point of view by shutting off the continuation of critical discussion or negotiation, and forcing the dialogue into a hardened quarrel of a dogmatic sort, the more evidence there is that he has committed a slippery slope fallacy.

The problem here is not just that Karaz's slippery slope argument is weak and unsubstantiated by the given evidence—and therefore open to challenge. That much is correct. But the deeper problem is that he shows evidence of an unwillingness to take the given evidence into account, or to look at the persuasive reasoning on both sides of the issue. He pushes so hard for the one side that his response does not follow the proper kind of sequence of moves needed to carry on the dialogue begun by Zarak. Without first even attempting to reply appropriately to Zarak's arguments, he goes ahead to cut off further discussion by advocating immediate action. When Zarak tries to respond to get the argument back on the track of the initial discussion, Karaz once again fails to reply by responding to the given argumentation. Once again, he simply pushes for direct action based on his own point of view, showing no willingness to respond to any challenges of the rightness of that point of view as applied to the given situation.

The slippery slope argument concerning the women's suffrage movement in case 3.6 seemed as if it could be easily classified as a fallacy in 1956 because the 'bad' consequences cited—'put women into trousers, reduce the birth rate, break up the home,' and so forth—seemed very unlikely at that time, no doubt. Now we don't think of these outcomes as bad, but to an extent that might have been hard to imagine in 1956, they have come about. Of course, the argument in case 3.6 is a weak one anyway, because it is doubtful that the event of women getting the right to vote was the single first step in a slippery slope that led to all these other developments. But still, from the perspective of 1989, it would not be possible to use case 3.6 as a clear example of the slippery slope fallacy in a logic textbook. The public climate of acceptance that defines what is possible or plausible as outcomes of the acceptance of a new policy or practice has changed.

The event of women's getting the vote, it is reasonable to assume, did make these other outcomes more likely, and was a step that made them happen sooner. In this sense, the slippery slope argument in case 3.6 was not an unreasonable argument from the point of view of those, at the time, who felt that these consequences were very bad. Nowadays, in the 1990s, our values have changed. The ideas of women wearing men's clothing, and of a reduced birth rate, are no longer rejected as bad. Of course the 'destruction of the family' is probably still regarded as a bad thing by many people, but high divorce rates, single-parent families, and the like, are now widely accepted, and reflect a different climate of opinion.

Why the argument in case 3.6 seems so bad that it may seem appropriate to call it 'fallacious' is, most of all, because values and social policies have changed. The idea that women should be denied the right to vote seems unthinkable, from a current perspective, and the 'horrible' outcomes cited are no longer regarded as bad, or considered as dangerous risks to be guarded against.

Any full slippery slope argument is based on presumptions about goals and values, and on presumptions about the climate of public acceptance at some period of time. These things change, however, and therefore so can the slippery slope argument, when it is used in a new situation, or a situation that has changed over time. Feedback and revision of premises are part of slippery slope argumentation. These factors are taken account of in the argumentation scheme below.

9. Argumentation Scheme for the Full Slippery Slope

The context of discussion for the full slippery slope argument characteristically concerns the adoption or acceptability of some policy or action that has broad social significance. It is therefore a kind of mixture, which can involve elements of the sorites, causal, and precedent argument features. It often involves a policy, or proposed change from a given custom, rule, or policy. Consequently, it involves precedents. But typically, it turns to a good extent on what people will take to be precedents, rightly or wrongly. It therefore involves not only public opinion, or group opinions of some sort, but also the causal seqence which leads from the acceptance of one opinion to an increased tolerance of a new opinion. Combined with these elements is the vagueness of language which often helps to make the slope difficult to resist. These features combine subtly to generate a more powerful many-pronged type of argumentation which is harder to pin down critically than any of its subarguments.

The full slippery slope is based on a sequence of cases $C_0, C_1, \ldots, C_n$. But any given pair $\{C_i, C_j\}$ in the sequence may be related in any of the three ways characteristic of the prior three types of slippery slope arguments. What most often links each pair of steps, however, is an argument for some form of social approval or public acceptance, transferring, it is argued, from each step to the next.

The context of discussion for the full slippery slope argument is a three-way interaction. The respondent has taken the point of view that some act he contemplates or proposes is or should be acceptable. What he usually means is that it is or should be generally acceptable to some third party, typically a social group who have a body of opinions that are presumptions they find plausible and will not dispute. For example, in case 5.5, this third party is presumably the people of Canada. This third party generally does not participate in the argument directly (although possibly they could, in principle). The second party is the proponent of the slope, who advances further opinions about what this group does or can be led to accept as normal or plausible. The second party, the proponent of the slippery slope argument, utilizes premises about the group's opinions in order to argue that the respondent's proposed policy will lead to the acceptance of other policies or practices by the group, which will lead in turn, through a sequence, to some horribly unacceptable outcome. By this technique of argumentation, the proponent seeks to imply that the respondent's original proposal is not acceptable to the group. The scheme he uses is outlined below.

Argumentation Scheme for the Full Slippery Slope

Initial premise:	Case C_0 is tentatively acceptable as an initial presumption.
Sequential premise:	There exists a series of cases $C_0, C_1, \ldots, C_{n-1}$, where each leads to the next by a combination of causal, precedent, and/ or analogy steps.

Group opinion premise:	There is a climate of social opinion such that once people come to accept each step as plausible, then they will also be led to accept the next step.
Unacceptable outcome premise:	C_{n-1} leads to an ultimate outcome C_n (the horrible outcome), which is not acceptable.
Conclusion:	C_0 is not acceptable (contrary to the presumption of the initial premise).

Two characteristics of the full slippery slope argument are especially distinctive. One is the use of the group opinion premise. In the most striking and important full slippery slope arguments, the group opinion is the opinion of the general public. In these cases, it is a shift in public opinion that is at issue. In such cases, the group opinion premise may be called the *public opinion premise*. The other characteristic is the mixing of the linkages in the use of the sequential premise—in a typical case, some links are causal, some are precedents, and others are pairs of closely similar cases of the kind found in sorites arguments.

Thus the account of the full slippery slope argument given by Govier (1982: 315)—see Section 1 above—needs to be modified. Clauses (3), (5), and (7) do not need to apply to each step of the full slippery slope argument. It is not characteristic of this type of argument generally that each and every link in the sequence is a causal link and a sorites-type link and a precedent link. Instead, these types of links are mixed in different combinations in a full slippery slope argument. At any given step in a sequence, all three kinds of link may be involved (as well as public opinion). But this is not always necessary. In some instances, for example, one link may be causal while another is based on a precedent relationship.

In some cases, particularly the shorter versions, it is hard to tell which type of slippery slope argument is involved. In other cases, a mixture of two or more types can be involved.

In practice, sometimes one type of slippery slope argument is dominant, but elements of another type are mixed in at specific points in the sequence. For example, in case 3.7, which concerned the decriminalization of marijuana, the emphasis was primarily on a causal linkage—physical addiction that leads to heavier drug use. But popular acceptance was also included as a factor in case 3.7*b* when it was said that the 'outbreak of this mind-bending drug is largely the result of casual acceptance and use of marijuana by our youth.' Thus decriminalization was cited as problematic at least partly because of its propensity to 'lead to higher marijuana acceptance,' which, it was feared, would lead to harder drugs being used more widely as well.

In case 3.7, the causal type of slippery slope is clearly the main theme throughout. But it is possible to discern, at some stages of the sequence, an admixture of use of the public opinion premise, characteristic of the full slippery slope argument. Even so, we should not classify case 3.7 generally as an instance of the full slippery slope argument. It should be classified as a causal slippery slope argument, but one that has some elements of the full type of slippery slope argument as well.

Another case in point is case 3.13, an ambiguous argument, but one that clearly has an important element of public opinion involved in the sequence, even though it is phrased in causal terms.

Generally, the best method of classification is to require that the full slippery slope argument should involve at least some elements of the four kinds of linkage—sorites, precedent, causal, and popular opinion. But it also seems best to allow that various combinations of two or three of these elements can occur in a slippery slope argument. In such cases, let us call it a combined slippery slope argument, as opposed to a full slippery slope argument, which must contain all four elements.

10. Critical Questions for the Full Slippery Slope

There are two primary critical questions for the full slippery slope argument. One is to ask how strong the argument is. This means examining the individual linkages in the sequential premise, and looking into the nature and extent of the evidence given to support each of the steps in the sequence. As with previous types of slippery slope argument, the chain of argumentation in the full slippery slope argument is only as strong as its weakest link.

The second question is to ask how strong the argument needs to be in order to fulfill its burden of proof. This means examining the language of the argumentation, especially key conclusion-indicator words like 'inevitably,' 'will happen,' 'might happen,' 'a short step to . . . ,' and so forth. The problems here are to determine what the conclusion is, and how strongly it is asserted as an alleged consequence of premises. Conclusions phrased as questions, or as projections concerning what might happen, should be judged as incurring a lighter burden of proof than those phrased in the language of 'must happen' or 'is an inevitable outcome.'

The problem of evaluation of a full slippery slope argument is one of matching the textual and contextual evidence (see van Eemeren 1986) for these two questions, asking: Is the evidence given strong enough to make a case for adequate support of the argument set by the standard for burden of proof? In making this evaluation, each individual case should be studied on its merits, in relation to the given textual and contextual evidence of the case.

For example, the language of case 5.2 is quite a bit stronger than that of the comparable argument in case 5.3. Therefore, the burden of proof standard for case 5.2 should be set higher than that of 5.3, as noted in the discussion in Section 1. Indeed, the burden of proof is so high in case 5.2 that it is one of those few cases that should properly be judged fallacious. Case 5.3 seems like a pretty bad argument too. But by the standards advocated here, it is not so bad that it should be called fallacious.

The third critical question is directed to the public opinion premise. This premise involves inherent uncertainties, because the full slippery slope entails plausible predictions towards the future, and it is a hazardous undertaking to try to predict public opinion (especially in a social context where rapid shifts of opinion are quite possible). Also, this premise sometimes involves an analogy to some past era or situation held to be comparable to the situation in question, in a certain respect. Judging a broad analogy of this sort requires the examination of broad socio-historic trends, patterns, and similarities. In some cases, this can potentially involve a massive compilation of evidence and interpretation of the trends and propensities indicated in it.

An example is the citation of the Nazi program of elimination of the 'socially undesirable' in the anti-euthanasia argument of case 5.1. Judging the evidential worth of this analogy in supporting the public opinion premise of the slippery slope argument in case 5.1 requires, to begin with, some understanding of what happened in the Nazi era. The reader will recall the discussion of this subject in Chapter 1.2, showing that there are historical controversies about whether or how there was a sequential progression from euthanasia for retarded or 'impaired' persons to the eventual mass killings of the concentration camps. Not only is the exact nature of this historical sequence controversial among historians of that era, but applying it to the present situation to suggest that a similar horrible outcome could occur is a tenuous analogy. Evaluating it requires asking the question of whether conditions in the present situation are similar enough to those of prewar Germany to justify the public opinion premise of the slippery slope argument. One can easily appreciate that this sort of comparative evaluation makes for a difficult question to answer. That does not mean that it is never worth asking, but when it is asked, it is important to see that answering it responsibly and fairly can mean assessing a large amount of relevant evidence. Small wonder then that the full slippery slope argument has so often been treated with suspicion and distrust as a fallacy. It is not an easy argument to support, and if presented in a brief text (the short form), it can be more of a teaser or provocation than a substantive argument. It should not be presumed, however, that the full slippery slope argument is inherently fallacious, or systematically wrong as an argument in every case where it is used.

In many cases of the full slippery slope argument, it is the way the argument has been presented that needs to be subject to scrutiny and criticism. In some cases, the problem is one of the use of language that is excessively laden with emotion to try to support a weak and incomplete argument. Case 5.3 can be cited as coming under this heading. In other cases, like 5.4, the argument is open to criticism because it has been represented in such a compressed form that the links in the sequential premise are not explicitly stated at all. The critical question to ask in this type of case is 'What are the missing links?' Only when this prior question of argument presentation is settled can the job of evaluating how strong the evidence is for each of the links properly begin.

In still other cases like 5.5, the problem is that an *ad hominem* attack has been substituted into the argument in an attempt to replace the function of the public opinion premise.

The way the public opinion premise is used in the full slippery slope argument represents a variant of the argument from popularity, which is in turn closely related to the *argumentum ad populum*. However, the way the public opinion premise is used is not a straightforward argument from popularity. It is a use that is distinctive of the full slippery slope argument.

In a full slippery slope argument, the proponent is trying to convince a respondent that a policy or proposal advocated by the respondent is not practically reasonable. The proponent's way of doing this is to cite bad consequences of the policy, and in particular, a chain of possible or plausible consequences that will ultimately lead to some horrible outcome. To carry out this burden of proof, the proponent has to visualize the future by postulating plausible sequences of events that may occur. This task also often involves citing analogies to similar cases, where such sequences of events have occurred in the past.

What is most often cited by the proponent as so worrisome is the factor of 'contagion,' that once one step is taken, a practice may become more and more popular, and lead to widespread accept-ance on a broad scale. The factor that propels the slide down the slippery slope in such a case is the acceleration of the popular acceptance of a trend by its increased practice, especially by influential 'role models.' The more people accept the practice, the more likely that it will become acceptable to an even greater number of people.

However, in some cases, such a progression will go only so far and then (at least temporarily) be stopped by a firm boundary or rule. In still other cases, the projected progression may not materialize at all. Judging a particular case involves an evaluation of how influential public opinion is in that case, and an evaluation of the subtleties of public opinion on the issue, and how it is likely to change or evolve in the future.

This broad type of evaluation is tricky at best, and often involves masses of empirical evidence that could be relevant. However, it can be narrowed down in a specific case where the full slippery slope argument has been used by concentrating on the weakest links in the sequence of argumentation. Surprisingly often, little or no evidence has been offered by a proponent to support these weakest links, and that lack of support is the area to which a reasonable critic should direct his questions.

The function of the argumentation scheme is to provide a general stencil that can be applied to particular cases of the full slippery slope argument in order to pinpoint the requirements of this kind of argumentation. If any of these requirements are missing, or inadequately supported by the right kind of evidence, a critic can reveal these weaknesses by asking the appropriate critical questions. If any appropriate critical question is not answered adequately by the proponent of the full slippery slope argument, the presumption should tilt towards the nonacceptance of the argument in the discussion. However, such a finding should not imply, by itself, that the original slippery slope argument is fallacious. It only means that the slippery slope argument is weak, and therefore may be rejected on the grounds that it has not been put forward in a manner that is adequate to meet reasonable standards of burden of proof.

A full slippery slope argument should only be judged fallacious if it is put forward in such a strong and inappropriate manner that it can be clearly shown to be used, in this particular case, as a sophistical tactic to try to prevent the asking of any appropriate critical questions in the subsequent course of the dialogue. In other words, in a fallacious case, the argument has been put forward in such a way that it is impossible for it to proceed further by reasonable dialogue which would fulfill its proper burden of proof. Clearly therefore, in such a case, there can be no question of a cooperative commitment, on the part of the respondent, to make a serious effort to fulfill the legitimate requirements of the burden of proof in the discussion. The tactic is one of opting out of the discussion by trying to close it off prematurely in a quick victory.

It should also be noted that the job of asking the appropriate critical questions often involves the asking of prior questions of interpretation and analysis of the argument relative to the particulars of the given case. The first step is to identify the proponent and respondent of the argument, along with any other essential participants in the dialogue. This information is extracted by inference from the given speech event in the particular case, and by identifying the normative model of dialogue that is appropriate. The questions to ask at this stage are the following. What kind of dialogue are the participants involved in? What is the purpose of the dialogue? What specific rules of dialogue are relevant to the proposed criticism of the given text of discourse? If it is a critical discussion, what are the points of view of both parties? Can the burden of proof on either side be assessed or identified? Answering these questions requires looking to the textual evidence of the given case, but it also involves normative questions of identifying the goals and rules of the type of dialogue that the participants are supposedly engaging in.

The first job is the practical task of confronting the particulars of a given case by interpreting and analyzing the given text of discourse, preparatory work most often badly needed before any intelligent and fair-minded attempt at evaluation of the argument as incorrect, open to criticism, or fallacious can be begun. One of the greatest weaknesses of execution in the current state of the art of informal (applied, practical) logic is that this task is too often overlooked or given inadequate consideration.

In many cases, adequate information to carry out this interpretative task fully is simply lacking. And therefore, practical advice should often take the form of general tactics for defending and attacking a slippery slope argument within the ebb and flow of the *pro* and *contra* argumentation in a particular case. These characteristic patterns of rebuttal, identified in Chapter 7, go beyond the posing of critical questions, in many instances. They function as affirmative counterattacking arguments in their own right which can be used to refute a slippery slope argument, or to secure it from attempted refutation.

The inherent defeasibility of the slippery slope argument has important implications concerning its evaluation when used as an argument in a particular case. The problem with the traditional approach to fallacies in the logic textbooks is that it fails to recognize defeasibility. It fails to recognize that even if you give a reasonably good criticism of an argument, like a slippery slope argument, it doesn't necessarily follow that the argument is fallacious, meaning that the argument is so bad or deeply wrong in structure that it is, once and for all time, refuted.

6

Analysis of the Dialectical Structure of Slippery Slope Arguments

IN the current literature two points of view on the slippery slope argument have dominated most studies of it. One is to see it as an informal fallacy. The general presumption in this approach is that the slippery slope argument is either inherently fallacious, or at least is such a suspicious argument that one should normally denounce it on sight as a fallacy. This presumption, although it is understandable, has led the textbook treatments to neglect serious research into the underlying structure of the slippery slope as a serious or important type of argumentation. For the real reason this argument is so convincing when used as a sophistical tactic is that, when used properly, it is a reasonable and highly persuasive argument.

The other point of view stems from the traditional dominance of deductive, formal logic. The general presumption in this approach is that the slippery slope argument—and almost all the literature in this tradition is directed exclusively to the sorites type—must be some type of deductive reasoning, albeit some mysterious and elusive type. The program of this formal approach has been to reduce the essentials of the slippery slope argument to some kind of many-valued deductive (semantic) structure which allows for truth-value gaps for reasoning in vague contexts.

Both these approaches have absolutely failed to come up with any practically useful method of evaluating slippery slope arguments. Perhaps that was not their objective. But at any rate, where these approaches have come up with interesting insights, it has only resulted in further puzzles that have demonstrated the inadequacy of their own theoretical framework to accomplish this objective. It is time to get out from under the dominance of these two stifling points of view, and take a more practical approach by looking to see how the slippery slope argument really works. The general theory proposed below is pragma-dialectical. By analyzing the underlying dialectical structure of slippery slope as an argumentation tactic which can be used to get the best of an opponent in dialogue, this theory opens up a new approach to the evaluation of particular cases of slippery slope argumentation.

1. The Six Basic Characteristics

There are six basic characteristics common to all slippery slope arguments. They can be summed up briefly as follows.

1. The respondent (defender) is committed to a particular proposition (or proposed course of action). The proponent (attacker) has the role of refuting or arguing against this proposition.

2. Using the respondent's proposition (the one he has expressed commitment to under (1) above) as an initial premise, the proponent applies a bridging relation over and over to lead the respondent to a further series of concessions.

3. Each single step in the sequence, taken by itself, appears to be a small, or not very significant step, and therefore appears relatively unobjectionable to the respondent.

4. There are contextual factors that aid in propelling the argument along the sequence. Vagueness removes the existence of any definite cutoff point. Climate of social acceptance may be another factor. These factors make it difficult for the respondent to resist.

5. The reapplication of the bridging mechanism in (2) generates new premises that tend to become less and less acceptable to the respondent as the sequence unfolds. Eventually the argument arrives at a final conclusion that is highly unacceptable (a horrible outcome) to the respondent.

6. Once past the point where the premises are still very acceptable for the respondent, the proponent continues appealing to case-to-case consistency to drive the argument forward.

The dialectical framework is similar to *reductio ad absurdum* argumentation. One participant is trying to refute a position or proposition held by the other. The *modus operandi* is the continued reapplication of a single step of argument into a linked sequence, where the conclusion of one step becomes the premise of a subsequent step.

These six essential characteristics can be described more fully as follows. The first characteristic is that all slippery slope arguments have two sides. The *attacker* or *proponent* of the slippery slope argument is pressing for a particular conclusion that he hopes to gain as a concession from the *defender* or *respondent*. The proponent's side 'pushes ahead' towards this conclusion, and the respondent's side tries to resist this pressure. There is a division of labor into two opposed roles.

The second characteristic is the means used by the proponent in trying to obtain his goal. In how it is used, this means could be compared to a lever or crowbar. In the slippery slope argument, it characteristically consists in a series of small steps used repeatedly, or sequentially, in order to force open a wide space or gap. The gap is between the initial, or base, premise—which is characteristically a proposition that is secure, that needs no argument for the respondent to be convinced of it—and the proponent's conclusion. The latter proposition is characteristically insecure, meaning that the respondent is initially inclined to doubt, or even to reject it.

The means or *modus operandi* of the slippery slope argument is the proponent's repeated use of the inductive step, in order to try to bridge the gap from the base premise to his conclusion. Thus there are three components or key points in the means—the base premise, the inductive step, and the proponent's conclusion. These three components are linked together into a pragmatic sequence of argumentation. It is through this sequence, or movement, that slippery slope argumentation takes shape.

The third characteristic of any slippery slope argument is the gradualism produced by a series of steps that are individually so small that they are likely to appear unobjectionable to the respondent. The key to understanding how the slippery slope argument functions as a lever for acceptance is that each single step in the argument appears to be such an insignificant difference or plausible step that the respondent could apparently not have any good reason to reject it as an illicit move from one case to another.

The fourth characteristic is that it is not just the smallness of each individual step that makes it appear to be unobjectionable. There is also something else about the context of the argument that makes it difficult for the respondent to resist the movement of the argument. This contextual factor varies. In the sorites argument, it is the vagueness of a key term or phrase. In the causal type of slippery slope argument, it may be the inherent openness of future contingencies. This fourth characteristic can be summed up by saying that there is no definite cutoff point in this type of argumentation sequence. As the sequence rolls along, there is no *single* well-defined point where the respondent can say, with clear evidence, 'No, that is definitely false.'

The fifth characteristic of slippery slope argumentation is the diminishing degree of plausibility of the premises as the argument moves away from the clear and towards the grey area—see Figs. 2.1 and 2.2. At each successive step, both the base premise and the inductive premise tend to become less and less plausible, less and less secure as concessions that the respondent can reasonably commit himself to. Normally, a reasonable respondent would have a threshold of minimum plausibility, and would not commit himself to a proposition where the argument backing it falls below this threshold. But when confronted with a slippery slope argument, it is difficult for him to dig in. For one thing, the reasonable minimum is impossible to pinpoint exactly because of the indeterminacy of context exploited by the slippery slope argument, which trades on vagueness or parameters that are impossible to measure or quantify exactly. For another thing, the difference between each pair of cases seems to be so minimal that it is difficult to pick any apparently nonarbitrary point to resist. If you resist too early, you can be criticized as overcautious or overdefensive. If you resist too late, you are already in too deep. Yet there is no single point which is the best point to begin resistance.

Of course, as the sequence of argumentation proceeds, the premises become less and less plausible to the respondent. It is clear that he has to begin resistance somewhere along the line. But in the transition stages, it doesn't seem to matter much whether he accepts them or rejects them. The evidence seems weak and could go either way.

The sixth characteristic is the 'whip hand' of consistency that the proponent uses to drive the argument forward. This is what makes it so difficult for the respondent to resist this type of argumentation. As soon as the respondent tries to dig in his heels and resist, saying, 'No, I don't accept that last step!', the proponent can question his consistency by saying, 'Well, you accepted the last step, didn't you? And the difference between these two steps is insignificant, isn't it? Therefore, unless you can give me a good reason why you accepted the last step, but now reject this step, I'll have to say that you are going back on your previous commitments, without any good reason.' If the respondent allows that he is being inconsistent, this makes his side of the argument appear weak and illogical. It is not a position he can put himself in without jeopardizing his side of the argument.

The last three components all work together. As long as there is no definite cutoff point, the proponent can use consistency to keep driving the argument forward towards his conclusion. The respondent keeps getting deeper and deeper into conceding conclusions that are less and less acceptable. But once the process has started, there seems to be no good way to resist the proponent's ratcheting procedure, worked along by the use of the two tools provided by the fourth, fifth, and sixth components. The proponent uses a 'carrot and stick' method of driving the respondent forward towards the proponent's conclusion. Toward the latter parts of the sequence, the use of the stick predominates.

The six characteristics above define the slippery slope argument as a distinctive type of argumentation. So defined, the slippery slope argument is a special kind of technique used by one participant in argumentative dialogue to try to modify the commitment of another participant. Utilizing this technique, one participant, the proponent, begins with a proposition that the other participant, the respondent, is committed to. Then by developing a sequence of inferences drawn from that commitment, the proponent tries to get the respondent to give it up, to reject his commitment to the original proposition in the sequence.

This technique can be used for legitimate purposes in dialogue, but it can also be used as a sophistical technique to try to get the best of a respondent unfairly. Used in this way to hinder the goals of reasonable dialogue by violating the rules of proper procedure, the slippery slope argument can be a mischievous trick of clever argumentation—a fallacy.

2. The Argument from Gradualism

The slippery slope argument is a variant of a more basic type of argument that could be called the *argument from gradualism,* which moves forward by a series of small steps in order to convince a respondent to accept a conclusion that, presented simply by itself, he would reject. Gradualism actually works in everyday life as a way of inducing or persuading people to actions or conclusions they would normally not be inclined to give in to. This kind of tactic of persuasion is well illustrated by the process of seduction, which works as follows. First, the person being seduced consents to some relatively innocent or apparently trivial actions that nevertheless represent a small compromise or first step. The seducer then proceeds by small steps to more and more compromising yet stimulating actions, until eventually the person being seduced gets so carried away that his or her normal resistance is thrown overboard. Having gotten past this ill-defined point in the process, the seducer proceeds towards his ultimate end.

How seduction works as a psychological process is not for us to say. It is enough to know that, at least in some cases, it does work very well. What is important for us to find out is the argumentation schemes that underlie the technique of gradualism when it is applied by a proponent to overcome the resistance of a respondent to carry out an action or to accept a conclusion when the two of them are engaged together in some form of reasoned discussion.

The slippery slope argument is an effective way of persuading someone to come to follow a course of action that is very difficult to accept, because gradualism is often an effective way of leading someone up to a distasteful conclusion in argumentation. Suppose the budget of a country needs severe cuts that the people will find very difficult to accept. One way to persuade them is to start with serious, but relatively smaller cuts in social programs, or tax hikes, that will get their attention, but that will not be so big as to be intolerable. Once this step is swallowed by the populace, the government's next step can be to move on to bigger cuts.

The same kind of gradualistic approach, however, can work to destroy a rule, standard, custom, or policy that ceases to be effective once it is not enforced strictly enough. Suppose there is a rule that essays have to be handed in by a certain day, but the professor does not enforce this rule strictly or equally, and often accepts late essays without penalty. Once this becomes known among the students, they will feel that they can relax somewhat, and do not need to work so hard to meet the deadline. Perhaps they can now afford the luxury of giving priority to other assignments where the deadlines are enforced with penalties. Naturally, there is a kind of erosion effect in these cases. Once small breaches of the rule are tested and found acceptable, larger infractions will be tested. As this process goes on, it becomes more and more difficult to fairly enforce the initial standard, until the rule becomes completely ineffective and is overwhelmed.

Gradualism is not the only effective means of persuading someone to accept a policy or conclusion that they would otherwise find unacceptable. It is just one argumentation tactic among many that are available. It is a useful tactic where the respondent can be led up by small degrees to accept a conclusion that he would not accept if it were presented to him in one step. The tactic is to work from some initial premise that he does accept, and then work by small degrees towards gaining assent to the conclusion he is inclined not to accept. The tactic is to overcome his defenses by small degrees.

Other ways of reasonably persuading a reluctant respondent could be equally effective in some cases, yet quite different as argumentation tactics. One way is to cite an authority that the respondent respects. (Walton 1987, ch. 7). Another way would be to attack the internal consistency of a supposedly reliable source that the respondent has based his acceptance of his conclusion on (Walton 1985a). Either of these two kinds of argumentation could be successful in different cases, depending on the respondent's views and his reasons for accepting them.

The gradualistic approach tends to be appropriate or successful where the respondent is committed to some proposition that can be used to bridge the gap towards acceptance of the conclusion he does not accept, by means of a series of gradual or sequential steps.

3. Slippery Slope as a Gradualistic Argument

The slippery slope argument is the negative version of the gradualistic type of argumentation which is used to lead a respondent to reject a conclusion (to dissuade) rather than to lead one to accept it (to persuade). The slippery slope bears the same relationship to the gradualistic argument as *modus tollens* bears to *modus ponens*. In fact, the gradualistic argument is characteristically a chain or linked sequence of *modus ponens* steps. The slippery slope argument is characteristically a kind of scare tactic type of argumentation that reasons backwards by a chain of *modus tollens* steps. Since the respondent presumably does not accept the 'horrible' conclusion which is the ultimate outcome of the sequence, he is led to reject even the first step which has set him on the slippery slope.

A pragmatic analysis of the argument from gradualism can be expressed as follows. The proponent starts with a *base step* or *initial premise* A_0, which represents a proposition that the respondent is committed to at the outset of the argument. Then he argues by means of the following kind of sequence, using a *conditional* or *inductive step*, $A_i \supset A_j$.

First step $\qquad\qquad\qquad A_0$

$\qquad\qquad\qquad\qquad\qquad A_0 \supset A_1$

$\qquad\qquad\qquad\qquad\qquad \overline{}$

$\qquad\qquad\qquad\qquad\qquad A_1$

Second step $\qquad\qquad\quad A_1$

$\qquad\qquad\qquad\qquad\qquad A_1 \supset A_2$

$\qquad\qquad\qquad\qquad\qquad \overline{}$

$\qquad\qquad\qquad\qquad\qquad A_2$

At each step, the conclusion of the previous subargument (step) becomes one premise of the next subargument. By repeating this process over a sequence of steps, the proponent eventually arrives at the conclusion A_n that represents the proposition that he is trying to persuade the respondent to accept.

*n*th step $\qquad\qquad\qquad A_{n-1}$

$\qquad\qquad\qquad\qquad\qquad A_{n-1} \supset A_n$

$\qquad\qquad\qquad\qquad\qquad \overline{\phantom{A_{n-1} \supset A_n}}$

$\qquad\qquad\qquad\qquad\qquad A_n$

The semantic structure of the argument from gradualism is basically that of *modus ponens*. Each single step has that logical form. But the pragmatic structure of the argument from gradualism is the linking together of a chain of these steps over a protracted context of argumentation.

The pragmatic distinction between the argument from gradualism and the slippery slope argument comes out once we go into the questions of the proponent's goal and how he uses these techniques of argumentation to carry out this goal. In the argument from gradualism, his goal is to persuade a reasonable respondent to commit himself to the conclusion A_n. In order to do this, he drives the argument forward, getting the respondent to accept the premises at each step, and using the *modus ponens* argument to get the respondent to accept the conclusion at each step. Proceeding this way, he drives forward towards the goal of securing the ultimate conclusion A_n as a proposition the respondent will accept.

The slippery slope argument, in its classical guise as it is standardly characterized by the tradition represented in the logic textbooks, is the backwards version of the same pattern of argumentation. In the slippery slope argument, the proponent's goal is to persuade a reasonable respondent not to accept the initial premise A_0, even though the respondent is initially inclined to accept A_0, or to go ahead acting on the presumption that A_0 is acceptable. To talk the respondent out of this, the proponent uses the same semantic structure of *modus ponens* steps to link A_0 to A_1, and so forth to a series of related steps. But the pragmatic structure of the proponent's argumentation tactics is quite different in the slippery slope argument. By the series of *modus ponens* steps, he links the argumentation to some horrible, disastrous, or absurd outcome A_n, which the respondent emphatically rejects as intolerable. Then by backwards reasoning, by a sequence of *modus tollens* steps of argument backwards through the same sequence of linked argumentation displayed in the structure of the argument from gradualism above, the respondent is forced to conclude that he must reject A_0.

For example, at the *n*th step, the respondent is directed to reason as follows: 'I strongly reject A_n. In other words, I am committed to $\neg A_n$. But I am convinced of the conditional, $A_{n-1} \supset A_n$. Therefore, by *modus tollens*, I must also become rationally committed to the proposition $\neg A_{n-1}$.' As he reasons backwards along the whole sequence of argumentation, eventually the respondent is led to the conclusion that he must accept the proposition $\neg A_0$. Hence, ultimately, the upshot of the slippery slope argument is that the respondent is persuaded to reject the proposition A_0 that he was originally inclined to accept.

Thus the slippery slope argument is a species of argument from gradualism in its underlying semantic and pragmatic structure. Essentially, the slippery slope argument is a kind of negative variant of the argument from gradualism. In the argument from gradualism, the proponent moves forward towards his goal of persuading the respondent to accept a proposition, using a chain of *modus ponens* subarguments linked together. In the slippery slope argument, the proponent moves backwards to dissuade the respondent from maintaining commitment to a proposition, by arguing that some unacceptable consequence shows why it must be rejected (see Section 7 below).

The different variants or types of both of these kinds of argumentation depend on how the conditional or inductive step is represented. For example, in the causal type of slippery slope argument, the conditional step is based on the causal relationship, which might be quite a different sort of relationship from that represented by the material conditional or hook utilized in the representation above. In many cases, however, the conditional involved in slippery slope argumentation is a presumptive might-conditional rather than a deductive must-conditional.

4. Presumptive Conditionals

In most cases, in slippery slope argumentation, the bridging conditional (if . . . then) relation that is applied repeatedly to build up the sequence premise is not really meant to be taken as a material conditional of the form $A \supset B$. For the material conditional is defined in such a way that the whole conditional, $A \supset B$, is false where the antecedent, A, is true, and the consequent, B, is false. As so often noted in many of our case studies of slippery slope argumentation, the conditionals used are projective conjectures meaning, 'If A is a condition that is realized in a particular situation, then B is an outcome or consequence that is possible or plausible.' In some cases, 'must' is used, rather than 'will' or 'might,' but these (former) cases tend to be the fallacious ones, where the conclusion was phrased in language that is inappropriately strong. The reasoning more characteristic of nonfallacious cases of slippery slope argumentation is a kind of plausible conjecturing based on the putting forward of defeasible presumptions that are meant to shift a burden of proof to the other side in a critical discussion of a projected course of action subject to deliberation or controversy.

In such a context, where the issue concerns a discussion of a best course of action in a particular situation, the appropriate linking relation is the presumptive conditional, $A \to B$, which reads: 'In this situation, the presence of A raises the presumption that B.' This interpretation leads to the following *rule for presumptive conditionals*. When a presumptive conditional is put forward by a proponent in a discussion, and in fact A is a reasonable presumption as applied to the case under discussion, then the respondent must proceed thenceforth in the discussion as if B were true, unless she can present evidence to the contrary.

Thus if A is a reasonable presumption, and $A \to B$ is also a reasonable presumption, then so is B. It does not follow that B is true, or that B has to be true, or anything of this sort. It only follows that B is tentatively true, meaning that it stands (as an assumption for the purpose of the discussion in which it occurs) subject to refutation by the respondent to whom it was directed in the discussion.

In presumptive reasoning then, a version of *modus ponens* is valid (presumptively valid, not deductively valid).

$$(MP) \quad A \to B$$
$$A$$
$$\overline{}$$
$$B$$

When an inference of the form (MP) is advanced by a proponent, it means that the respondent must hold to B as a presumption henceforth unless she can show either that $A \to B$ is not an acceptable presumptive conditional that holds in this situation, or that A is not a presumption that holds in the situation. This means that B then follows as a defeasible conclusion which tentatively stands, subject to rebuttal. It does not follow that B is true, known to be true, or anything of that sort. B is only a reasonable presumption.

Similarly construed, *modus tollens,* utilizing the presumptive conditional, is also a valid principle of presumptive reasoning.

$$(MT) \quad A \to B$$
$$\neg B$$

$$\underline{\hspace{3cm}}$$

$$\neg A$$

Although presumptive reasoning utilizes argument forms like *modus ponens* and *modus tollens* that are familiar from deductive logic, the presumptive conditional has different properties from the material conditional.[1] For example, the following principle holds for the material conditional (as a tautology).

$$(A \supset B) \supset ((A \wedge C) \supset B)$$

But the failure of this property is characteristic of the presumptive conditional. And generally, the following form of inference, called the *monotonic property,* fails to hold in presumptive reasoning.

$$(PP) \quad A \to B$$

$$\underline{\hspace{3cm}}$$

$$(A \wedge C) \to B$$

A logic in which (PP) fails is said to be *nonmonotonic*. This failure is a key characteristic of presumptive reasoning which highlights its defeasible (rebuttable) nature. A presumptive conditional is always tentative or provisional in the sense that it holds only subject to the possibility of rebuttal by new evidence that may come forward at the next stages of a discussion. As new facts come into the discussion at a next stage, the presumptive conditional may fail to hold at that stage.

Ullman-Margalit (1983: 147) gives a comparable account of the presumptive conditional where she analyzes the relation 'A raises the presumption that B' as meaning, 'All subjects involved shall proceed as if B were true until they have sufficient reason no longer to so proceed.' She sees presumptive inference as different from either deductive inference or inductive inference.

The difference between presumptive and probabilistic consider-ations[2] is well brought out by an example used by Ullman-Margalit (1983: 158). The law in criminal cases sets a high burden

[1] Note the comparable properties of the relation called 'provisoed assertion' by Rescher (1977: 6–17).

[2] Rescher (1976: 28–39) has shown very clearly the distinctions to be made between reasoning based on probability and presumptive reasoning based on plausibility.

of proof—the accused must be proved guilty of the crime 'beyond reasonable doubt.' This burden of proof means that during the conduct of the trial, there is a presumption in place against presuming guilt, i.e. the presumption is that the defendant is not guilty. But even if, statistically speaking, it should turn out that most individuals charged are in fact guilty of the crimes they are accused of, this probability does not negate or even weaken the legal presumption or the procedural rationale behind it.

Case 6.1:

. . . if the relevant class is taken to be that of persons charged and even if it turns out that most of the people in this class are actually guilty of the crimes attributed to them, the presumption in favor of proceeding as if the person charged is innocent may nevertheless be retained and defended; it may fly in the face of the probabilistic consideration. (p. 158)

Another case in point would be the Gricean conversational presumptions of sincerity and truthfulness. Such presumptions are justified because they are useful to facilitate the goals of a cooperative discussion. The reasonableness of such presumptions in a particular case, however, could be consistent with a high probability of insincerity or untruthfulness in a range of cases of discussions of this type. Probability is not irrelevant to the usefulness of such presumptions, but, in itself, it is neither necessary nor sufficient to invalidate or defeat the reasonableness of them in a case.

5. Presumptive Argumentation

A presumption is a kind of assumption or concession made in an argument in order that the argument can go forward even though there is not enough evidence to justify accepting the assumption as something that is known to be true. Presumptions are always tentative. They can be cancelled or retracted if subsequent argumentation shows that they no longer hold.

Presumption is a practical notion that enables action to go ahead, even if it is on a provisional basis, instead of being impeded by having to wait for inquiries that will come up with definite or established knowlege of a doubtful matter. However, a presumption is not just any assumption, freely made and accepted in an argument. Presumptions do relate to evidence.

A presumption is a kind of assumption put forward by one party in an argumentative discussion, where the other party to the discussion is not absolutely free to accept or reject the proposition in question. The second party is obliged to accept the proposition, according to standards of politeness in a cooperative discussion, unless he can give evidence that the proposition is false, or good reasons why it would not be proper to accept it.

There are two parties to a presumption. Once the first party, the proponent, has put the presumption forward in an argumentative discussion, the second party, the respondent, has a choice of accepting it or not. But if he does nothing, that means he accepts it. And once a presumption is in place, it holds for the rest of the discussion unless, by the agreement of both parties, it can be withdrawn.

An example of a presumption is given in the following case, where a memo was sent out from the head of circulation of a university library to all department chairmen, containing the following statements.

Case 6.2:

The Library Staff are reviewing the policy of keeping old university exams on file for student use. It has been found that the majority of exams are more than 10 years old. For some departments, we have only 2–3 exams. Please discuss this with other members of your department. Please report back to me by September 22, 1986. *If no response has been received by this date, it will be assumed that you are in favor of disposing of the practice of keeping university exams.*

In this case, the presumption is made explicit in the last (italicized) sentence of the memo. Unless the department chairman sends back a response by the date specified, it will be presumed that the department favors the practice of disposing of the old exams. The use of presumption in this case makes things easier for the department chairman, who only has to write a reply if there are significant objections by individuals in his department. It also expedites action for the library staff by making it possible for them to go ahead with their proposed action of disposing of the exams, unless they hear that there are significant objections that require further discussion of the situation.

Notice that the presumption put forward in case 6.2 has the form of a negative conditional. This form of conditional presumption is associated with the *argumentum ad ignorantiam*[3] (argument to ignorance), a kind of argumentation traditionally classified as an informal fallacy. This type of argumentation has the following form: if there is no evidence (i.e. if there is absence of knowledge) that a proposition is true (false), then we may conclude that this proposition is false (true) (Walton 1989: 44; see also Woods and Walton 1989, ch. 11). But contrary to the tradition, this kind of argumentation can be reasonable, if it is taken as a conditional presumption, i.e. if what is concluded is taken as a presumption, based on a condition that can make it a reasonable (but rebuttable) inference in an appropriate particular situation.

The most charitable and constructive way to interpret many of the cases of slippery slope arguments we have examined is as instances of presumptive argumentation. These arguments are basically intended to warn someone not to take a first step of contemplated action because, as things stand, there are reasons to believe that consequences may follow which may in turn lead towards some horrible outcome. If such arguments are interpreted as being intended to be deductively valid or inductively strong, it is easy to sneer at them, or portray them as 'fallacious.' However, if, as has often seemed more appropriate and constructive, we interpret them as leading to presumptive conclusions that are inherently open to rebuttal, they are no longer so easily portrayed as arguments that are obviously fallacious. True, such arguments are often weak and tentative, by their nature, but it only makes sense to classify them as fallacious (in the proper sense of this word), if the argument has been posed in such a strong or unduly aggressive fashion that it closes off all possibility of rebuttal in the discussion.

To get a better insight into the slippery slope argument as a kind of reasoning that can be stronger or weaker in different cases, we need to understand its structure as a technique properly (or improperly) used to shift a weight of presumption towards a

---

[3] The *argumentum ad ignorantiam* was introduced in Ch. 1.6. A fuller description of this kind of argumentation can be found in Walton (1989: 43–9).

conclusion in a critical discussion. Hence we turn to a closer study of the dialectical structure of slippery slope argumentation.

6. The Composite Nature of Slippery Slope

The slippery slope argument is a composite of two simpler types of argument, the argument from gradualism and the argument from consequences. In some cases, it involves other types of subargument as well, like the argument from analogy and the argument from popular opinion.

In another way as well, the slippery slope is complex. When carefully analyzed, it can be shown to involve three participants, and not just two. When you look at the context of dialogue of the particular cases of the slippery slope argument we have studied, you can see that they are always put forward by a speaker who is warning some other person, by using a negative argument from consequences, not to do something. The person being warned is the respondent. The person doing the warning, the proponent of the slippery slope argument, could also be called 'the warner' of the slippery slope argument. He is warning the respondent, 'Don't take this step, because if you do, you will be led forward to some horrible outcome.' But led forward by whom or what? The answer can vary in different cases. It could be nature, in the causal slippery slope argument. It could be popular opinion, in the full slippery slope argument. It could be some third person, who will be your 'enemy' and will drive you to destruction by dragging you along and down a slippery slope.

When the deeper structure of the dialectical context of slippery slope argumentation is examined more carefully, then, we see that the argumentation used involves a 'warner' who is using a negative

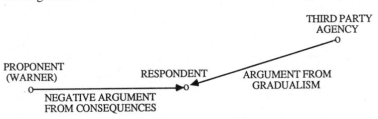

Fig. 6.1   Dialectical structure of the slippery slope argument

argument from consequences to warn a respondent that some third party (who acts in conjunction with the proponent of the slippery slope argument) is using or will use the argument from gradualism to drive him (the respondent) towards some dangerous conclusion. The warner is essentially saying, 'Don't do it, i.e. whatever the respondent is contemplating, or he (the third party agency) will drive you to destruction!'

The argument from gradualism is essentially a two-participant type of argumentation. The proponent pulls the respondent gradually along a continuum towards the conclusion that he (the proponent) wants to convince the respondent to accept. The argument from consequences is also a two-participant type of argumentation. In the positive argument from consequences, the proponent is trying to convince a respondent to do something because this action will have good consequences. But the slippery slope argument contains a negative argument from consequences where the proponent is trying to dissuade a respondent from doing something on the grounds that it would have bad consequences. The slippery slope argument essentially combines these two arguments. One party is warning a second party (by an argument from consequences) that some third party (a real or hypothetical proponent) will drag him along by an argument from gradualism, or by some gradual process, towards a conclusion that will be disastrous for him (the second party). Thus the slippery slope argument is a composite of two arguments and three parties.

A genuine slippery slope argument requires all three of these characteristic participants to be engaged in the roles attributed to them above, involving the use of the argument from gradualism and the argument from negative consequences. In some cases, we are presented with something that appears to be a slippery slope argument, but is not really, because it lacks some of these necessary features.

In one of these types of case, we are presented with a sequence of events which has a slopelike development—for example, a gradual sequence of developments where a person or group becomes accustomed to a new way of doing things. In case 1.5, for example, it was stated that under the Nazi regime euthanasia gradually 'evolved' from voluntary euthanasia for the terminally ill into the killing of anyone deemed 'useless' or an enemy to the state. As described in Chapter 1.2, case 1.5 was part of a larger sequence of argumentation that compared the possibilities implicit in the present-day situation to the case of the Nazi euthanasia program in the past.

But is the text of case 1.5, in itself, an argument? On superficial examination, it may appear to be a slippery slope argument. But it is not (in itself) a genuine slippery slope argument. It does not exhibit the characteristic three-participant structure of the slippery slope argument where one party is warning a second party about the negative consequences of being driven along a sequence of commitments by a third party.

The most plausible interpretation of the text of case 1.5 is that it is a proposed explanation of how the Final Solution of the Nazi police state came about. It was said to come about through a causally related sequence of steps where each stage became an institutionalized practice and then led to the acceptance of the next stage in the sequence. It is not an argument—at least, not a slippery slope argument, but a particular historical explanation of how the Holocaust came about in Nazi Germany.

Of course, the text of case 1.5 is subject to various interpretations. One possible interpretation of what is being said is that the Nazis were persuading the rest of the German people to go along with these programs by gradually getting them used to each stage in order to get them prepared to go along with the next stage. This interpretation has some aspects of a slippery slope argument, because at least you have one party persuading another using the argument from gradualism.

But even this interpretation is not fully adequate to justify classifying case 1.5 as a slippery slope argument, because it lacks the 'warning' function of the use of the argument from negative consequences. This warning function only comes in when we take into account how case 1.5 is being used as an analogy in a larger sequence of argumentation that includes consideration of the argument of cases 1.3 and 1.4.

The most plausible interpretation, therefore, is that case 1.5 by itself is not a slippery slope argument. It is an attempted historical explanation. In other words, a description of a series of events which gradually led to some horrible outcome is not, in itself, a slippery slope argument. Indeed, it may not even be an argument at all. In order to have a slippery slope argument, the use of the argument from gradualism must be combined with the use of the negative argument from consequences to get the characteristic three-party structure of argumentation where one party warns another about the dangerous outcome implicit in a sequence of events.

7. The Forward and Backward Movement

The slippery slope argument works by a kind of forward and backward movement. First, the proponent moves the argumentation forward in a series of *modus ponens* steps. This forward-moving sequence uses the argument from gradualism. The proponent develops a movement in the sequence of argumentation suggesting 'This is what might eventually happen.' Then, in a second stage, the proponent moves the argumentation backward, once the ultimate 'horrible outcome' conclusion has been reached. At this point, the argument begins to move backward, in a series of *modus tollens* steps. The proponent uses this backward movement to pose the suggestion that is the real conclusion of his line of argumentation: 'You don't want that to happen do you? You had better reconsider!' The final 'horrible outcome' is cited as

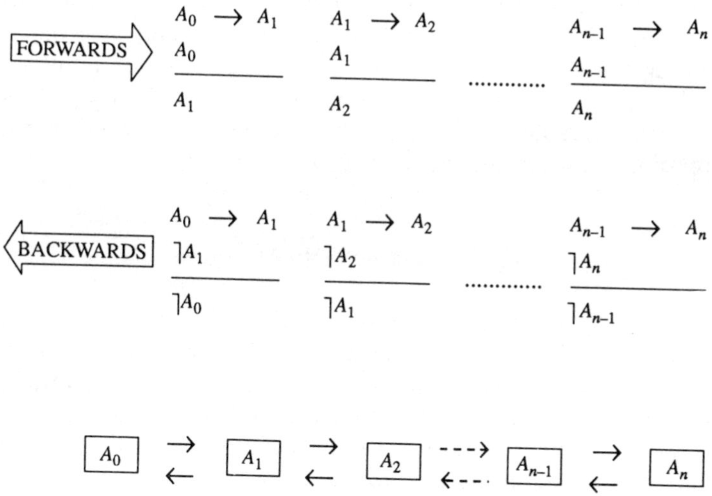

$$
\boxed{\text{FORWARDS}}\!\!\!> \quad
\begin{array}{c} A_0 \rightarrow A_1 \\ A_0 \\ \hline A_1 \end{array} \quad
\begin{array}{c} A_1 \rightarrow A_2 \\ A_1 \\ \hline A_2 \end{array} \quad
\cdots\cdots \quad
\begin{array}{c} A_{n-1} \rightarrow A_n \\ A_{n-1} \\ \hline A_n \end{array}
$$

$$
<\!\!\!\boxed{\text{BACKWARDS}} \quad
\begin{array}{c} A_0 \rightarrow A_1 \\ \rceil A_1 \\ \hline \rceil A_0 \end{array} \quad
\begin{array}{c} A_1 \rightarrow A_2 \\ \rceil A_2 \\ \hline \rceil A_1 \end{array} \quad
\cdots\cdots \quad
\begin{array}{c} A_{n-1} \rightarrow A_n \\ \rceil A_n \\ \hline \rceil A_{n-1} \end{array}
$$

$$
\boxed{A_0} \; \substack{\rightarrow \\ \leftarrow} \; \boxed{A_1} \; \substack{\rightarrow \\ \leftarrow} \; \boxed{A_2} \; \substack{- -> \\ \leftarrow - -} \; \boxed{A_{n-1}} \; \substack{\rightarrow \\ \leftarrow} \; \boxed{A_n}
$$

Fig. 6.2 Forward and backward movement

a reason for not taking the initial course of action that starts the slippery slope.

Along the top of Fig. 6.2, proceeding from left to right, the argumentation moves forward, starting at the initial premise A_0, which is advanced as a tentative supposition. Then by the series of *modus ponens* steps, the argumentation moves towards the ultimate conclusion A_n. At the point of having reached the conclusion A_n, the backward movement begins. The proposition A_n is a 'horrible outcome' that the respondent presumably wants to avoid at all costs. Therefore, the proponent argues that he (the respondent) must also reject A_{n-1}, and so forth, until, by a sequence of *modus tollens* steps, the respondent is guided backward, ultimately to the rejection of the initial supposition, A_0. This backward movement, from A_n back to A_0, is represented by the chain of arguments of the *modus tollens* form proceeding from right to left along the bottom of Fig. 6.2.

Once this structure is revealed, we can see the distinctive character of the slippery slope argument, and we can see why it is different from other arguments from consequences, other causal arguments, and other arguments that exploit vagueness and popular opinion. The distinctive feature is that the basic *modus ponens* and *modus tollens* steps are linked together, and they are applied over and over again, first in one direction, then in the opposite direction.

Now seeing this underlying structure we can also appreciate that this type of argumentation is in principle reasonable as a way of shifting a burden of presumption in a critical discussion. Where each step in the sequence is presumptively valid, the whole chain or sorites argument can also be presumptively correct and appropriate in contributing to the goal of the discussion.

8. The Mechanism of the Movement

The slippery slope argument is a method that can be used to dissuade someone from taking a particular course of action by arguing that once he takes this first step, he will be driven towards some final outcome that will be very bad for him. It is the nature of this 'being driven towards' that is the key mechanism of the slippery slope argument as a tool of persuasion. The idea is that once the person in question takes a first few steps, he will be more and more pulled along in a 'sticky' sequence that will be harder and harder to resist, until, eventually, he will have lost all control over the situation. Then with great speed or force he will be pulled along to the very bad outcome, once he has gone past the point where escape is possible.

The key mechanism that is characteristic of this type of argumentation was already revealed by the way the sorites argument works. The proponent drives the argumentation forward by a series of small steps. At first the respondent could easily resist, but there is no need for him to resist—there is no cost or penalty for making concessions at these early stages. But because of the vagueness of a key term, there is no single 'logical' point where resistance should begin, and consistency between each step and the next drives the argument forward. There is no clear, single best point of resistance going into the grey area. And there is no clear, single best point of resistance going out of the grey area and into the dangerous area where it becomes more and more plausible that a falsehood is being conceded by the respondent.

The message of the proponent to the respondent in a slippery slope argument is the following: 'You had better not start, because once you start it will get harder to stop, and eventually (but at no single, well-defined point), you will not be able to stop at all, until you reach the very bad outcome I am warning you about.' The proponent of the slippery slope argument is taking the stance of giving advice to the respondent: 'Better not to take this first step, because once you take it, things will go in a bad direction, and if you go very far, things will run out of control.' The conclusion is a kind of warning or imperative not to take a particular course of action.

Of course there can be many warnings or negative arguments from consequences of this type that are possible. What is especially characteristic of the slippery slope argument is the repetitive mechanism that is used to drive the argument along a sequence of actions or events. And the sequence has a characteristic tripartite pattern. The white zone is the area where the respondent is not yet in trouble, where it is clear that he can give an affirmative response to requests for commitments without being

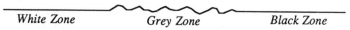

| White Zone | Grey Zone | Black Zone |

Fig. 6.3   Tripartite pattern

committed to anything that is definitely bad, wrong or false. In the grey zone, however, it is not clear whether one's commitment to a proposition is good or bad, right or wrong, true or false. Once into the black zone, it is clear that things are bad, and getting worse.

The function of the slippery slope argument is to enable the proponent to pull the respondent along through the white zone, and get him 'over the hump' of the grey zone, and into the black zone. The grey zone is used to produce a 'fragmenting' or 'pulling apart' of commitment. In the white zone, it is clear that the respondent should definitely say 'yes' when asked to make concessions for the sake of argument. But in the grey zone, it is not clear that the respondent should say 'no.' Accustomed to making concessions, he may think 'Why not?' and say 'yes.'

The slippery slope works by creating a presumption in favor of accepting a proposition, especially in the grey zone, where the existing evidence is indeterminate, and the respondent's choice could easily go either way. The suggestion is that if the respondent is being cooperative and helpful he will make the concession that the proponent has put forward, unless he (the respondent) can give some reason why he should not do so. In other words, the use of the slippery slope argument appears to put the burden on the respondent to present evidence why something is *not* the case, if he is not going to concede that (for all he knows) it is the case. There is a suggestion, by a kind of Gricean implicature, that the respondent should continue to make concessions similar to the kinds of concession he has been making all along, if he is cooperating in the discussion, unless he can give some definite evidence against the acceptability of the next concession he is asked to make.

Now of course the respondent may be able to present exactly this sort of evidence. And if he can, then that is the end of the slippery slope argument. But more typically he cannot, especially in the grey zone, or when dealing with conjectures that admit of very little in the way of solid or decisive evidence, one way or the other. And here the slippery slope argument exerts a subtle pressure, by making the respondent appear impolite or unco-operative if he refuses to make a concession when he has no clear or definite evidence that the proposition in question is false.

This is a kind of argumentation that is not always fallacious, but it is always tricky and subtle, and needs to be handled with care. It seems a slender and weak argument in many cases, because it is only based on presumptions. But it can be quite powerful enough to cause you to lose an argument, or fail to establish your case.

9. When Is a Slippery Slope Argument Fallacious?

The slippery slope is by its nature a partial type of argument based on rebuttable presumptions. It is rarely if ever a conclusive and nondefeasible argumentation. The reason for this is that it is basically a species of negative argument from consequences. This type of argumentation is always based on projections or conjectures about the possible or plausible future consequences of some proposed line of action that is being considered. Often such projections are long-term, and therefore when a slippery slope argument phrases its conclusion in terms like 'inevitable' or 'can't be stopped' or 'must happen,' there are always strong grounds for suspecting that you are dealing with a fallacious case.

A negative argument from consequences in practical reasoning is never overruling, decisive, or complete, in itself. It can always be counterbalanced by a positive argument from consequences, or by other countervailing considerations which may be relevant. In some instances, like cases 2.6 and 8, the slippery slope argument can even be questioned critically by posing a countervailing slippery slope argument that goes in the opposite direction.

For these reasons, the slippery slope argument is best seen as a kind of argumentation that, while it has genuine weight to shift a burden of proof, is normally not a strong enough consideration to settle or close an issue, by itself. When the proponent attempts to treat it this way, however, by trying to close off the discussion prematurely by browbeating the respondent into silence, we can say that the slippery slope has been used as a fallacy in this particular case. However, in order to document a charge of fallaciousness—which should be regarded as a very strong form of criticism of an argument—evidence from the text of discourse in any particular case must be cited. It must be shown that the conclusion that the proponent is attempting to put forward as the one the respondent should concede, as the conclusion of the slippery slope argument in question, is inappropriately strong for the argument.

The implications of this way of characterizing the fallacy of slippery slope are clear, for example, in cases 2.6, 2.6*a*, and 2.6*b*. In case 2.6, Bertha has used a slippery slope argument against Bob's contention that a baby in the womb must be defined as a living person. However, she merely uses the argument to challenge or throw doubt on Bob's previous argument, and she commits no fallacy. Similarly, in case 2.6*a*, where Bob turns Bertha's argument around by using a countervailing slippery slope argument against her, he commits no fallacy. Bob is using the argument to throw doubt on the possibility of finding a single point between birth and conception where the fetus may be said to become a person.

However, if we attach the statement of case 2.6*b* as the conclusion of the argument in case 2.6*a*, the situation is very different. Here, the strong phrase 'we are forced to' prefaces the definite conclusion that the beginning of human life must be located at conception. This conclusion is far too strong to be supported by the slippery slope argument alone, and is inappropriate. That conjoined with the use of the strong language by the proponent, a kind of move to try to close the issue beyond further discussion, indicates that in this case it is justifiable to say that a slippery slope fallacy has been committed.

By contrast, in other cases that have been classified as instances of the fallacy of slippery slope by the textbooks, according to the analysis proposed here these cases are not classified as fallacious (even if they are very weak arguments to be sure). In case 3.5, for example, the proponent is so worried about possible side-effects of laughter that we quite rightly think his argument is ridiculous. This person is advocating a level of caution that seems absurdly high in the kind of normal social situations we are accustomed to in daily life. Laughter may occasionally lead to fisticuffs and worse. But this kind of outcome is rare or unusual enough that it would be excessively cautious to worry unduly about it, in the absence of some special reason to think one is in a dangerous or potentially explosive situation where laughter would be inappropriate.

Nevertheless, although case 3.5 is an absurdly weak slippery slope argument, to the point where we rightly think it is ridiculous, by our analysis it would not be correct to classify it as an instance of the slippery slope fallacy. To see why, we must pay careful attention to the wording of the argument.

Notice that St John of Chrysostom is not warning just about the effects of laughter *per se*, but about 'unseasonable laughter.' And he is not saying that laughter always or inevitably leads to fisticuffs and the like, but only that laughter 'often' leads to 'foul discourse,' which, in turn, can lead to worse things. His conclusion is that if you would 'take good counsel' for yourself, you should avoid not only 'foul words' and the like, but also 'unseasonable' or inappropriate laughter.

This advice may have been more suited to an era where settling grievances on the spot with a sword was more commonplace than it is now. But in a contemporary context St John's advice seems absurdly out of place. What we should say then, for sure, is that his argument is extremely weak because it fails to show how each of the steps in his attempted slippery slope argument really leads to the next step with any degree of likelihood or plausibility that would be strong enough to sustain the argument. While there certainly can be negative side-effects of inappropriate laughter, there are also many positive effects of laughter. To be too restrained on the cautionary grounds proposed by St John in case 3.5 would be an overly cautious policy.

Therefore, the argument in case 3.5 should be evaluated as a very weak one, which fails to give a strong enough argument for the conclusion it proposes. And although it is a slippery slope argument, it should not be classified as an instance of the slippery slope fallacy. For in this case, there is not enough evidence to show that the slippery slope technique is being used as a tactic to try to close off the discussion or prevent any further consideration of the subject. Rather, it could well be in this case, as far as we know from the evidence, that the slippery slope was used to offer a kind of cautionary advice on how to act. This use of slippery slope argumentation is, in principle, reasonable and appropriate. However, the argument is weak in this case, because the proponent has failed to present a convincing slippery slope argument because the linkages he proposes are implausible and only weakly substantiated at best.

We can contrast case 3.5 with case 3.8 where the allegation was made convincingly by the report in the *Newsweek* article that the slippery slope argument was being used as a scare tactic to 'hype' a 'myth' of 'instant and total addiction.' The allegation made here was that the slippery slope argument was being used as a sophistical tactic to scare young people away from trying crack. Unfortunately, according to the article, the use of this tactic backfired badly once young people began to see evidence for themselves that many crack users were only using the drug in a more sporadic way, and that some of them were able to give it up. The tactic backfired because the drug is very dangerous and addictive, according to the *Newsweek* article, but once young people detect the exaggeration of the claim of the extent and nature of this addiction, they will skeptically reject the whole slippery slope argument against it—a bad error, but one brought on by the original misuse of the slippery slope argument by its proponents.

The best way to understand the claim being made in case 3.8 is to interpret it as alleging that a slippery slope fallacy has been committed by those who exaggerated the addictive properties of crack to persuade young people not to experiment with it. The slope was a fallacy precisely because it was a sophistical tactic, an argument pushed ahead in an excessive and exaggerated way so it would function as a scare tactic. Instead of engaging in the proper type of discussion to show people how and why crack is dangerously addictive, the short cut was taken of skipping the evidence and raising an alarm by appealing to fear. Instead of replying to the legitimate critical questions and making a carefully argued and properly substantiated case about the real, and somewhat insidious, dangers of crack, the scare tactic was pushed forward to shut down any discussion of the issue before it could begin. The presumption pushed forward was that crack was totally and instantly addictive, so that any discussion of possible or real exceptions was ruled out.

Now in case 3.8, we do not have the original texts of arguments used by those who supposedly propounded the thesis of instant and total addiction (except as reported by the *Newsweek* article). So our concurrence with the *Newsweek* conclusion that these arguments made the claims they are reported to have made must be regarded as conditional upon the examination of the specific texts of the original slippery slope arguments. Here we are saying that the *Newsweek* article has made a particular type of charge. The charge is open to questioning or rebuttal by those who allegedly used the scare tactic of the slippery slope. But granting the assumption that the *Newsweek* claims are accurate reports of the arguments that were put forth—and this seems a plausible assumption to proceed with as a premise—we can conclude that case 3.8 is a good illustration of how the slippery slope works as a fallacy. At least we can say that the type of argumentation criticized by the article fits our requirements of, and is a good illustrative example of the use of the slippery slope argument as a sophistical tactics type of fallacy.

Throughout our analyses of the four types of slippery slope argument, it has been emphasized that there are various characteristic types of critical question that are appropriate for any instance of a slope argument. Whether a particular slippery slope argument is fallacious or not depends on how it has been used in the dialogue. Thus there is no context-free semantic failure of one proposition (a conclusion) to follow from other propositions (premises) that we can fix on and say: 'This failure of inference is the slippery slope fallacy.' A slippery slope fallacy occurs where a slope argument is used and where the proponent has pursued a tactic of trying to hinder unfairly or shut off one or more of these appropriate critical questions, as judged from his performance in the dialogue.

Hence the quest for a single, simple error of reasoning or invalid inference that is the slippery slope fallacy is a misguided inquiry. The slippery slope argument is best not viewed as a single error of reasoning or invalid inference, but as a characteristic sophistical tactic or approach when using a slippery slope argument to try, unfairly, to get the best of an opponent in a critical discussion. And the use of this tricky tactic can manifest itself, depending on the type of slippery slope argument involved, in attempts to suppress or avoid one critical question, or in some cases even more than one of the critical questions that are appropriate for that particular argument.

Windes and Hastings (1965: 226) was quoted in Chapter 3.10 above to show how an affirmative advocate of a policy can reply to a critical attack which employs negative argumentation from consequences, like the slippery slope argument. The advocate can modify his proposal, he can refute the allegation of harmful consequences, or he can point out countervailing positive conseqences of the policy he defends. In such a case, the defender against the slippery slope attack is going even further than asking critical questions. He is shifting the burden against his attacker even more strongly by posing positive, countervailing argumentation which could actually refute the slippery slope argument, rebutting it even more strongly than merely questioning or challenging it by asking questions.

Now note that there are various ways the defending respondent can reply by countervailing argumentation. Not one of these ways is identical with the unique demonstration that a slippery slope fallacy has occurred. Nor need we always say, in every case, if such a rebuttal has successfuly taken place, that the proponent of the slippery slope argument (whose argument has been refuted) has committed a slippery slope fallacy. He has only committed a slippery slope fallacy if he has unfairly tried to prevent the rebuttal by closing off the discussion, or by trying to puff up his slippery slope argument to make it appear so final and irrefutable that any further consideration of the issue would be pointless.

It follows then that the project of studying slippery slope arguments by dividing them into only two classes of cases, the fallacious and the reasonable (correct) ones, is inherently simplistic and misguided, to a great extent. For although it is important to be able to recognize those extreme cases that are fallacious, the bulk of the work really lies in evaluating the broader range of cases that are neither perfectly good nor perfectly bad. These cases, that appear to constitute the majority of those we have studied, are arguments that tend to be weak and in need of analysis, clarification, and critical questioning, but are not so bad that they rightly deserve to be called fallacious.

A slippery slope argument should only properly be evaluated as fallacious where the proponent has pressed forward with his slippery slope argument so hard in the dialogue that the tactic is used in such a way as to cut off or preempt the asking of the right critical questions by the respondent. The fault, in such a case, is to be found not just in the reasoning—the set of propositions that make up the premises and conclusions of the slippery slope argument. It is to be found in the way that the proponent has advanced the slippery slope argument in the context of the dialogue.

A weak slippery slope argument is one where critical questions have not been answered adequately, and gaps in the argument have been left open. A fallacious slippery slope argument is one where the proponent has used a tactic of shutting off the opening for the asking of critical questions by the way he has put forward his argument—as judged by the evidence in the text of discourse and the context of dialogue. The job of pinning down an argument as a case of the slippery slope fallacy is therefore best seen as a pragma-dialectical evaluation of how the argument has been used in a context of dialogue. It follows that the slippery slope fallacy is a sophistical tactics type of fallacy, as opposed to simply being an error of reasoning.

A slippery slope argument that is not in accord with the goals of dialogue, and breaks the rules for that type of dialogue, is an incorrect or faulty slippery slope argument. But it is not necessarily a fallacious slippery slope argument. It could be simply a logical blunder, a weakly supported slippery slope argument. A slippery slope argument that goes against the goals of a dialogue, that blocks or hinders the dialogue by the use of a systematically obstructive tactic, is a fallacious slippery slope argument. It is an incorrect argument, but also a particularly bad sort of one. It is a fallacy because of its use of a deceptive tactic that blocks the further legitimate progress of the dialogue.

The use of argument that is fallacious in a dialogue shows an uncooperative type of attitude on the part of an arguer. He is not entering into the spirit of the dialogue. It is not just that he is violating any particular rule of the dialogue intentionally. Rather he is presenting his argument in an aggressive, deceptive, or obstructive way that shows he is not sincerely taking part in moving the dialogue forward towards its proper goals. He may appear to be making the right sorts of move, but the evidence shows that he is employing tricky tactics that do not really give his opponent a fair chance to make the right rational moves in response. He is undermining the dialogue by peremptorily blocking it, throwing it off its proper course.

According to this view of fallacy, an allegation that an argument is fallacious is quite a serious charge. It has to be possible to back it up by appropriate textual evidence, if the charge is challenged by the alleged perpetrator of the fallacy. Thus not every objectionable or inadequately supported argument is fallacious. A fallacy, in this sense, is a serious abuse of a technique of argumentation, an underlying systematic flaw or sophistical tactic that is not only tricky and slippery, but serious—it throws a discussion badly off its proper course.

As a result of these findings, we will advocate a new approach to the evaluation of slippery slope arguments in Chapter 7. This new approach will proceed by a more careful route, instead of starting by immediately classifying a slippery slope argument as fallacious or nonfallacious.

10. A New Approach Opened Up

The new approach to the evaluation of slippery slope arguments to be advocated in Chapter 7 is based on the thesis that, as critics of argument, we should take care to resist a simplistic inference. Just because a slippery slope argument is presented in a weak or incomplete form that makes it open to requests for clarification and to critical questions which ask for further support, the argument need not necessarily be classified as fallacious. Making the unjustified leap from the one finding to the other could even be described as a kind of higher-order fallacy in evaluating slippery slope argumentation.

A key thesis argued for in Chapter 6 was that the slippery slope argument is not necessarily fallacious. Although it can be used fallaciously—and very effectively at that—it is not, in itself, an inherently fallacious type of argumentation.

The slippery slope argument is a species of argumentation that can be used quite legitimately, in a discussion, to shift a burden of proof to an opposed point of view. Part of the tactics of this kind of argument may be, for example, to take advantage of the vagueness of a word or phrase in a discussion. But this is not in itself fallacious. Terms and phrases are very often vague, or used in a vague manner, in discussions in natural language. There is nothing wrong with that, in itself. And it can be quite acceptable to take advantage of this vagueness to press ahead with a clever argument that exploits it, even in the most logical and carefully reasoned critical discussion.

On the other hand, it can be quite reasonable to criticize a slippery slope argument, or to defend an opposed position against it. This can be done without calling the slippery slope argument a fallacy, as well. Yet in some cases, when the slippery slope argument is pressed ahead too hard, it can and should properly be called fallacious.

A corollary follows in the form of a second thesis which has also been argued for here. This thesis is that the slippery slope argument should not be judged according to a standard whereby it is required to be either (*a*) a deductively valid argument, or (*b*) a conclusive argument that settles a case beyond rebuttal. At least it is correct to say, consistently with the position advocated here, that the slippery slope argument, in most cases, is not meant to be taken as a conclusive argument. Rather, it is a kind of argument that can, in some cases, be used reasonably to shift a burden of presumption in a discussion, and, in other cases, can be used incorrectly, or be open to criticisms. In some cases, it can even be subject to such serious objections that it can rightly be judged fallacious, especially, of course, when it purports to be conclusive.

To sum up the findings of the analysis, the slippery slope is a kind of argument that can sometimes be used correctly and sometimes incorrectly. Whether it has been employed correctly or not in a particular case depends on how it has been used in the context of dialogue, in accord with the requirements of the appropriate argumentation scheme.

The usual or characteristic context of dialogue where slippery slope arguments are used is a kind of persuasion dialogue where both participants have adopted or advocated a particular point of view. One participant has claimed that a particular proposition or thesis is right and the other doubts this claim, or even opposes it by advocating the opposite thesis. The other participant has the role of doubting or questioning whether that same proposition is right, or can be justified by arguments that are strong enough to make it acceptable. In still other cases, the second participant has the role of trying to show that the proposition in question is not right, i.e. that it is definitely wrong or unacceptable.

In addition, however, the context of dialogue typically concerns the rightness or wrongness of an action or policy for actions. Thus it characteristically takes the form of practical reasoning and is a species of argumentation from consequences.

One contrast that seems immediately apparent is that the sorites type of slippery slope argument evidently has to do with truth and falsehood whereas the other three types of slippery slope argument have to do with the goodness or badness of contemplated actions. In the sorites argument, notably in case 2.3, the argument is designed to show that the initial premises are false. In the causal, precedent, and full slippery slopes, the argument is designed to show that some contemplated action or policy is impractical, unwise (prudentially), or otherwise bad, because it leads to some outcome which reveals this bad aspect of it. In short, it seems that the sorites argument is a more cognitive type of slippery slope, whereas the other three types are more practical in nature.

This apparent contrast can now be revealed, to a large extent, as an illusion. For the sorites type of slippery slope argumentation can now be seen to be really more practical than it may have initially seemed in Chapter 1.2.

One has to be careful to appreciate that case 2.3, the argument that concludes that every person is short, is not an instance of the slippery slope fallacy. It is not even really a slippery slope argument, as it stands, because it lacks the proper dialectical elements of the slippery slope argument required by the analysis given in Chapter 6. Accurately described, case 2.3 is an instance of the sorites paradox which has been especially constructed for the pedagogical purpose of showing how you can get into trouble (i.e. be led by deductively valid arguments to a patently false conclusion) by starting with premises that contain vague terms, even if these premises initially appear harmless and not implausible. Case 2.3 is a technical presentation of a logical paradox, and is not meant to be a slippery slope argument in the full sense of this concept explicated in Chapter 6.

However, the kind of argumentation displayed in the sorites paradox in case 2.3 clearly can be used in a slippery slope argument. An instance is case 2.6, where Bertha has used this type of argument to rebut Bob's argument that the baby in the womb must be defined as a living person. Bertha utilized the vagueness of Bob's term 'living person' in order to case doubt on the workability of his classification of the unborn fetus as a living person. She argued that if the fetus is a living person in the later stages of its development in the womb, it has to be a living person in the early stages as well, because Bob hasn't given any clear, single point to draw the line between any two pairs of stages in the development of the fetus which appear to be otherwise indistinguishable. Bertha adds that she thinks classifying a fetus as a living person in these early stages, i.e. especially at conception, is 'an absurd view'. It follows that Bob's classification of a fetus as a living person is an unworkable approach—because it leads to a false or indefensible outcome, it is not a tenable argument (according to Bertha's criticism).

Is Bertha claiming that Bob's hypothesis that the baby is alive in the latter stages is *false* (because it leads to an absurd, or clearly false consequence)? Or can she be interpreted as claiming that Bob's attempt to apply the concept of a living person to the case of a fetus is an unworkable approach to definition and classification, as it stands, because it leads to a consequence that demonstrates its unworkability and untenability (unless Bob can find a clear and tenable place to draw the line)? If the second interpretation is the more reasonable— and it does seem so after the analysis and discussions of this Chapter —then the sorites slippery slope argument can also be seen to have a practical nature which makes it seem more similar to the other three types of slippery slope argument.

More carefully interpreted, sorites slippery slope arguments concern an arguer's right to use or apply definitions of key terms in a way that support his own side of a contested dispute. But empirical concepts are inherently open-textured and character-istically vague, as they are used in natural-language argumenta-tion. Hence the issue is not truth or falsehood of propositions *per se*, but the defensibility or workability of definitions or classifica-tions that are put forward in presumptive arguments that are open to challenge.

When it is said that the slippery slope argument is used correctly, that does not mean that it has to be formally valid, in some system of two-valued or many-valued logic composed of a system of truth-values and quantifiers, as it was presented in the text of discourse in the particular case in question. Nor when a slippery slope argument is fallacious or incorrect does it only mean that it is not valid in some semantic system of this sort. A slippery slope argument is used correctly when it contributes cooper-atively to the goals of an interactive critical discussion, according to the rules of conduct appropriate for a discussion of this type. A slippery slope argument should be open to criticism if it violates, or otherwise deviates from, one or more of these rules. And finally, a slippery slope argument can be properly said to be fallacious if it is used by its proponent as an argumentation tactic which is a charateristic type of mechanism of deception to illicitly try to fool or entrap the other party with whom he is engaged in discussion, and thereby triumph unfairly.

The evaluation of whether a particular slippery slope argument is correct or not should proceed by identifying the appropriate argumentation scheme for that type of argument, and then judging, in relation to the given textual and contextual evidence, where the burden of proof should lie. If all the appropriate premises have been supported with sufficient evidence, the burden is on the respondent to pose critical questions. If the respondent has posed appropriate critical questions for that argumentation scheme, the burden is on the proponent to reply adequately to those critical questions.

Basically the slippery slope is a reasonable kind of argumentation because of parameters of argumentative discussions in natural language that are inherently open and contestable. In the sorites type of slippery slope argument, key terms in the argument are always inherently open to disputation. One side has the right to propose a definition that will make a key term more precise. But the other side always has the right to challenge such a definition, especially if it is 'unfriendly' or contains presumptions that appear prejudicial to the side of the objector. Even despite these rights, however, it is true that both sides will generally try to use language in a way that supports their own side of a dispute. This tendency to use 'friendly' or 'loaded' terms is natural, and is generally unobjectionable (within limits, and subject to exceptions, in specific cases), precisely because natural-language argumentation has to utilize terms that are inherently open-textured, and subject to various interpretations.

A dramatic example would be the Middle East conflicts about territorial borders. One side describes its participants in an incident as 'freedom fighters' and the other side's participants are called 'terrorists' or 'guerrillas.' The other side uses precisely the opposite terminology. Use of argumentatively loaded terminology is not always this radical. Often the implications of key terms in an argument are much more subtly shaded. But this kind of example shows how participants in an argument characteristically use language in a way that tends to support their own side of a disputed issue.

This tendency is not inherently bad or fallacious in itself. Only if persistence in it, despite reasonable objections, becomes dogmatic, does it harden into an obstacle to resolving a dispute. The employment or application of a definition of an empirical concept in natural-language argumentation is therefore a practical matter of the workability of the definition, and such a move can properly be criticized as unfeasible using the sorites slippery slope argument.

The causal type of slippery slope argument is made possible by the fact that the possible causal consequences of any projected future line of action are potentially endless. Any attempt to weigh them is inherently open, a matter of conjecture or intelligent guesswork. Circumstances can always change, and alter the parameters of even a very confident prediction. Discussing an example of the causal type of slippery slope argument, Schauer (1985: 381) writes: 'a persuasive slippery slope argument depends for its persuasiveness upon temporally and spatially contingent empirical facts rather than (or in addition to) simple logical inference.' The context of dialogue is characteristically a critical discussion concerning the practical wisdom of policies for action on a particular issue or problem. The question is whether the balance of presumption favors a particular policy, or projected course of action, or not.

In order to resolve such a conflict of opinions, the plausible future consequences of the proposed course of action have to be weighed *pro* and *contra*. Presumptive argument and burden of proof are the best tools for evaluating arguments, like the slippery slope argument, that can be used quite appropriately in this context. But sometimes what is criticized is a definition or classification of a term that occurs in an argument. When it is the definition itself that is criticized as unworkable, then the type of slippery slope argument used is of the sorites variety. But in other cases, it could be another kind of speech act, like an explanation, that occurs in an argument, and is criticized by using a slippery slope attack. In still other cases, as in the causal, precedent, and full types of slippery slope argument, the fuzziness of a definition is just a part of what propels the slippery slope along. In these cases, vagueness is only part of the problem.

7

Practical Advice on Tactics

USING the argumentation schemes for the four types of slippery slope argument presented in Chapters 2 through 5, along with the analysis of the dialectical structure of slippery slope arguments given in Chapter 6, a rational critic can criticize an instance of this type of argument as weak or faulty in specific respects, posing critical questions about the unsupported premises. But in some cases, this approach is not good enough to rebut the argument.

In a case to be studied in this chapter, a slippery slope argument was open to this kind of criticism because required premises were left out, yet the argument turned out to be surprisingly strong. Its opponents could not refute the argument, and it turned out to be a major factor in winning a case in the U.S. Supreme Court. Subsequent public commentary brought out some of the missing premises, but that just seemed to make the argument all the more powerful and convincing.

In light of such evident limitations of the methods of critical analysis, is there any practical advice that can be given on how a respondent could try to counter a slippery slope argument which has been used against his side in a given instance he confronts? This task involves seeing how the structure of the slippery slope argument fits into the ebb and flow of *pro* and *contra* argumentation in a particular case. In what type of situation does slippery slope arise? What is its deeper, underlying nature as a special strategy of argumentation? What tactics can be used to counter it? General answers to these questions are given in this chapter. Practical advice is also offered, but the limits of its usefulness, as applied to particular cases, are explored.

1. Effective Refutation

The result of the analysis put forward in this monograph is that many examples routinely classified as instances of the slippery slope fallacy by the logic textbooks will now have to be reclassified as nonfallacious. It will not follow that these cases are therefore always perfectly good slippery slope arguments, or as good as they could possibly be. And indeed, an important thesis of the monograph is that we need to be much more careful to distinguish between slippery slope arguments that are fallacious, and those that are weak or incomplete in various respects.

Slippery slope tends to be an inherently weak or inconclusive type of argumentation, because it warns of possible developments that might occur. The argument has force because it claims that these developments would be extremely bad if they did occur. But future developments being what they are, one is never certain that they will occur. They may not. Hence slippery slope arguments are always open to rebuttal, and are, in general, best regarded as defeasible arguments, based on presumption, rather than conclusive arguments.

However, it does not follow that slippery slope arguments cannot be decisively refuted in some cases. No longer can we refute a slippery slope argument by simply calling it a 'fallacy,' or merely saying that it is an instance of the slippery slope fallacy. But we can, in some cases, decisively refute a slippery slope argument by attacking it with tactics suited to the particulars of its deployment in a case of dialogue. The slope argument works by altering given presumptions in a discussion. A refutation checks or reverses these forces of presumption to block the argument effectively.

Ideally, there should be no practical problem of evaluating a slippery slope argument, given the foregoing analysis of this type of argument. All you need to do is to identify which of the four types your given slippery slope argument is, and then test it against the appropriate argumentation scheme for that type of slippery slope argument. It ought to be that simple, but it isn't.

Why not? There are several reasons. One is that you typically have to interpret the given argument to see whether it is really a slippery slope argument, who the participants are, what the premises are, and what the conclusion is supposed to be. But in some cases, this job of interpretation is by no means trivial.

Second, even once the argument has been interpreted as a slippery slope argument, and you can see, at least broadly, what its premises and conclusions are, you may still have a large job on your hands of giving an analysis of these premises that is definite and clear enough to make evaluation possible.

Consider a case of the short form of the slippery slope argument like case 5.4, where opponents of mandated parental leave argued that this policy is 'the first step down a long road that will end with mandated paid leaves.' In this 'short form' version, the sequential premise of the argumentation scheme is not expressed explicitly. It is merely sketched out, using the analogy of a 'long road.' The specific steps in the linked sequence of connecting cases are not indicated. This means that a rational critic should appeal to the argumentation scheme for this type of argument by asking the proponent to fill in the missing steps. Only then can the argument be rationally and carefully evaluated on its merits.

But here we come to an important point. The background presumptions already in place in the context of dialogue in case 5.4 may already support the sequential premise, as far as the audience or respondent of the argument is concerned. Even though the sequential premise has not been explicitly spelled out, that may not matter very much as far as the convincingness of the argument in case 5.4 is concerned in a particular situation.

From a more practical point of view then, if a critic wants to do a really effective job of criticizing this argument, he must attack it more forcefully, for example, perhaps by giving some convincing reason why this 'first step' will only go so far, and will not end in the bad outcome of mandated parental (paid) leaves. At least this outcome would certainly be perceived as 'bad' from the point of view of people in the business community, or taxpayers, who have to pay for mandated parental leaves. Presumably, these people are going to be very worried by the slippery slope argument in case 5.4, and are going to be inclined to accept the argument as convincing, even if the middle steps of the slope are not precisely filled in. Indeed, the argument may be all the more scary for them, because the middle steps are left out. To convince them to change their minds, raising a general critical question will hardly do the job of refuting the argument effectively.

In approaching the task of evaluating an argument, it is useful to distinguish two points of view. From the point of view of the objective critic of the argument, it is enough to find the critical weaknesses in the argument by posing the appropriate critical questions. But from the point of view of the involved participant in argumentative dialogue, that may not be enough, in some cases. It may be necessary for this individual to defend himself against the argument by countering it strongly enough to rebut it. For even asking exactly the right critical question may still leave the argument as effectively convincing for the audience it was directed to. Much may depend on the forces of presumption in a particular case.

It is possible to identify the appropriate argumentation scheme with its set of conditions and then say to the objective critic, 'Here, take these, and if the slippery slope argument meets all these conditions, it is correct, whereas if it fails to meet any of these conditions, it is incorrect.' But basically, the reason why this kind of approach is not appropriate for the involved participant is that each case is different in its given context of dialogue from every other particular case of a slippery slope argument. Analyzing the correctness or incorrectness of the use of a slippery slope argument in a particular case is a pragmatic task which demands sensitivity to the individual situation of a given case. In approaching each case, the given context of dialogue has to be interpreted and evaluated on its own merits. It might not do it justice to approach an individual argument in a purely stereotyped way that takes no account of the real context of discussion in which it has been put forward.

On the other hand, this pragmatic aspect of the task does not mean that we are trapped in a hopeless situationism as rational critics in approaching slippery slope arguments. For each slippery slope argument arises out of a given problem or conflict of opinions, and is a means of trying to resolve that conflict by a collaborative process of entering into dialogue for the purpose of constructive discussion of the issue posed by the conflict. There are standard ways of arguing, and responding to arguments, that are characteristically used when the situation makes a slippery slope argument useful. And it is possible to classify and study these standard techniques, and to see how they can be rightly and wrongly used in particular situations. This is in fact the function of the argumentation schemes.

How an argumentation scheme is employed in a particular case depends on the proponent's strategy, the means he is using to carry out his goal in the discussion. And the strategy is implemented, in a particular case, by tactics that are suited to the special needs and given dialectical situation of that case. To respond effectively to a slippery slope argument, and defend your side of a disputed case against it successfully, you have to know something about argumentation tactics.

In the case of the slippery slope argument, there are several characteristic types or patterns of tactics that can be used to attack it and to defend it. In this chapter, an account of these tactics is given which will prove very useful as practical advice for anyone confronted by a slippery slope argument. And, for that matter, a knowledge of these tactics is also very useful for anyone who wants to use a slippery slope argument, or defend it against rebuttals.

These tactics arise, and are useful, only within the framework of practical reasoning for the given case. To evaluate a particular slippery slope argument in a given case, you have to reconstruct the various parameters of the practical reasoning as they are expressed, or unexpressed but potentially available, in that case. What this means is that the slippery slope argument, by its nature, is used to dissuade an agent from a 'first step' in a course of action he is contemplating. To evaluate the prudential wisdom of this first step, the would-be-dissuader must know or find out something about the agent's goals, about the possibility of the projected course of action, about alternative possibilities, and so forth. Five factors in particular are cited in the next section.

2. The Framework of Practical Reasoning

Presumptive conditionals can be of various kinds. They can be causal conditionals, they can rest on case-by-case analogies between a precedent and subsequent case, or they can be based on predictions about the popular acceptance of a new trend that is becoming an established practice among a group. Indeed, in some cases, instances of all three kinds of presumptive conditional can be chained together in a sequence of practical reasoning. This mixing of the three types of conditional is characteristic of the full slippery slope argument, where the prediction or suggestion is that one thing is likely to lead to another, by a sequential linkage of a chain composed of all of these types of conditional.

Practical reasoning can encompass all three kinds of presumptive conditionals, in some cases. The paradigm case of practical reasoning utilizes the causal conditional, as we saw in Chapter 3.4. But this restriction is not necessary to practical reasoning in general, shown in the case studies of Walton (1990) often to involve a mixing of different kinds of conditional in the sequence. What is characteristic of all such conditionals, however, as they are used in practical reasoning, is their presumptive nature. They are not truth-functional conditionals, and they do not involve a tight connection to the effect that the consequent *must* (absolutely) follow from the antecedent. Rather they are rebuttable conditionals to the effect that there is a practical weight of presumption that the consequent may plausibly follow from the antecedent, all else being held constant.

In judging any slippery slope argument as weak or strong, right or wrong, therefore, we have to look at the context of the practical reasoning in the given case. This context always has the following elements. There is a respondent, who is considering bringing about some state of affairs, A. Should he take this step or not? It is presumed, if not stated in the text of discourse of the given case, that the respondent has some goals or values—states of affairs he holds to be desirable (good) or undesirable (bad). In general, the respondent has some goal, G, or perhaps a set of goals he is committed to.

Next, there is a proponent of the slippery slope argument, and this proponent has taken up the stance of arguing that the respondent would be prudentially unwise to bring about A. The reason given by the proponent is that A would lead by a sequence of presumptive conditionals linked into *modus ponens* steps, after the fashion outlined in Chapter 6.7 to some horrible (dangerous, very bad) outcome, B. This part of the practical reasoning context of argumentation corresponds to the proponent's use of the negative side-effects premise, which in turn corresponds to the fourth question in the list of matching critical questions for practical reasoning given in Chapter 3.4.

These four critical questions can also be expressed within a set of premises stating presumptions that have to be met before the respondent can come to the conclusion that he ought practically to carry out the action of bringing about A. Thus we can express the practical inference that represents the respondent's reasoning as follows.

(P1) I have a goal G that I would like to implement, if possible.

(P2) As far as I know, in the given circumstances, bringing

about at least one of a set of alternatives $\{A_0, A_1, ..., A_n\}$ is necessary in order to bring about the realization of G.

(P3) I have selected one member, A_i, of the set of alternatives in (P2) above as the most acceptable way to bring about G, in the circumstances.

(P4) Nothing that I can't change prevents me from bringing about A_i, as far as I know.

(P5) As far as I know, there are no negative side-effects of bringing about A_i that are so bad that they would outweigh the positive value of bringing about G.

(C) Therefore, I ought practically (prudentially) to bring about A_i.

Practical reasoning of this sort is defeasible in the sense that the conclusion is only reasonable on the basis that all five of (P1) through (P5) are reasonable presumptions in the given situation. As soon as that changes, for any reason, the conclusion may have to be withdrawn. Thus practical reasoning is a kind of temporary, presumptive argumentation that can be overturned or refuted if new intelligence comes in to the effect that the particular circumstances of the given situation (as the respondent knows it) have now changed.

Another uncertainty introduced in realistic cases of practical reasoning is that a reasoner who is contemplating some step generally has a multiplicity of goals. He may want to bring about some particular goal G_1, but then it may be drawn to his attention that bringing about G_1 by some particular means he has been considering will also bring about some other state of affairs, B. Moreover, it may become clear to him that B is very bad for him, in the sense that B will interfere with or run contrary to some other goal, G_2, that he also values very highly. For example, earning money may, in a particular situation, be found to be very unsafe, interfering with the goal of self-preservation. In such a case, a rational person may be torn by conflict in trying to decide which is the most prudent course of action.

In this type of conflict, there is room for argumentation, as the respondent deliberates internally, and perhaps also discusses the situation with someone else. In such a case, as Windes and Hastings (1965: 226) put it, there are two sides. A critic may ask:

'What if some of the consequences are not beneficial and are downright dangerous?' playing the role of a 'negative advocate.' On the other side, 'the [positive] advocate lists and proves the benefits which will result from his proposition.' (p. 227). Such a conflict could take the form of a debate, where each advocate tries to persuade an audience that his side has the greater weight of presumption behind it.

Practical reasoning, as a kind of argumentation, occurs in several different contexts of dialogue. For example, it can occur in an expert consultation type of dialogue, where a layperson asks an expert in a domain of knowledge, 'What is the best, or a good way to do this?' It can occur in political debate on public policy or legislation on a controversial issue. It can occur in a critical discussion to resolve a conflict of opinion on values or moral controversies. And of course it can occur in deliberation on choosing a prudent course of action in personal decision-making.

Practical reasoning also occurs in legal argumentation, where it is characteristically involved with problems of interpretation and enforcement of laws, and questions of whether a new rule will have precedents that may be favorable or unfavorable. Legal argumentation is a special context, because the legal rules of evidence, and other legal rules governing the conduct of trials, have been codified in an explicit and institutionalized fashion.

When evaluating a slippery slope argument in a particular case, you need to see (*a*) how it fits into the larger framework of practical reasoning, of which it is a part, and (*b*) how the practical reasoning exhibited in the case fits into the larger context of dialogue. The project of evaluation is, to a significant extent, one of fitting the slippery slope argument into the ebb and flow of the particulars of this larger dialogue setting.

3. The Tactical Framework

Tactics arise out of the application of strategies to a given, particular situation. Whether a tactic is useful depends both on the strategy and on the purpose of the strategy. But it also depends on the nature of the particular situation to which that strategy is applied. As an argumentation strategy, the slippery slope has the purpose of convincing someone not to do something—it is a kind of refutation. But it is a very special type of refutation that will work well only in cases where a gradual continuum can come into play, linking the respondent's proposed first step with some bad eventual outcome.

The slippery slope argument is the negative counterpart or antithetical argument to the positive argument from gradualism. But the key thing to realize is that both types of argument work or function most effectively in the same kind of argument situation. This similarity is reflected in the four basic elements that these two types of argumentation have in common. These four elements are: (1) the tactical basis—the initial type of situation that makes a type of argument useful; (2) the strategy which an argument is designed to carry out; (3) the tactic that is used to apply the strategy to its tactical basis in a given case; and (4) the preparatory, opening-up move which makes it possible to set the operation of the tactic into motion. These four elements make up the *tactical framework* for using the slippery slope argument. The tactical framework is a set of conditions implicit in a particular case that are favorable for the successful use of slippery slope argumentation.

The slippery slope argument arises as a logical response to counter an opposed type of argumentation which can either be put forward explicitly by an opponent in dialogue or can be a threat inherent in a particular case which is present through the forces of presumption in the context of dialogue. In some cases, both these types of precipitating factor can be combined. For example, in case 1.5, the danger of voluntary euthanasia for the terminally ill was argued against, using a slippery slope argument that cited a historical interpretation of how the Holocaust came about in Nazi Germany. In the discussion of this case five identifiable steps in the sequence through which the Nazis carried out their program of 'life unworthy of life' were identified, as cited by Lifton (1986: 22). By suggesting a comparison between the present situation and the conditions of the pre-Nazi period in Germany, this slippery slope argument warns that the same thing, or something comparable, could happen again. We noted in Chapter 1.2 that this sequence of actions, as it came to be realized in the Third Reich, as described by Lifton, is not itself a slippery slope argument, although it did appear to us that there were some elements of slippery slope argumentation implicit in it. We can now define and locate these elements.

The first element is the *tactical basis,* or originating situation out of which slippery slope argumentation arises as a way of advancing a particular type of argumentation tactic that is useful to resolve a conflict or deal with a problem that has been posed. This element characteristically arises at the confrontation stage of argumentation, and it prepares the way, or opens up a situation as 'ripe' for the use of a slippery slope argument.

In the instance of the euthanasia argument in case 1.5, this *tactical basis* is provided by the initial plausibility of the analogy to the Nazi era, which suggests that one thing could lead to another. In this case, the tactical basis that prompts the argument is the suggestion that there is the possibility (or plausibility) of a natural development, a situation in which once people become accustomed to accepting one stage of a development, they might naturally become accustomed to accepting various other stages which will lead the situation in a certain direction. The slippery slope argument then arises as a way of defending against this development, should it be felt by one party in the dialogue that the direction of this development could be dangerous—something to take up opposition against.

The other party in the dialogue could quite possibly feel that the direction of this line of development is good, or at any rate is acceptable, and should not be opposed. In the example of the euthanasia dispute, consider the case of someone who is generally for euthanasia, at least to the extent that she supports voluntary euthanasia with consultation with one's physician, along the lines currently practiced in Holland. But the problem is that in trying to convince Canadians to adopt this type of policy she encounters all kinds of resistance, based on fears that 'killing' is bad, and so forth —even 'killing' oneself when one is terminally ill, by taking a lethal dose of a drug. In this type of situation, such a person might adopt the tactic of arguing—somewhat after the first stages of the argument in case 5.1, that the current practices of allowing nonutilization of aggressive therapy, for example in allowing patients not to take chemotherapy in some cases, is already a widely accepted (and acceptable) practice in Canadian hospitals. Such a person might then argue that it is a very short step from the existing practices to allowing patients to take medications that might have the effect of shortening life. By stressing that this is a natural development of the existing practice, this advocate of euthanasia could argue positively that euthanasia (at least in some safe and acceptable form) ought to be accepted, and allowed as a general policy, as an option for those who want it.

Now it is just this kind of pro-euthanasia argumentation, which tries to push us forward from one step to another along a natural sequence of developments, that the slippery slope argument opposes. The function and *raison d'être* of the slippery slope argument is precisely to oppose this positive argumentation, or even the force of presumption that makes it possible or plausible, in a particular case. This first element then functions as the tactical basis, the structure inherent in the given situation giving rise to the problem or possible conflict of opposed opinions, out of which the slippery slope characteristically arises as a relevant and useful kind of argumentation.

The second element is the use of a dividing strategy by the advocate of positive argumentation in this type of case.

Several types of attack and defense strategy in formal games of dialogue were presented in Walton (1984: 137–61). One type called the *dividing strategy* (p. 135) works by taking a premise that your respondent would not be likely to accept, as it stands, and breaking it up into parts—for example, by using disjunctions or conjunctions—and then trying to convince him separately to accept each part.

In the type of situation appropriate for the use of slippery slope argumentation there is a tactic that Perelman and Olbrechts-Tyteca (1971: 282) called the *device of stages,* which they describe as a technique of splitting up a whole interval or passage to some end of argumentation into partial ends or 'stages.'

It is often found to be better not to confront the interlocutor with the whole interval separating the existing situation from the ultimate end, but to divide this interval into sections, with stopping points along the way indicating partial ends whose realization does not provoke such a strong opposition. Though the passage from point A to C may cause difficulties, it might happen that no objection may be seen to passing from point A to B, from which point C will appear in a quite different light. We may call this technique the *device of stages*. The structure of reality conditions the choice of these stages but never imposes it.

Dividing strategies are quite common in all kinds of argumentation, but the device of stages applies to a kind of case where a sequence or whole complex of argumentation can be divided into smaller parts or stages, for the purpose of convincing a respondent to accept these parts piecemeal, even where he would not accept the whole complex if it were presented to him all at once. Depending on what kind of end and interval are involved, the device of stages can be applied as an argumentation tactic in various ways.

In a type of situation that typically gives rise to slippery slope argumentation, the device of stages is applied using the *tactic of gradualism* which can also be called the *tactic of the continuum,* a tactic to push forward over a gradual development or continuum by repeated use of the device of stages over a sequence. This tactic exploits concessions in argumentation by applying a repeatable process of working by small steps. It is a kind of argumentation by small degrees which gradually move the line of argument forward.

The third element is the possibility of using the tactic of gradualism, which is one particular type of device of stages. The fourth element is the *wedge technique,* a preparatory, opening-up move for getting the respondent ready for later developments by securing acceptance of an initial case(s). This tactic could also be called the 'foot in the door' or 'camel's nose in the tent' argument. It is used to begin the process of going ahead with the first step in applying the tactic of gradualism. It is a small but necessary and significant part of the mechanism of applying the tactic of gradualism.

When all these four elements are present in a particular case, the right conditions are there for slippery slope argumentation to arise naturally and function successfully. In many cases, it is not just the given situation itself that creates the right tactical framework for slippery slope argumentation. It is that plus the argumentation itself that has already headed in a particular direction which makes it amenable to extension by the use of a slippery slope.

You can usually get a good idea of whether a slippery slope argument would be a useful tactic in a given situation by asking whether the argument from gradualism would apply to that situation. And indeed, the tactical situation for the use of the slippery slope argument can be summed up by noting that the slippery slope argument is always the opposed counterpart, the negative version of the (positive) argument from gradualism.

Note, however, that the argument from gradualism is not itself always as simple as it may appear, for the tactic of gradualism can be used in different ways. One variant of the argument from gradualism, the *positive gradient argument*,[1] uses the tactic of gradualism to convince a respondent to go ahead and take a first step towards a goal that the respondent should not be opposed to, i.e. that is in his real interest. For example, I might convince you to take the first steps in a fitness program by arguing that even though the process is painful at first, it quickly gets better and better as you become fitter.

On the other hand, some instances of the argument from gradualism are different from the positive gradient argument, because the tactic of gradualism is used as a deceptive device to get somebody to accept something that they should be opposed to, or that is not in their real interest, by first getting them to accept an initial step. Here the use of the wedge tactic is to convince someone by small stages to accept a policy that they should or would not normally accept if it were presented to them all at once.

For example (to elaborate on the situation in case 1.6), suppose a governing political party needs to raise government funds to offset a rising national deficit, and they decide to introduce a value-added tax (VAT) on all items and services purchased in the country. Knowing that the voters would never accept a 15 percent VAT, which is the average in other countries, and which is needed to solve the deficit problem, they hit on the tactic of introducing a 3 percent tax as a first step. Their plan is that two years later, once the tax is in, and the controversy about it has died down, they can raise it higher and higher, by tolerable degrees, until they can finally get it up to their target goal of 15 percent.

Now in this case, presumably the people on whom this tactic is being used ought to be opposed to the 15 percent VAT. And if so, the argument from gradualism in this case is different from the species of it used in the positive gradient type of case. In the VAT case, the tactic of gradualism is a deceptive tactic used to persuade someone in a tricky way by getting them to go along with something by overcoming their opposition in a series of small stages, making the task of persuasion easier.

---

[1] I am indebted to Robert Druce for introducing this term during a discussion at NIAS.

The best tactical advice would seem to be, in many cases, to be ready to confront a slippery slope argument or an argument from gradualism through anticipating its use by recognizing the existence of the tactical framework for this kind of argumentation in a particular case.

4. The Prisoners' Voting Case

In some cases, an argument starts out by drawing an analogy between two classes of things in a situation that invites extending the analogy to a third class of things. Once these initial steps have been made, the argumentation may then be open to extension to further cases, providing a tactical basis for the use of the slippery slope argument.

In some cases, the tactic framework arises out of the dialogue between both participants. One party starts the argument by furnishing some elements, and the second party then contributes further steps that open the way for the potential use of a slippery slope argument.

A case of this sort can be reconstructed from two examples presented in Walton (1989). In the first example, case 7.1, a lawyer argued that prisoners should have the right to vote. His argument was that the current law, which denies prisoners the right to vote, is inconsistent. The current law, he argued, excludes those who are in jail (even for a minor offense) from voting, while it allows someone on parole or awaiting sentence (perhaps for a serious crime) the right to vote.

Case 7.1

A lawyer for three prison inmates claimed that the law denying all sentenced prisoners the right to vote is irrational. The lawyer argued that the present law does not make sense because it excludes those who are in jail from voting, but allows those who are out on parole or awaiting sentence to vote. He also argued that the law makes no distinction between prisoners convicted for serious crimes and those in prison for minor infractions of the law. The lawyer argued that, if lawmakers want to exclude prisoners from the democratic process, they must ensure that the reason is sufficiently important to override the constitutional right to vote. He concluded that the burden of proof must be on the state to show why prisoners should be denied this fundamental civil right. (Walton 1989: 254–5)[2]

The lawyer's argument here is based on drawing a comparison or analogy between two kinds of case. He argues that there may be no relevant difference between the case of a prisoner in jail, and one on parole or awaiting sentence, as far as their right to vote should be concerned. Thus the lawyer argued that the current law is inconsistent by treating these two similar cases differently. Moreover, he argued, the law makes no difference where there is a relevant difference, namely between those in prison for serious crimes and those in prison for minor infractions. On this basis, the lawyer is challenging the burden of proof which currently is used by the state to exclude prisoners from voting.

This argument presses for consistency by comparing two cases where it is alleged there is no relevant difference between them. It is not a slippery slope argument, but it could be used as a wedge technique, along with a device of stages, to argue for extending voting privileges even further.

Exactly this strategy was used by another individual who objected to the lawyer's argument. This person tried to refute the argument of case 7.1 by extending it a step further to the case of politically aware teenagers who are not old enough to vote. Arguing from this further parallel, this new argument appeared to question the conclusion that prisoners should be given the right to vote.

Case: 7.2

In recent mock elections held in high schools, teenagers have shown themselves politically aware and capable of expressing their views in a civilized fashion. On this evidence, it is reasonable to have more confidence in the ability to reason and sense of honesty and fair play of many seventeen-year-olds, and less cause to be vigilant of their motives or integrity than you could say for many of those adults convicted of crimes. 'In our haste to create a fair and equitable society for all, does it really make sense to extend the right to vote to criminals and degenerates in our jails but not to our young people? Why should anyone whose

[2] This case was originally based on information in the article by Paul Moloney 'Voting Right Denial Called Unfair to Prisoners,' *Winnipeg Free Press*, Mar. 5, 1986, p. 3.

birthday falls one day too late be any less entitled to vote than someone else who has been found guilty of committing a crime and has been exiled out of society behind bars?' (Walton 1989: 255)[3]

This argument contends that once we allow convicted prisoners voting privileges, wouldn't we also have to allow our young people the same privileges? This argument extends the analogy to yet another case, that of minors. It therefore carries the argument for consistency raised in case 7.1 one step further.

This argument immediately raises a problem of interpretation. What is the conclusion? Is it supposed to lead us to conclude that we ought to adopt the policy of allowing teenagers the right to vote? Or is it really a backhanded way of suggesting that we ought not to allow prisoners the right to vote, because if we did that, we would have to allow teenagers the right to vote too? The second construal interprets the argument as a kind of indirect speech act.

Interpreted either way, the argument in case 7.2 provides a problem which blocks the proposal put forward in the argument of case 7.1. Right now, teenagers do not have the right to vote. It would be very difficult, presumably, to convince a majority to accept a general policy of allowing teenagers to vote, for this proposal is a radical step, and it would lead to many problems. We can presume, in other words, that such a proposal would have to overcome many serious objections.

The strategy of the second interpretation of the argument in case 7.2 seems like a kind of partial *reductio ad absurdum* tactic. Most of us would find difficulties in the policy of allowing minors the right to vote, and be resistant to accepting such a conclusion without pretty strong justifications for it. By consistency then, this new argument logically impels us to go back and question whether we ought to make the first step of allowing the right to vote to convicted prisoners.

Thus the respondent to the argument posed by the proponent of case 7.1 has carried the original argument one step further. In effect, the respondent has brought forward a tactical basis for a slippery slope argument which could potentially be used to try to refute the first argument. He suggests that once we extend the right to vote to prisoners, what reason could we have for not

---

[3] This case was quoted from Roger Young, 'Readers Forum: No Vote for Convicts,' *Winnipeg Free Press*, Mar. 22, 1986, p. 7.

extending this right to teenagers? But once this suggestion has been raised, the tactical framework for extending the argument is in place. Why not extend the same right to other comparable groups, who seem equally if not more deserving? But of course the suggestion is that we are now on a kind of slippery slope. We are disinclined to want to start extending the right to vote this freely, perhaps for various reasons. But if so, then we have to question the wisdom of allowing the first step of giving the right to vote to convicts.

To rebut this challenge, the proponent of the original argument of case 7.1 could show that there is a relevant difference between the two cases. And we should note that there is plenty of room for this sort of refutation. For the proponent of the argument in case 7.2 has shifted the basis of the comparison significantly. He has shifted the argument around to concentrate on the 'ability to reason and sense of honesty and fair play' of many teenagers, to contrast with the 'criminals and degenerates in our jails.' This represents quite a shift from the issue of the argument of case 7.1, which was not based on the prisoner's honesty or ability to reason.

When these two cases are presented in the order above, the argument of the second one can be seen to function as a tactical response to the argument of the first case. The first case proceeds by drawing an analogy between two kinds of prisoner. The second case extends that analogy further.

The conclusion of the argument in the first case is that prisoners should have the right to vote. But the second case can be interpreted as arguing that if prisoners should have this right, then teenagers should have it too. Is the conclusion of the second case then that teenagers should have the right to vote? This is a possible interpretation, but it does not represent the real strategy of the argument.

By extending the argument to the situation of teenagers, the argument of case 7.2 creates the tactical framework for a slippery slope. Suppose we grant the right to vote to teenagers. At what age should we draw the line—17, or 16, or what? Or is the argument only suggesting that we give the right to vote to those teenagers who are 'politically aware and capable of expressing their views in a civilized fashion'? But once again, there is a problem—how do we draw this line? The argument has landed us in a situation where, no matter how we draw the line, it is bound to be problematic.

But it seems that the strategy of the argument is precisely to show the problematicity of extending voting privileges. Citing 'our haste to create a fair and equitable society,' the argument concludes with the question why 'anyone whose birthday falls one day too late' should be less entitled to vote than someone who has been found guilty of committing a crime. The suggestion is that extending voting rights to criminals is hasty and arbitrary. The conclusion of the argument of the first case is being rejected, on the basis that its acceptance could lead to an absurd, untenable, or highly problematic situation, once its full implications are brought out.

Thus the strategy of the argument of the second case proceeds by setting up a tactical basis for slippery slope argumentation by using a *reductio ad absurdum* type of argument. However, it is not the same as the familiar type of *reductio*, where a proposition is reduced to absurdity by deducing a contradiction from it. In this instance, an argument is shown to be questionable by showing that it starts a sequence that can be extended to a situation that is highly problematic and difficult to deal with—where there is no clear solution that would not be arbitrary. By extension, then, the original argument is shown to be problematic, and open to reasonable doubts. By means of using this slippery slope *reductio*, a burden of proof is shifted back onto the original proposal. The suggestion is that unless the original proposal can deal fairly and adequately with this severe problem, it ought to be dropped until further notice, as a policy that is currently practical or feasible, to be put into place.

5. Six Tactics to Counter a Slippery Slope

In the kind of conflict situation in which slippery slope argumentation arises, the negative advocate stresses how bad one particular outcome is, and marshals his arguments to support as strong a weight of presumption as possible that this outcome is a serious risk of the course of action that the positive advocate proposes to embark upon. There are six basic tactics that the positive advocate can use to counter these attacks. All six of these tactics apply to disputation concerning the argument from consequences generally, but some of them also have special subtactics applicable to slippery slope arguments in particular.

1. *Claim that the negative consequence won't really follow.* This tactic is to positively attack the claim of the negative advocate by citing reasons to suppose that the negative consequence will not be an outcome, contrary to his claim that it will be. As Windes and Hastings (1965: 226) put it, 'The advocate can refute the attack, contending that the harmful consequence will not follow.' As noted below, however, the use of this tactic may have to be backed up strongly, if it is to be effective in winning an argument. Note also—as shown by case 5.6—that citing a definite cutoff point in the sequence may not be enough. Such a move can be refuted, in some cases.

2. *Cite the uncertainty of the future.* This tactic is to argue that we don't really know that the negative consequence will follow, and therefore we should not worry about it so much that it causes undue hesitation, or leads us to do nothing at all. Perelman and Olbrechts-Tyteca (1971: 284–5) expressed the method of this tactic very clearly when they wrote: 'Stress will be laid on the ambiguity of development and, consequently, on the arbitrariness of seeing only a single possible direction.' This tactic is softer than the first tactic, which claims that the negative advocate's claim is false. This second tactic only claims that we don't know whether the negative advocate's claim is true or not—we can't tell because any attempts to predict the future consequences of our actions are always 'guesswork' at best, etc. In other words, why worry about something you can't be sure about anyway?

3. *Modify the goal to eliminate the negative consequences.* For example, if the negative advocate argues that having a social policy of euthanasia would result in people eventually being eliminated without any say in the matter, the positive advocate could change his argument, saying that he is only in favor of 'voluntary euthanasia.'

4. *Stress positive consequences, arguing that these outweigh the negative consequence.* This tactic involves conceding the claim that the negative consequence is a real risk, but rebutting the negative value of this risk by countering with the positive value of all the good consequences that are likely to result. Like tactic (1), this is a positive attack which can be used to refute the case of the negative advocate, not just to throw doubt on his contention.

5. *Choose some alternative means of achieving the goal, one that does not have the negative consequence.* In practical reasoning,

there is always a set of alternative means of attempting to carry out a goal. Some of these may not have the negative consequence as such a likely outcome, or in such a bad form. A subtactic of this tactic is to keep to the same general line of action you were considering, but eliminate one link in the sequence of reasoning, or replace it with an alternative, so the negative consequence is made less of a risk. Windes and Hastings (1965: 226) express this subtactic by saying that the positive advocate can 'overbalance with advantages any disadvantages of the action, demonstrating that the benefits are more important and extensive.'

6. *Argue that not taking the action in question (or taking an opposed course of action) will have even worse negative consequences.* For example, in response to the slippery slope argument in case 3.5, where it was argued that to laugh or 'speak jocosely' could ultimately lead to 'foul deeds,' 'blows,' or even murder, you could argue that always repressing your natural feelings by never laughing could lead to even worse results. Everyone would be sad, uncommunicative, depressed, and we would have psychological disorders and mental illness on a wide scale, expressed in antisocial behavior, and even violence and war, once deprived of a healthy release of our stronger emotions.

There are two especially interesting subtactics of tactic (6). One is to produce a counterslope that is as bad as (or ideally worse than) the original slope in its negative consequences.

An excellent example of this kind of tactic is quoted from Schauer (1985: 381) in case 7.3 below.

Case 7.3

OBJECTOR. If you allow Pawtucket, Rhode Island, to erect a nativity scene on public property, then it is only one small step to allowing organized prayers and religious services on public property, and then the next step is involvement of public officials in those services, and then official endorsement of particular religious denominations, which is exactly what the establishment clause was originally designed to prevent.

DEFENDER. If you allow the courts to stop Pawtucket from erecting the nativity scene, then the next step is allowing the courts to prohibit any mention of religion at all, including studying the Bible as literature in schools and hanging Giotto paintings in publicly funded museums, and then the courts will prohibit any public official from mentioning religion, and before long the courts will even prohibit fire and police protection of church buildings.[4]

Of course this tit-for-tat rejoinder is not the normal or expected response to a slippery slope attack. But it is interesting to see that it is possible.

The tit-for-tat tactic is also possible for other kinds of argumentation—for the dilemma, a counterdilemma can be produced; in reaction to an argument from analogy, a counteranalogy can be devised; in response to an *ad hominem* attack, another *ad hominem (tu quoque)* reply can be mounted. However, although such clever replies can be highly effective, it is not possible to devise them (especially, on short notice), in all cases. They are, in fact, fairly rare as rejoinders to these kinds of argument and seem to be feasible only in some cases, and require considerable craft and artifice to construct.

The second subtactic of tactic (6) is a variation of the first one, which replies by producing a counterslope where the negative outcome is worse, arguing that we are already on this counterslope, and if we don't do anything at all, the worst consequences will come about. According to Perelman and Olbrechts-Tyteca (1971: 286), Demosthenes was particularly fond of this kind of argument, and used it, in the case below, to argue against those who counseled against going to the aid of the city of Megalopolis when it was threatened by Sparta. They argued that Megalopolis was an ally of Thebes, and therefore no steps should be taken to aid it. Demosthenes' reply was the following argument.

Case 7.4

If the Lacedemonians take Megalopolis, Messene will be imperiled. If they take Messene too, I predict that we shall become allies of Thebes. Is it not then a far more advantageous and honorable course to spontaneously welcome the allies of Thebes, thus thwarting the cupidity of the Lacedemonians, than to shrink from protecting a city because it is an ally of Thebes, and so sacrifice it, only to have to rescue the Thebans themselves later and, in addition, be afraid for our own safety?[5]

---

[4] Schauer (1985: 381) used the facts of an actual court case, *Lynch* v. *Donnelly* (104 5. Ct. 1355—1984) to construct the stylized dialogue of case 7.3.

[5] This quotation was attributed by Perelman and Olbrechts-Tyteca (1971: 286, n. 67) to Demosthenes, *For the People of Megalopolis,* §§20–1.

According to Demosthenes' reply, it was best to take that first step after all, because the consequences of not taking it would be an even worse slippery slope.

Incidentally, case 7.4 (and case 5.11 as well) shows that the slippery slope is not always or necessarily a conservative argument, used to preserve a status quo. It can, in some cases, be used to argue for taking positive action.

Clearly then, the use of tactic (6) can take various forms. One might simply argue that taking the action in question would have worse consequences than not taking it, without using a counter-slope argument to show how these worse consequences are supposed to come about. Or one might use a counterattacking slippery slope to respond to a slippery slope argument. Or one might argue that *any* alternative course of action would lead to worse consequences. What all of these tactics have in common is that they attack the opposite (negation) of the policy of taking the step under consideration on the basis that this opposed course of action would have worse consequences than the step in question.

Tactic (1) is perhaps the most direct and obvious way to oppose a slippery slope argument, but this tactic involves a positive claim that may have to be backed up with a solid defense if it is to work very well, in many cases. Generally, the best and strongest approach, if it can be managed, is to 'draw the line' by citing a particular point on the continuum where the argument from gradualism stops, and then to defend this stopping point by giving good reasons why the argument can only go that far.

For example, in case 2.6 (including 2.6*a* and 2.6*b*), the abortion dispute between Bertha and Bob, the dialogue was deadlocked. Bob opened with a slippery slope attack, and Bertha responded with a counterslope (tactic (6)). Both had equally strong arguments, and as a result, neither argument gained an ascendancy that could resolve the dispute. A good tactic to break the deadlock would be for one side or the other to take the initiative and make a case for the beginning of personhood at some point on the continuum other than the two poles of conception and birth, rejected by the other side.

For example, if one of them were to argue that a fetus becomes a person at the last point of the first trimester, it would break the deadlock. But of course this argument would have to be backed up by good reasons for picking this point, or else the other party might still insist that this point is arbitrary, using the slippery slope argument again.

Clearly, tactic (1) is a very important one, but its effective use in particular cases involves the use of subtactics and good judgment in applying the tactic to the particulars of the given case.

6. Applying the First Tactic

The first tactic is the most normal and direct method of attacking a slippery slope critically, but there are important questions about how it is best applied. The sequential premise typically offers a multiplicity of premises. Which one(s) should you attack?

There seem to be two kinds of advice that can be given here. One strategy is to attack the weakest link in the chain of a slippery slope argument. The other advice is to start at the beginning of the sequence of slippery slope argumentation, i.e. to attack the earliest steps first. The second strategy could be summed up in the maxim: 'Start at the top and work downwards.' Both are global approaches that involve judging the sequence as a 'flow' of argumentation.

Actually, there are several choices open. First, you can attack the initial premise (a local strategy) or you can attack the sequence, taking a more global perspective on the whole sequence of argumentation.

These tactics can also be combined. One good strategy that sometimes seems applicable works in two stages. First, look over the whole sequence of argumentation and try to determine the weakest point. Second, having chosen a particular subargument to attack, focus your attack on one of the premises. You can attack the simple premise, the bridging premise, or both.

Yet another strategy is to attack the transitive closure of the bridging relation in the sequence. For example, in the causal argument, causality might be held to 'fade out' over a prolonged sequence of events. This strategy is a semiglobal approach.

Note that the slippery slope argument is based on principles of plausible reasoning. It is a linked argument, at each local level, and a serial argument in its overall (global) structure. To criticize it, you may have to go over the whole sequence of argumentation and look for the weakest point or points. Then having found a particular subargument to concentrate on, you can attack either the simple premise or the bridging premise, whichever is weaker (less plausible). Or you can attack both, if both are weak.

In the case of the sorites argument, both premises are plausible at first in the sequence, then move towards the grey area, where the premises are not plausible, but not implausible either. It is better to attack in the grey area, rather than wait until the premises become highly implausible, e.g. a man who is 6 feet in height is short.

But this seems to contradict the advice given in the paragraph above. According to that rule, it is better to attack the local premises that are weakest, i.e. least plausible.

What is disguised here, however, is the fact that once the respondent starts to concede premises that are even slightly implausible, he has begun to lose the argument. His best strategy should be not to let the slippery slope argument get even this far. He should attack it as soon as the premises are no longer plausible.

There are really two principles at work. First, the respondent should attack the slippery slope argument at its weakest links, i.e. in the subargument where the premises are least plausible. But second, depending on the order of questioning posed by the proponent, the respondent should also attack the slippery slope as early as possible in the sequence of argumentation. The reason is that if he waits too late to begin raising critical questions, he has become 'implicated' or committed to the argument to some degree, and will have trouble extricating himself from this commitment. For the proponent can attack him on grounds of the consistency of the respondent's commitments.

Everything depends on the order of questions put by the proponent, however. Characteristically, in the causal argument, the proponent presents the slippery slope all at once, and then the respondent can reply by questioning any stage he chooses. In the classical way of presenting the sorites argument, however, the proponent asks the respondent to reply to each step one at a time, beginning with the initial premise and proceeding downwards by question and reply, one local argument at a time. The proponent waits until the respondent replies affirmatively at each step, before he goes on to the next question. In this type of discussion, the respondent has to be a lot more careful to choose the right point to begin resistance. For at each step, he is making a commitment. In the causal argument, such a step by step, orderly extraction of commitments does not seem to be the usual way the slippery slope is presented. The causal argument could be presented this way in some cases, but normally it is not.

Even in the causal slippery slope argument of the usual type, however, it may be better to attack it in the earliest stages first. As the argument goes on and on towards its conclusion, it gets more and more dangerous for the respondent's side. As a question of practical advice, therefore, it may be better in most cases for the respondent to try to cast doubt on the early stages of the sequence first.

This advice applies even more markedly to precedent types of slippery slope argument, where it may be crucial to stem the flow of precedents early on. In fact, it is in the nature of some precedent arguments, like the speeding-ticket case (case 4.1), that to resist the slippery slope effectively, the respondent has to firmly attack the very first step pleaded in the series, or else have a strong argument for treating it as an exception to the rule. It seems that the best general advice for a respondent in the precedent type of slippery slope argument would be to try to mount resistance at the earliest possible stages, even at the first step if possible.

The strategic options are summed up in Fig. 7.1. Although all these different options are available, there are reasons to believe that no general rule can be formulated that will fit every particular case exactly. For in some cases, the best point of attack for a respondent may depend on the respondent's own position on the issue of the particular discussion.

Consider the slippery slope argument against euthanasia of the type cited in Walton (1987: 209), quoted in case 5.1. Where should a reasonable respondent attack this kind of argumentation? Here no general solution would appear to be applicable, because it depends on where the respondent wants to draw the line. This in turn would seem to depend very heavily on the nature of the respondent's position on the issue of euthanasia, on what acts or omissions he thinks are permissible or impermissible, according to his point of view as expressed in the previous discussion.

The tactics outlined in Fig. 7.1 and Section 5 above do not represent all possible ways of successfully attacking a slippery slope argument in every case. Other ways of criticizing slippery slope arguments have already been indicated in the lists of critical

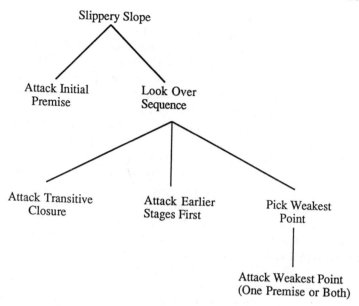

Fig. 7.1 Options in responding to slippery slope

questions for each of the four types of slippery slope argument analyzed in Chapters 2 through 5. Moreover, each case is unique to some extent, and many different kinds of specific error and weakness can crop up in a case. We have already noticed, for example, the affinity slippery slope arguments have with other kinds of traditional informal fallacy, like the *ad hominem, ad verecundiam,* and *ad populum* arguments. It is also true that many slippery slope arguments are supported by arguments from analogy. And often the most significant bone of contention is whether analogous cases support or undermine the slippery slope argument.

7. The Case of Texas v. Johnson

A good way to begin preparation of your defense against a slippery slope attack is to keep in mind the characteristic critical questions for each type of slippery slope argument. These are the sets of critical questions listed at the end of each of the four previous chapters. These critical questions are always a good place to start, and provide a good way of putting any slippery slope into a pragmatic perspective. The structure they offer provides a template for organizing a strategy for responding in any particular case. The next step is to go on to consider the six tactics. But they do not exhaust all relevant considerations in a particular case. Much has to depend on the specifics of the arguments offered to support a slippery slope argument in an individual case, and such factors can vary considerably from case to case, as we have seen.

Actually applying this tactical advice to the specifics of a particular case is no trivial job, in many cases. You may need to do a lot of serious research and thinking about the specific ways and means available of mounting a workable defense in the particular situation you are dealing with. Indeed, in some cases, mounting a successful defense may even require special expertise in a field of knowledge, like law or medicine, for example.

The slippery slope argument is most powerful and effective when it is a kind of surprise attack which takes advantage of some new development that has not been widely anticipated. Coping with this development may take time and ingenuity. So mounting an effective defense against the slippery slope may require not only ingenuity, but also substantial research into a specific problem.

In the following case, a slippery slope argument was used as part of the argumentation to make a case for one side, and it proved extremely effective. The other side did not oppose the slippery slope argument strongly enough, and it appears that this failure was a decisive factor in the outcome of the case. This case not only illustrates the critical and tactical problem of countering a slippery slope effectively in a particular tactical framework—it is an extremely interesting case of the effective use of the slippery slope argument in its own right.

The case concerned the burning of an American flag by Gregory Lee Johnson during a political demonstration in Dallas to protest policies of the Reagan administration. Johnson was convicted of desecration of a venerated object, but the Texas Court of Criminal Appeals reversed the ruling, arguing that Johnson's act was 'expressive conduct,' protected by the First Amendment's guarantee of freedom of speech. The Texas Court of Criminal Appeals argued that Johnson's conduct was a form of 'symbolic speech' intended to convey a political message and that, as such, it should be protected by the First Amendment, which includes, under the heading of 'speech,' acts like organized demonstrations and the distribution of literature.

In the majority opinion of the court, delivered by Justice William J. Brennan, Jr. in the case of *Texas* v. *Johnson* (1989 WL 65231 (U.S.), 57 U.S.L.W. 4770), it was argued that Johnson's act was not in itself disruptive, or a breach of the peace, and should not be prohibited as 'an expression of an idea,' according to the First Amendment, 'simply because society finds the idea itself offensive or disagreeable.'

The Supreme Court majority opinion backed up the Appeal Court ruling, stressing that Johnson's act was an overtly expressive act, and that it comes under the First Amendment protecting free speech. The court conceded that the government has an interest in regulating actions like flag-burning that many people find offensive, but argued that this interest was not strong enough in this case to warrant creating an exception to the First Amendment. Justices Thurgood Marshall, Harry A. Blackmun, Antonin Scalia, and Anthony M. Kennedy joined in this majority opinion. The four remaining justices disagreed, filing dissenting opinions. Chief Justice William H. Rehnquist filed a dissenting opinion, with which two other justices concurred, and Justice J. Stevens filed a separate dissenting opinion. Thus the majority opinion passed, five to four, holding that Johnson's conviction for flag desecration would not stand.

In delivering the opinion of the court, Justice Brennan cited the precedent case of *Schacht* v. *United States,* where it was ruled that an actor could wear a uniform of one of the U.S. armed forces while portraying someone who discredited that armed force by opposing the war in Vietnam. The rationale linking the Schacht case and the Johnson case was expressed by Justice Brennan in these words.

Case 7.5

We perceive no basis on which to hold that the principle underlying our decision in Schacht does not apply to this case. To conclude that the Government may permit designated symbols to be used to communicate only a limited set of messages would be to enter territory having no discernible or defensible boundaries. Could the Government, on this theory, prohibit the burning of state flags? Of copies of the Presidential seal? Of the Constitution? In evaluating these choices under the First Amendment, how would we decide which symbols were sufficiently special to warrant this unique status? To do so, we would be forced to consult our own political preferences, and impose them on the citizenry, in the very way that the First Amendment forbids us to do. (*Texas* v. *Johnson* 1989: 10)

The argument in case 7.5 is quite clearly an instance of the precedent type of slippery slope argument. It appears to be the type classified in the summary of varieties of precedent slippery slope arguments (Chapter 4.10) as the arbitrary results argument, the variant where a first step in a slippery slope is said to lead to a series of unclear or arbitrary decisions about what to include. Justice Brennan is arguing that subsequent decisions—whether to prohibit the burning of state flags, copies of the presidential seal, or the Constitution, and so forth—would lead to a situation where the individuals making these decisions would be imposing their own political preferences on the citizens. This would be an intolerable outcome in a free country, and in fact, Justice Brennan concludes, would be in violation of the First Amendment.

Like all slippery slope arguments, this one is based on a prediction of how future cases are likely to turn out or be decided. It is therefore not in itself a perfectly solid or incontrovertible argument. But it did seem to make a reasonable point that should rightly have been considered in deciding the case of *Texas* v. *Johnson*. Any decision made by the Supreme Court is an important precedent that is binding on lower courts. Therefore, it is very reasonable to try to anticipate the direction of the implications of a decision for future cases, to the extent that such predictions are possible and significant.

Of course the argument presented in case 7.5 is a short form of the precedent slippery slope argument, and not all the steps are filled in. But even so, enough of a line of argumentation was given to carry some weight of presumption in evaluating the Supreme Court's argument as a whole. The slippery slope argument of case 7.5 was just one subargument in the network of argumentation used by Justice Brennan to support the majority opinion in this decision. But although it was only a small part of a long sequence of argumentation, clearly it had quite a strong influence on the outcome of the case. This impact was also reflected in the wide media coverage and subsequent public discussion of the slippery slope.

Chief Justice Rehnquist delivered a dissenting opinion, in which Justices White and O'Connor joined (*Texas* v. *Johnson* 1989: 13–19). This argument stressed the patriotic value of the flag as a stirring symbol that united the U.S., quoted poetry (including the national anthem) at some length. The overall strategy of the argument was directed to denying that burning the flag can be counted as expressive conduct. The main argument for this was to the effect that the flag is not merely a 'point of view' or political belief.

Case 7.6

The American flag, then, throughout more than 200 years of our history, has come to be the visible symbol embodying our Nation. It does not represent the views of any particular political party, and it does not represent any particular political philosophy. The flag is not simply another 'idea' or 'point of view' competing for recognition in the marketplace of ideas. Millions and millions of Americans regard it with an almost mystical reverence regardless of what sort of social, political, or philosophical beliefs they may have. I cannot agree that the First Amendment invalidates the Act of Congress, and the laws of 48 of the 50 States, which make criminal the public burning of the flag. (*Texas* v. *Johnson* 1989: 16)

Rehnquist's argument was emotional and patriotic, but it did not attempt to directly attack or counter the slippery slope argument posed by the other side. His argument was, of course, indirectly relevant, because if the flag-burning was not 'expressive conduct,' then the slippery slope argument would not work. However, he did not try to attack the slippery slope argument directly by, for example, using any one of the six tactics outlined in Section 5 above.

Justice Stevens filed a separate dissenting opinion (*Texas* v. *Johnson* 1989: 20–6). But unfortunately, parts of this opinion seemed to run counter to the argument of Justice Rehnquist's opinion. For Justice Stevens argued that the flag is a symbol.

Case 7.7

The message conveyed by some flags—the swastika, for example—may survive long after it has outlived its usefulness as a symbol of regimented unity in a particular nation. So it is with the American flag. It is more than a proud symbol of the courage, the determination, and the gifts of nature that transformed 13 fledgling colonies into a world power. It is a symbol of freedom, of equal opportunity, of religious tolerance, and of goodwill for other peoples who share our aspirations. The symbol carries its message to dissidents both at home and abroad who may have no interest at all in our national unity or survival. (*Texas* v. *Johnson* 1989: 20)

But this argument that the flag is a symbol seems inconsistent with the main thrust of Justice Rehnquist's argument to the effect that burning the flag is not 'expressive.'

Thus it seemed that while the dissenters raised a powerful emotional argument, they did not really address their argument to the logic of the slippery slope argument posed by the other side. Evidently this lack of a unified and targeted response must have played an important role in the outcome of the case, for in its absence, the slippery slope argument brought a powerful unity to the argumentation behind the majority opinion.

Of course we do not know what form the actual discussions among the justices took, but it is also possible to gauge the power and effectiveness of the use of the slippery slope argument in this case by looking at its impact on public opinion.

8. Public Reaction in the Flag-Burning Case

The Supreme Court decision was widely offensive to popular patriotic feeling in the U.S., and in the wake of this public reaction, George Bush proposed a constitutional amendment to overrule the court decision.

On the one side of this dispute, many politicians came out strongly in agreement with the popular opinion to condemn the court ruling. On the other side, some felt that a constitutional amendment was not an appropriate way to deal with the problem. Critics, according to an article in *Newsweek,* cited dangers inherent in the wording of a ban that outlaws 'physical desecration' of the flag (Jacoby and Clift 1989). Such a ruling might lead to all kinds of legal cases that might be difficult to decide. At one point, the slippery slope argument was explicitly mentioned by name.

Case 7.8

Then there's the slippery slope that frightened the court: if we ban flag-burning, the justices asked, shouldn't we also 'prohibit burning . . . the Constitution'—or even the Texas state flower? As those who back the ruling point out, it's both difficult and treacherous to make exceptions to the First Amendment: start with the flag, and Congress could soon be banning all kinds of unpopular political protest. (Jacoby and Clift 1989)

Now from one point of view, the argument in case 7.8 clearly represents a slippery slope argument. President Bush has proposed an amendment to the Constitution, and then critics (taking up the role of the respondent in the slippery slope argument) have condemned this move on the grounds that it may lead to problematic cases which may have to be decided in an arbitrary way that will make the amendment difficult to enforce or to live with. Finally, it could lead to Congress banning 'all kinds of unpopular political protest.'

But this is not the same slippery slope argument cited in case 7.8, even though the slippery slope actually cited is attributed to the Supreme Court. Evidently in their deliberations, according to *Newsweek,* the justices of the court were 'frightened' by the possible consequences of ruling flag-burning as a crime. Their worry, according to the report in case 7.8, concerned analogous, similar cases that they would, sooner or later, have to rule on if they made this ruling. Would they have to declare that burning the constitution is illegal? Or what about burning a state emblem? Their worry evidently was that taking the first step of banning desecration of the flag might commit them to banning a lot of similar actions. But banning these other actions as crimes, the prohibition of which would have to be enforced, could be inappropriate or problematic for all kinds of reasons.

This argument cited does seem to have many of the leading characteristics of the same slippery slope argument in the Supreme Court case. But who is the proponent? And who is the respondent? One possible interpretation is that some members of the court (the majority opinion) were against making flag-burning illegal and some (the dissenters) were for it. Then those against it have the role of the proponent, and those for it have the role of respondent in the slippery slope argument, according to the analysis of Chapter 6.

But is this the interpretation that the *Newsweek* account is putting forward? Or is it Congress who is the proponent, in this account, while the American people are the respondents?

It seems that what is being said is that those who are supporters of the Supreme Court ruling are worried that the Congress might be led to intolerable subsequent rulings once they, the Congress, have made flag-burning an exception to the First Amendment. On this interpretation, it seems as if the supporters of the Supreme Court decision are the proponents and the Congress is the respondent.

But this interpretation doesn't seem to be quite right either. For according to the first sentence of case 7.8, the Supreme Court is worried about its own decision of whether to ban flag-burning or not. It seems that they are worried about the consequences of their own decision as a court ruling, and not just about what Congress might or might not do.

This case is complicated by the factor that there seem to be two slippery slopes involved. One is the legal slippery slope argument attributed to the Supreme Court. The other is the broader, political slippery slope suggested by citing the dangers to all U.S. citizens implicit in a constitutional amendment to ban 'physical desecration' of the flag by Congress.

Case 7.9

The dangers inherent in any ban will become clear when Congress starts grappling with specific language. Does the 'physical desecration' outlawed by Bush's amendment include walking on the flag? What about sewing it on the seat of your pants? . . . Nor would the danger be confined to one ideological camp.'Conservatives would set a horrible precedent by turning the Constitution into a political tool,' said the right-leaning *Washington Times* last week. (Jacoby and Clift 1989)

As shown in the quotation in case 7.9 the *Newsweek* report was concerned here with the possible consequences of the amendment proposed by President Bush to Congress. The nature of the slippery slope, however, is very similar to the characteristics of the slippery slope argument in the Supreme Court deliberations. It is a problem of 'specific language,' and the problem is posed by a sequential development of similar cases, like sewing the flag 'to the seat of your pants' or walking on the flag.

By looking at the public reactions to this use of the slippery slope argument, we can see how powerful it was, and how difficult it would be to refute it. The public reactions to the case expressed in the media showed how plausible it was to fill in more steps in the sequence of the slope. Although the slippery slope argument expressed in the Supreme Court majority opinion of Justice Brennan was very brief, taking up only a short paragraph, the reactions to it by the public indicated how fertile this argument was in suggesting other links that could easily be filled in by respondents to the argument. Evidently, this particular situation of prosecuting flag-burning as 'expressive conduct' presented a highly appropriate tactical basis for the effective use of a slippery slope argument.

The broad public reaction to this case was largely negative, and it was cited as one of a number of cases where the Supreme Court had made decisions that were at odds with public opinion. Once the Supreme Court had ruled against making flag-burning a crime in *Texas* v. *Johnson,* there was very wide coverage of the controversy in the media, but the issue often seemed to be treated as a joke. The feeling often conveyed was that the reasoning behind the Supreme Court decision was another example of questionable or even ridiculous legal argumentation.

One of these commentaries was much more astute and revealing, however. In the Doonesbury cartoon by G. B. Trudeau (*Winnipeg Free Press,* August 12, 1989), Zonker asked Mike what he thinks about the flag-burning amendment.

Case 7.10

MIKE. I'm, for it. Aren't you?

ZONKER. Sure! How could anyone be *for* flag burning?

MIKE. Beats me. Of course, 'physical desecration' is a tricky business . . . .
For instance, will it be illegal to burn a paper flag? Or to tear up a photo of a flag? How about cutting a cake decorated with a flag? And what about flag clothing? Are you a patriot if you wear a flag T-shirt, but a felon if you wear flag pants? And what does that make Uncle Sam? And what about art—who decides whether a flag painting is a desecration or an homage? Also, what about other national symbols, like the eagle or the Statue of Liberty? Or state flags? Or the confederate flag? All sacred to somebody—should they be protected? Also, since burning is the only sanctioned way of disposing of a worn-out flag, aren't we really outlawing an idea instead of an act? And, if so, what other ideas do we outlaw?

This particular presentation of the substance of the slippery slope argument in the flag-burning case, though meant to be somewhat ironic, is in fact quite a detailed and revealing exposition of one interpretation of the sequence premise. Mike's reply cites quite a number of problematic cases which could represent problems in delimiting the concept of physical desecration.

Another very favorable feature of Trudeau's portrayal of the argument is the device of having Mike express each problematic stage in the form of a question. Not only is this a particularly perspicuous expression of the slippery slope argument on the flag-burning issue because of the detailed and plausible way the steps in the sequence are filled in, but the format of putting each stage as an interrogative is highly appropriate and consistent with the conjectural and question-raising nature of slippery slope argumentation as a correct and useful kind of practical reasoning in deliberation.

Particularly, the way of phrasing the final step in the sequence as 'outlawing an idea instead of an act' is a very nice way of linking the sequence of argumentation to abstract considerations like freedom of speech, clearly an important legal consideration but one the public seemed to find hard to take very seriously as a real danger, judging from other commentaries on the issue. Another revealing aspect of this interpretation is that it shows how the sequence of questions is brought up by the vagueness of the phrase 'physical desecration,' showing the sorites element of this slippery slope.

In some ways, the reactions to the slippery slope argument in the Johnson case were typical of the classic (standard) treatment of this argument in the logic textbooks. Superficially, it was treated as an obvious 'fallacy,' another instance of the Supreme Court falling into conundrums of abstruse and sophisticated legal labyrinths of argumentation instead of using common sense. But if you take a harder look at the original text of the argument in the exact words it was put forward in the majority opinion, you can begin to appreciate the real power of it as a genuine argument with legitimate rational force. In the situation, with good reason, it was extremely difficult to refute, precisely because it was so appropriate.

How could it have been refuted, using any of the six tactics of Section 5 above? In his reply Justice Stevens was clearly on a good line of approach when he tried to argue that Johnson was being tried for 'desecration,' as separate from 'expressive conduct' (*Texas* v. *Johnson* 1989: 23). But the arguments of the dissenting opinion did not go far enough to tell us, generally, how these two things can be clearly separated. Their arguments which tried to make a case that Johnson's act was not 'expressive conduct' were not plausible. This tactic went nowhere.

What was needed was to dig in by giving some clear dividing line between 'desecration' and 'expressive conduct' so that, in subsequent cases, acts could be prosecuted under the first category satisfactorily while drawing a sharp line between this and the second category. How this could be done is in fact, however, a substantive legal problem which would involve citing and dealing with the whole relevant range of related cases in law. In short, knowledge of general tactics for using and defending against the slippery slope argument offers only a kind of generalized insight or rough guide on how to proceed with a line of argumentation in a particular case. Filling out the particular steps in your argument in that case is a substantive job in its own right.

What we can say in this case is that the slippery slope won the argument because the response was tactically ineffective. Even though it was expressed in a compressed or 'short form' version by Justice Brennan, it was a successful argument because it was appropriate to the situation, and because it backed up the premises of the argumentation scheme for the precedent type of slippery slope argument strongly enough to fulfill the requirements of burden of proof for the context of the dispute. Thus it was neither a fallacious nor a perfectly conclusive argument. It was simply good enough for the needs of the particular discussion— good enough to demand an adequate response that was not forthcoming.

9. Pinning the Fallacy Down

There are three stages in judging the strength or weakness of a slippery slope argument in a given case—identification, analysis, and evaluation. The identification stage has three parts. First, identify the basic components of the context of dialogue—the proponent of the slippery slope argument, the respondent, the thesis at issue, and the tactical situation. Second, identify the type of slippery slope argument—sorites, causal, precedent, or full type. Also, at this stage, identify the elements of that type—for example, if it is a sorites type, or a full type, identify the vague term that helps to generate the slippery slope. Third, identify the key propositions, namely the initial premise, the sequential premise, other premises, and the conclusion.

Another important task of argument identification is the specification of the time frame of the slippery slope argument. As we saw (in cases 3.5 and 3.6, for example), the temporal factor of the prediction and the historical situation of the case may be crucially important to identify prior to any critical evaluation of the argument.

The analysis stage involves studying the given text of discourse in the context of dialogue in order to specify the background presumptions which need to be filled in. The most important of these is the specification of the type of dialogue and, if it is a critical discussion, the burden of proof should be clarified. Once some analysis of reasonable requirements of burden of proof is given, the question needs to be asked (*a*) whether the conclusion does follow with a sufficient degree of plausibility from the premises, or (*b*) what needs to be filled in, by way of additional assumptions, to make it follow. In the full slippery slope argument, the public opinion premise needs to be specified. In the sorites, the definitions of the key terms in the context of the dispute need to be analyzed. In the causal type of argument, the causal situation or field needs to be specified. In the precedent type of slippery slope argument, the rule and precedents need to be clarified and stated.

At the evaluation stage, a critic needs to arrive at an evaluation of how strongly the premises support the conclusion in light of the argumentation scheme and its requirements, and also in light of the appropriate burden of proof for the dialogue. The question here is a three-part one. Is the argument strong enough to meet these requirements? Or is it too weak, in certain respects? Or is the failure bad enough that the case can rightly be classified as an instance of the slippery slope fallacy?

In answering these questions of evaluation, several subquestions should be asked. How strongly has the slippery slope argument been pressed forward by the proponent? Look carefully at the language (indicator words) of the outcome premise—is it expressed as a 'must,' 'may,' or 'will' prediction? Is the conclusion inappropriately strong, a 'logical leap' like that of case 2.6*b*? Have tactics of coercion been used by the proponent, e.g. 'You have no choice!' Have scare tactics been used, in a heavy-handed attempt to exaggerate the dangerous outcome, well beyond the evidence? What is the attitude of the proponent to critical questioning in response to his slippery slope argument? Are critical questions allowed, and responded to properly? Or are they brushed aside without real consideration? Are tactics used to prevent or stifle peremptorily the asking of legitimate critical questions? Evidence to support incriminating answers to these questions builds up a case for backing a charge that the slippery slope fallacy has been committed.

The problem is that in many cases where allegations of someone's having committed a slippery slope fallacy have been made, there is not enough textual and contextual information given to pin down this charge in an unconditional way. Again we might note the difference between cases 3.5 and 3.8. In case 3.5, the warning against 'unseasonable laughter' could have been used as a scare tactic to try to intimidate people into suppressing their display of emotions. If so, it could be a case of a slippery slope fallacy. But the evidence of the text, taken together with what we can surmise about the historical and dialectical context of the case, is insufficient to make such a charge plausible. On balance, there is too little evidence to classify this instance of the slippery slope argument as a fallacy. By contrast, in case 3.8, there is enough evidence to build up a good prima facie case to back the charge that the slippery slope argument cited here was being used as a scare tactic of a kind that would fit our requirements for a fallacious slope argument very well. The actual text quoted in cases 3.8*a* and 3.8*b* are, of course, by themselves insufficient to document and pin down the charge against the reported offenders finally and decisively. Yet even so, it is possible to arrive at a conditional evaluation, based on plausible presumptions, provided they are correctly seen as being open to rebuttal. The general problem is that further research must turn to the detailed study of loner cases where more text and context is presented.

In this book, our primary goal has been to provide reasonable criteria for the evaluation of slippery slope arguments. But carrying out this task has revealed that prior identification and analysis of the slippery slope argument is typically a necessary and important part of arriving at an evaluation that is based on the relevant evidence furnished by the text and context of discourse in a given case. Therefore, as we have seen, the job of proving that a particular instance of the slippery slope argument is fallacious or not (pinning the fallacy down) has turned out to be a lot more work, in most cases, than the rather superficial treatments of the textbooks have suggested.

10. Underlying Structural Characteristics

The textbooks can move towards a more balanced and adequate account of the slippery slope argument by recognizing more clearly that it is a technique of argumentation that can be used reasonably in some cases and unreasonably or improperly in other cases. Although this type of argument is sometimes employed so badly and sophistically that its use in a particular case can be called fallacious, more often it is only a weakly or inadequately supported argument that should be criticized, but not classified as a fallacy. Plausible arguments are always on the borderline of questioning, in general, because their conclusions are reasonable presumptions rather than items of established knowledge. When it is used correctly, the slippery slope argument is characteristically a plausible argument which correctly functions in a context of dialogue by shifting a burden of proof from one side of an argument to the other.

The method for evaluating a particular instance of the slippery slope argument as strong or weak, therefore, is to identify the appropriate argumentation scheme and check to see whether the requirements for that argumentation scheme have been met in a particular case. The four argumentation schemes for the slippery slope argument have been set out, in Chapters 2 through 5. For each scheme, there is a matching set of critical questions.

The methods used to analyze the slippery slope argument in this monograph have been pragmatic—called 'pragma-dialectical' by van Eemeren and Grootendorst (1984). As these pragmatic methods of research in argumentation continue to be improved and refined, our knowledge of the slippery slope argument will continue to deepen and mature.

But the big move forward needed to analyze the slippery slope fallacy is to think of a fallacy as not just a violation of a rule of reasonable dialogue, but as a dynamic tactic that has been used incorrectly, to shift a burden of proof illicitly in a reasonable dialogue. It is a kind of tactic of argumentation that has been used in such a way that it goes against the goals of dialogue that the participants in the argument are supposed to be taking part in. What is especially distinctive about the slippery slope as a method of argumentation is its use as a tool of practical reasoning. It needs to be clearly seen that the slippery slope argument is a tool of human deliberation that is used to test and evaluate the prudential reasonableness of a proposed line of action by discussing its plausible consequences. It is a species of negative argument from consequences, a type of argumentation that is used every day in normal human deliberations about politics, planning of all sorts, and even in personal human decision-making. There is nothing immoral or fallacious about this kind of argumentation *per se*. It is simply a tool that can be used for good or bad purposes. Used wrongly, it can be a fallacious kind of argumentation.

An underlying structural characteristic of all slippery slope argumentation is that it is a species of case-based reasoning. It proceeds by steps of analogy between one case and another. Another underlying structural characteristic is that it is a species of practical reasoning in a context of dialogue where one party is trying to persuade another party not to pursue an action that the other party is contemplating and is committed to going ahead with. These two characteristics tie in together, making a kind of argumentation that has not been studied very intensively in logic or allied disciplines. In fact, practical reasoning has not yet been widely recognized as a fundamentally important kind of reasoning that is central to argumentation as a discipline. Case-based reasoning is now getting more recognition as its importance to artificial intelligence has become apparent. But in the past, logic has been too preoccupied with deductive and inductive models of argument to even systematically recognize practical reasoning as a significant model of argument in its own right.

Viewed as a component of practical reasoning, the function of slippery slope argumentation as a genuine and legitimate technique to be used in reasoned dialogue has now been revealed. It is a method of taking a respondent's commitment to an action or policy, and by deploying an argument from gradualism, leading the respondent by a series of small steps towards a conclusion that is unacceptable (intolerable) to him. Especially in the causal, precedent, and full slippery slope arguments, the method is used by evaluating the possible or plausible consequences of the respondent's proposed course of action. The slippery slope is essentially a negative argument from consequences. The bad consequences are brought out in order to dissuade the respondent from a course of action. Using the slippery slope argument to warn someone of the dangerous consequences that can be anticipated to flow from his or her commitments to action is a common and quite legitimate kind of argumentation.

Unfortunately, informal logic has not in the past—nor is it yet—oriented towards studying actions, practical reasoning, and case-based reasoning as legitimate normative models of correct (and incorrect) argument.[6] This must change if further headway in understanding the logic of the slippery slope is to be made. But there is every indication that it will change, and that the slippery slope argument will achieve greater recognition as a universal technique of argumentation that can often be quite correct and reasonable.

[6] Michael Scriven made this same point, arguing that actions need to be taken into account in informal logic, in his paper 'The Philosophy of Ordinary Logic' at the Third International Symposium on Informal Logic at Windsor on June 15, 1989.

References

ARISTOTLE (1955), *Aristotle*, Loeb Library (London: Heinemann).

BARRY, VINCENT E. (1976), *Practical Logic* (New York: Holt, Rinehart and Winston).

BLACK, MAX (1970), *Margins of Precision* (Ithaca, NY, and London: Cornell University Press).

Brockhaus Enzyklopädie (1974) (Wiesbaden: F. A. Brockhaus).

CAMPBELL, RICHMOND (1974) 'The *Sorites* Paradox,' *Philosophical Studies*, 26: 175–91.

CHASE, STUART (1956), *Guides to Straight Thinking* (New York, Evanston, Ill., and London: Harper & Row).

CICERO (1951), *Academica* 93, trans. H. Rackham, Loeb Library, xix (Cambridge, Mass.: Harvard University Press).

CLINTON, HENRY LAUREN (1897), *Celebrated Trials* (New York: Harper).

COPI, IRVING M. (1986) *Introduction to Logic* (New York: Macmillan).

CRIGHTON, SUSAN (Producer) (1990), *Family Matters*, Transcript of a Panel Discussion on Research on Human Embryos Televised on BBC-1, Feb. 21.

DEMORGAN, AUGUSTUS (1847), *Formal Logic* (London: Taylor and Walton).

DIGGS, B. J. (1960), 'A Technical Ought,' *Mind*, 69: 301–17.

Duden: Das Grosse Wörterbuch der Deutschen Sprache (1981) (Mannheim: Bibliographisches Institut).

ELIOT, LANCE B. (1986), 'Analogical Problem-Solving and Expert Systems,' *IEEE Expert* (Summer), 17–31.

ENGEL, S. MORRIS (1976), *With Good Reason* (New York: St Martin's Press).

FINE, KIT (1975), 'Vagueness, Truth and Logic,' *Synthese*, 30: 265–300.

FOGELIN, ROBERT J. (1972), *Understanding Arguments* (New York: Harcourt Brace Jovanovich).

—— (1987), *Understanding Arguments*, 3rd edn. (San Diego, Calif.: Harcourt Brace Jovanovich).

FRANKEL, MARK, THOMAS, RICH, and MORRISON, JANE (1989), 'Harmonizing World Taxes,' *Newsweek*, Nov. 27, pp. 42–7.

GILBERT, MICHAEL A. (1979), *How to Win an Argument* (New York: McGraw-Hill).

GOLDING, MARTIN P. (1984), *Legal Reasoning* (New York: Knopf).

GOLDMAN, ALAN H., (1987), 'The Force of Precedent in Legal, Moral, and Empirical Reasoning,' *Synthese*, 71: 323–46.

GOVIER, TRUDY (1982), 'What's Wrong with Slippery Slope Arguments?' *Canadian Journal of Philosophy*, 12: 303–16.

GRICE, H. PAUL (1975), 'Logic and Conversation,' in Donald Davidson and Gilbert Harman (eds.), *The Logic of Grammar* (Encino, Calif.: Dickenson).

HAMBLIN, CHARLES (1970), *Fallacies* (London: Methuen).

HAMEL, E. (1967), 'Casuistry,' in *New Catholic Encyclopedia*, iii (New York: McGraw-Hill).

HARDIN, GARRETT (1985), *Filters Against Folly* (New York: Viking Penguin).

HINTIKKA, JAAKKO (1989), 'Rules, Games and Experiences: Wittgenstein's Discussion of Rule-Following in the Light of his Development,' *Revue Internationale de Philosophie*, 43: 279–97.

HURLEY, PATRICK J. (1982), *A Concise Introduction to Logic* (Belmont: Wadsworth).

JACOBY, TAMAR, and CLIFT, ELEANOR (1989), 'Congress – Rallies around the Flag,' *Newsweek*, July 10, p. 19.

JACQUETTE, DALE (1989), 'The Hidden Logic of Slippery Slope Argument,' *Philosophy and Rhetoric*, 22: 59–70.

JOHNSON, RALPH H., and BLAIR, ANTHONY J. (1983), *Logical Self-Defense* (Toronto: McGraw-Hill Ryerson).

JONES, TREVOR (ed.) (1967), *Harrap's Standard German and English Dictionary* (London: Harrap).

JONSEN, ALBERT R., and TOULMIN, STEPHEN (1988), *The Abuse of Casuistry* (Berkeley: University of California Press).

KAHANE, HOWARD (1971), *Logic and Contemporary Rhetoric* (Belmont: Wadsworth).

KANTROWITZ, BARBARA, and WINGERT, PAT (1989), 'Parental Leave Cries to Be Born,' *Newsweek*, June 15, p. 65.

KERFERD, G. B. (1981), *The Sophistic Movement* (Cambridge: Cambridge University Press).

KEYSERLINGK, EDWARD W. (1979), *Sanctity of Life or Quality of Life*, Study Paper, Protection of Life Series (Ottawa: Law Reform Commission of Canada).

KING, JOHN L. (1979), 'Bivalence and the *Sorites* Paradox,' *American Philosophical Quarterly*, 16: 17–25.

KLEIN, HANS E. (ed.) (1988), *Case Method Research and Application: Selected Papers of the Fifth International Conference on Case Method Research and Case Method Application*, distribution by World Association for Case Method Research, Needham, Mass.

KNEALE, WILLIAM and MARTHA (1962), *The Development of Logic* (Oxford: Oxford University Press).

KOLODNER, JANET L., SIMPSON, JR., ROBERT L. and SYCARA-CYRANSKI, KATIA (1985), 'A Process Model of Case-Based Reasoning in Problem

Solving, *International Journal of Computing and Artificial Intelligence* (Aug.) 284–90.

LAMB, DAVID (1988), *Down the Slippery Slope*, (London: Croom Helm).

LEVINSON, STEPHEN C. (1983), *Pragmatics* (Cambridge: Cambridge University Press).

LEWIS, CHARLTON T., and SHORT, CHARLES (1969), *A Latin Dictionary* (Oxford: Clarendon Press).

LIFTON, JAY (1986), *The Nazi Doctors: Medical Killing and the Psychology of Genocide* (New York: Basic Books).

LITTLE, J. FREDERICK, GROARKE, LEO A., and TINDALE, CHRISTOPHER W. (1989), *Good Reasoning Matters!* (Toronto: McClelland & Stewart).

LYONS, DAVID (1984), 'Formal Justice, Moral Commitment, and Judicial Precedent,' *Journal of Philosophy*, 81: 580–7.

MACCORMICK, NEIL (1978), *Legal Reasoning and Legal Theory* (Oxford: Oxford University Press).

McGRATH, PETER, 'The Lessons of Munich,' *Newsweek*, Oct. 3, p. 37.

MARTZ, LARRY (1990), 'A Dirty Drug Secret: Hyping Instant and Total Addiction Doesn't Help,' *Newsweek*, Feb. 19, pp. 44–5.

MOORE, CHRISTOPHER W. (1986), *The Mediation Process* (San Francisco, Calif.: Jossey-Bass).

NELSON, BENJAMIN (1973), 'Casuistry,' in *Encyclopaedia Britannica*, v (Chicago: Benton).

ODEGARD, DOUGLAS (1965), 'Excluding the Middle from Loose Concepts,' *Theoria*, 31: 139–45.

PERELMAN, CHAIM and OLBRECHTS-TYTECA, L. (1971), *The New Rhetoric: A Treatise on Argumentation*, trans. John Wilkinson and Purcell Weaver (Notre Dame, University of Notre Dame Press).

RACHELS, JAMES (1986), *The End of Life* (Oxford: Oxford University Press).

RESCHER, NICHOLAS (1976), *Plausible Reasoning* (Assen-Amsterdam: van Gorcum).

—— (1977), *Dialectics* (Albany: State University of New York Press).

RIGTER, HENK (1989), 'Euthanasia in the Netherlands,' *Hastings Center Report*, Supplement (Jan.–Feb.), 31–2.

ROBINSON, RICHARD (1953), *Plato's Earlier Dialectic* (Oxford: Oxford University Press).

ROHDE, DAVID W., and SPAETH, HAROLD J. (1976), *Supreme Court Decision Making* (San Francisco, Calif.: Freeman).

ROSTAND, JEAN (1973), *Humanly Possible: A Biologist's Notes on the Future of Mankind* (New York: Saturday Review Press).

RUDINOW, JOEL (1974) 'On the Slippery Slope,' *Analysis*, 34: 173–6.

SAINSBURY, R. M. (1988), *Paradoxes* (Cambridge: Cambridge University Press).

SCHAUER, FREDERICK (1985), 'Slippery Slopes,' *Harvard Law Review*, 99:361–83.

SCRIVEN, MICHAEL (1976), *Reasoning* (New York: McGraw-Hill).

SEARLE, JOHN (1969), *Speech Acts* (Cambridge: Cambridge University Press).

SIDGWICK, ALFRED (1914), *Elementary Logic* (Cambridge: Cambridge University Press).

SIMPSON, JR., ROBERT L. (1985), *A Computer Model of Case-Based Reasoning in Problem Solving*, Ph.D. thesis, Technical Monograph GIT-ICS-85/18, School of Information and Computer Science, Georgia Institute of Technology.

STOLJAR, SAMUEL (1980), *Moral and Legal Reasoning*, (New York: Barnes & Noble).

SULLIVAN, PAUL (1982), 'The Real Issue Is Repression,' *Winnipeg Sun*, Aug. 27, p. 11.

Texas v. *Johnson* (1989), Syllabus, Transcript of U.S. Supreme Court Case 1989 WL 65231 (U.S.), 57 U.S.L.W. 4770.

ULLMAN-MARGALIT, EDNA (1983), 'On Presumption,' *Journal of Philosophy*, 80: 143–63.

VAN EEMEREN, FRANS H. (1986), 'Dialectical Analysis as a Normative Reconstruction of Argumentative Discourse,' *Text*, 6: 1–16.

—— and GROOTENDORST, ROB (1984), *Speech Acts in Argumentative Discussions* (Dordrecht and Cinnaminson, NS: Foris Publications).

—— —— (1987), 'Fallacies in PragmaDialectical Perspective,' *Argumentation*, 1: 283 301.

—— and KRUIGER, TJARK (1987) 'Identifying Argumentation Schemes,' in Frans H. van Eemeren, Rob Grootendorst, J. Anthony Blair, and Charles A. Willard (eds.), *Argumentation: Perspectives and Approaches* (Dordrecht and Providence, RI: Foris Publications).

VON WRIGHT G. H. (1972), 'On So Called Practical Inference,' *Acta Sociologica*, 15: 39–53; repr. in J. Raz (ed.), *Practical Reasoning* (Oxford: Oxford University Press, 1978); also repr. in G. H. von Wright, *Practical Reason* (Ithaca, NY: Cornell University Press, 1983).

WALLER, BRUCE N. (1988), *Critical Thinking* (Englewood Cliffs, NJ: Prentice-Hall).

WALTON, DOUGLAS N. (1980), 'Why is the *Ad Populum* a Fallacy?' *Philosophy and Rhetoric*, 13: 264–78.

—— (1983), *Ethics of Withdrawal of Life-Support Systems: Case Studies on Decision Making in Intensive Care* (Westport, Conn.: Greenwood Press).

—— (1984), *Logical Dialogue-Games and Fallacies* (Lanham, Md.: University Press of America).

—— (1985a), *Arguer's Position* (Westport, Conn.: Greenwood Press).

—— (1985b), 'Are Circular Arguments Necessarily Vicious?' *American Philosophical Quarterly*, 22: 263–74.

—— (1987), *Informal Fallacies* (Amsterdam: Benjamins).

—— (1989), *Informal Logic* (Cambridge: Cambridge University Press).

—— (1990), *Practical Reasoning* (Savage, M.: Rowman and Littlefield).

—— (1991), *Begging the Question* (New York: Greenwood Press).

WEISS, STEPHEN E. (1976), 'The *Sorites* Fallacy: What Difference Does a Peanut Make?' *Synthese*, 33: 253–72.

WHATELY, RICHARD (1836), *Elements of Logic* (New York: William Jackson).

WHITE, DAVID E. (1985), 'Slippery Slope Arguments,' *Metaphilosophy*, 16: 206–13.

WILENSKY, ROBERT (1983), *Planning and Understanding: A Computational Approach to Human Reasoning* (Reading, Mass.: Addison Wesley).

WILLIAMS, BERNARD (1985), 'Which Slopes Are Slippery?' in Michael Lockwood (ed.), *Moral Dilemmas in Modern Medicine* (Oxford: Oxford University Press).

WINDES, RUSSELL R., and HASTINGS, ARTHUR (1965), *Argumentation and Advocacy* (New York: Random House).

WITTGENSTEIN, LUDWIG (1958), *The Blue and Brown Books*, ed. Rush Rhees (Oxford: Blackwell).

WOODS, JOHN (1987), '*Ad Baculum*, Self-Interest and Pascal's Wager,' in Frans H. van Eemeren, Rob Grootendorst, J. Anthony Blair, and Charles A. Willard (eds.), *Argumentation: Across the Lines of Discipline* (Dordrecht: Foris Publications).

—— and WALTON, DOUGLAS (1989), *Fallacies: Selected Papers 1972–1982*, (Dordrecht: Foris Publications).

Index